This is Strobist® Info

YOUR SETUP GUIDE TO **FLASH** PHOTOGRAPHY

DUSTIN DIAZ

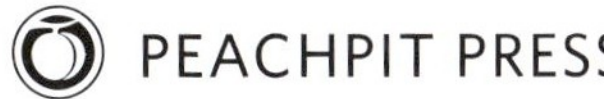

THIS IS STROBIST® INFO: YOUR SETUP GUIDE TO FLASH PHOTOGRAPHY

Dustin Diaz

Published by Peachpit Press. For information on Peachpit Press books, contact:

PEACHPIT PRESS

1249 Eighth Street
Berkeley, CA 94710
(510) 524-2178
Fax: (510) 524-2221

Find us on the Web at www.peachpit.com
To report errors, please send a note to errata@peachpit.com
Peachpit Press is a division of Pearson Education

Editor: Ted Waitt
Production Editor: Lisa Brazieal
Interior Design: Mimi Heft
Compositor: WolfsonDesign
Indexer: James Minkin
Cover Design: Mimi Heft
Cover Images: Dustin Diaz

ISBN-13 978-0-321-80354-2
ISBN-10 0-321-80354-X

9 8 7 6 5 4 3 2 1

Printed and bound in the United States of America

To Erin

She's pretty cool.

CONTENTS

INTRODUCTION

I swore on my mother's grave that I would never write a book again. With that said, Mom, I am terribly sorry for even insinuating that you weren't alive. I'll send you a copy once this is over, and I'll await that embarrassing phone call where you're all like, "Mijo, what was that all about?" And I'll be like, "Oh, yeah. Sorry about that. I didn't have a clever opener so I just went with it."

Nevertheless, this wasn't yet another painful experience to complete. Luckily, I had an amazing wife (Erin), a patient editor (Ted Waitt), and a plethora of friends (an excuse to mention JR and Ashley) who helped push me along (or took me away) to complete this book. Pro tip for first-time authors: Don't write a book immediately after having a first child and switching jobs. Just don't.

To the point—you see, this was all a big misunderstanding with one thing leading to another. And it all happened like this.

BACKSTORY

In 2006, I bought my first SLR camera, a Nikon D40. I took a lot of terrible photos. Like...just badly terrible. In 2007, I added more to that terrible collection. In 2008, I decided I liked taking terrible photos so I bought more lenses, figuring that would improve my ability to be a terrible photographer. Unfortunately, near the end of the year I caught a bug that made me care about taking good pictures. Then finally came Christmas 2008, when I decided to do one of those cheesy 365 "photo a day" projects for 2009. Long story short, it became stupidly successful. I wrote some things about lighting and drew some diagrams. I learned a lot of things, many hardships were had, and I am now a better person. Years later, I wrote a book about it. The End.

ON STROBIST® INFO

Just to be up front, Strobist® is part of the David Hobby Hair Club for Men brand. If you haven't been there, I highly recommend you take a visit back to the old town and know your flash roots. Visit strobist.com for more information.

But seriously, if it weren't for David pouring in countless hours of blood, sweat, and beers, I can honestly say I'd be doing something else other than pretending to act like I'm a writer. David Hobby is *the* Godfather of Flash Photography.

THIS BOOK

Considering this book made it into your hands one way or another, it's highly unlikely you'll ever read this introduction thing. For example, chicken butt banana brains! Am I right? Given that this book is filled with full-page, high-resolution beautiful photos (just sayin') accompanied by detailed setup shots, there seems very little reason to bother reading about gear, light travel, and the inverse square law. And to your defense, I'm right there with you! Photos speak a thousand words! But for what it's worth, in the spirit of terseness and not wasting your time, you'll be a thousand times better off reading the accompanying text chapters before trying to decipher the photo diagrams. So if you're learning about flash photography for the first time via this book, first off, good choice, and secondly, don't skimp out on the words. Everything from aperture settings to softboxes to rock music is covered, helping you streamline your way to becoming a professional flash diagram decoder and allowing you to recreate any image shown in this book. So just read the text, for you and for me. Together. We can make a difference. Now queue the happy music and read on.

one! Lights, Camera, Action

Or I suppose I should say, "Lights, then lenses, then a camera, then action," but really, you could put the action anywhere in that equation. But to the point: the key to a happy pocket and jumping into flash photography is to seek after these items in the order listed. Invest wisely first in lights, then lenses, then gold, then cameras. When your priorities shift from drooling after the next big camera to buying more flash speedlights, you won't regret having that extra light or two in your bag. Also, if you caught that gold reference, good on ya.

Of course, this is easy for the guy who's already jumped into debt buying really expensive cameras and lenses before even considering buying a flash. Nevertheless, were I forced to start all over again, I would first invest in lighting equipment, then build up a small lens collection, then shop for a camera. Obviously it's a bit counterintuitive since you can't take pictures without a camera and a lens...or can you?! No. You can't. But more than likely, anyone reading this, at minimum, has a decent (d)SLR and the kit lens that came with it. That's perfect! Start there! Plus, cameras these days are pretty much way more awesome than they need to be. So even if you have what Nikon or Canon calls the "entry-level beginner's pre-school toddler camera," it probably has a good-sized sensor, shoots multiple frames per second, makes movies, breakfast, and cleans your home. No joke.

ON ACQUIRING LIGHTS

When talking about "making lights a priority," the whole gamut comes along with it, including stands, clamps, modifiers, gels, triggers, power clowns, and more. But don't fret; it's a beautiful world you can easily get lost in, and before you know it, you'll seriously reconsider your first-born over a few more speedlights and some softboxes. Wait, no. Don't do that. I got that all wrong! Except, actually, well, not all wrong. After all, you still have to get all this "stuff," but with my 12-step program, you'll be keeping your first-born *and* have a happy pocket. (God, I can't wait to see how well this book translates into multiple languages. I mean, why would pockets be happy? Why does it take 12 steps? In fact, I skimmed ahead, and I don't see 12 steps?)

SPEEDLIGHTS

Without a doubt, when it comes to cameras, lenses, and speedlights, I have a bias toward buying Nikon and Canon gear. It's not that other systems aren't great or can't provide solutions that fit your needs, but I've found that by sticking with Nikon or Canon you'll have higher chances of compatibility between devices like remote triggers, umbrella adapters, and light-modifying contraptions to fit your speedlights. So with that said, my recommended purchase guide at the time of this writing is as follows.

LOW-END: CANON 430EX II, NIKON SB-700

Perfect as a first-time durable off-camera lighting solution. Both feature simple interfaces to change modes, power settings, and zoom the flash heads. Both come with carrying cases and take standard double-A batteries, minimizing trips to specialized electronic stores for batteries that couldn't normally be found at 7-Eleven.

HIGH-END: NIKON SB-900, CANON 580EX II

For more (brighter) power and faster recycling times, these make excellent solutions if you're willing drop a little more cash. As a side note, I own six SB-900s and one 580EX II. And although Nikon didn't ask me to say this (I mean, I wouldn't mind 17 more SBs), the SB-900 is truly one of the greatest speedlights of all time. There are some old-schoolers out there who claim it's the older, more expensive SB-800, but with the versatility, savvy product packaging, and intelligence of the SB-900, it wins hands-down. This badboy comes with a carrying case for the light itself, a cubby for extra batteries, and room for the sample gel pack. Not to mention, it was the first speedlight with the easy dial interface and no-fuss gel-clamp solution. (Basically, any other speedlight out there requires you to get a little clever with arts and crafts.) But I digress, since Nikon will more than likely not give me 17 of them.

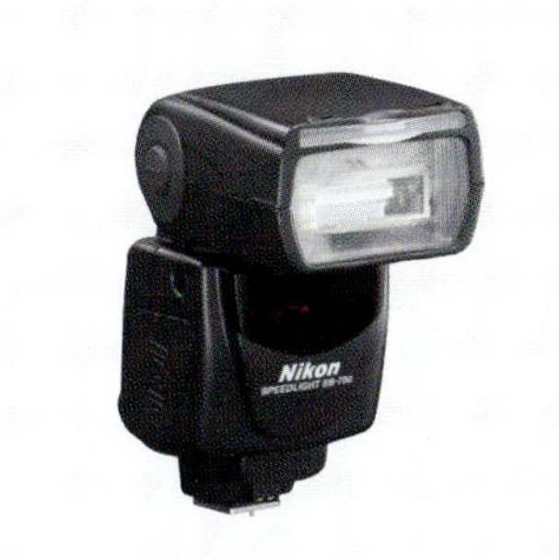

The Nikon SB-700

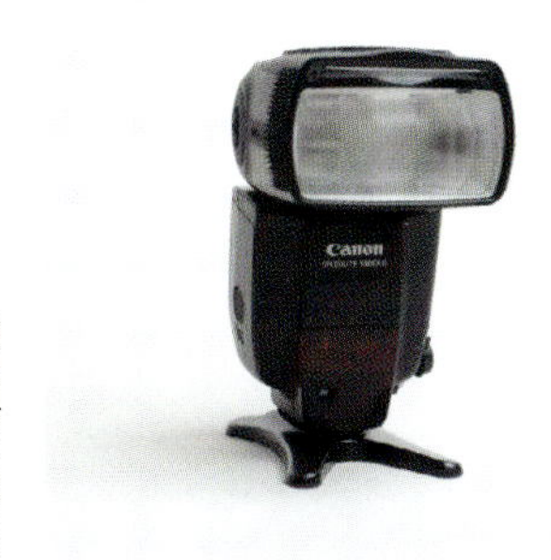

The Canon 580EX II

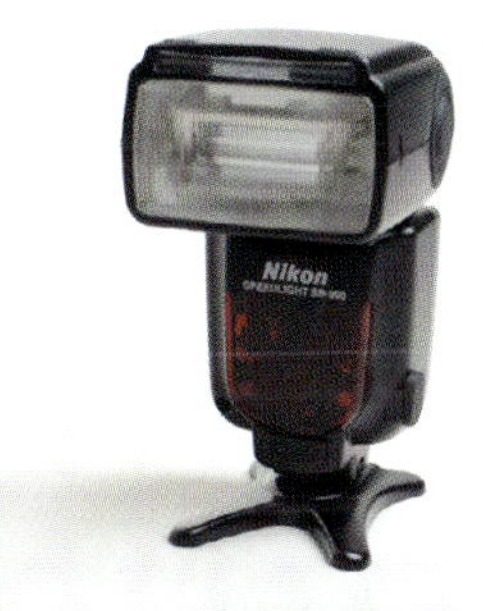

The Nikon SB-900 flash, as well as the case, diffusion dome, filter set, filters, and stand that come with it

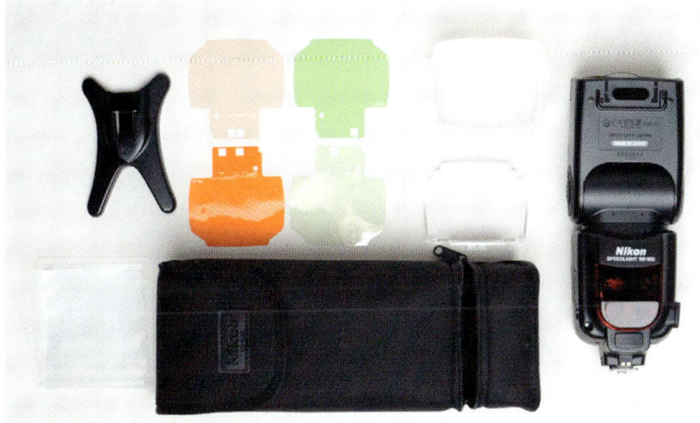

RADIO TRIGGERS

I'll skip the pretense that you should start your off-camera ventures with a corded solution. Anyone recommending a system that attaches a light to your camera via hardwire needs to be shot. Because, quite frankly, they suck, and for the same price range you can jump straight into (wireless) radio triggers. They are, indeed, more awesome, and they won't get in your way. So just do it this way. I promise.

CACTUS V4 TRANSMITTERS AND RECEIVERS

An excellent start, with high compatibility across the major brand flashes and cameras. Buy one transmitter for your camera and one receiver for each flash. Includes a solid set of 16 channels, but expect these to only be reliable indoors, as you'll notice some shortcomings when heading outside. At the time of this writing, they're running for about $20 US each.

The Cactus V4 transmitter and receiver

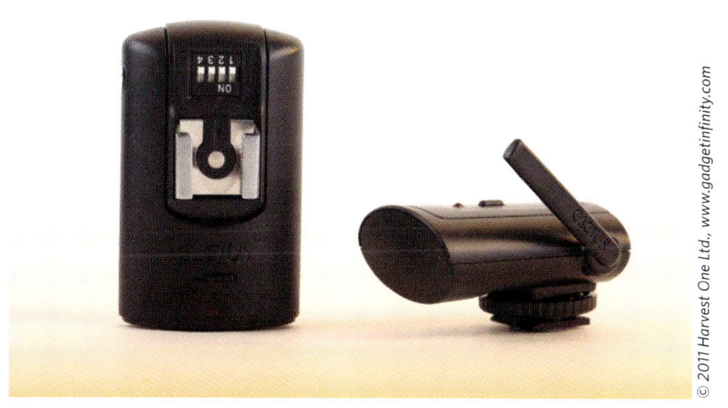

CACTUS V5 TRANSCEIVERS

Superior range, same high compatibility, and they fair much better outside due to the higher 2.4 GHz frequency. Price difference is negligible.

RADIO POPPER JRX

These little duders are pretty rad. Extremely high range. They also contain 16 channels, but range is no longer a question. This means they will not require line-of-sight for triggering, and sunlight distractions will not cause problems (as they sometimes can). They're compatible with both Canon and Nikon systems. I'd say these are highest on my recommended list, currently running around $80 US for the transmitter, $100 for each receiver, or $170 for the pair.

POCKETWIZARD PLUS II

Without a doubt, these are the most rugged. Any one I've ever owned, I've dropped on the street a dozen times, and they've continued to work. They're a little more on the expensive side, but you can count on these guys never failing you. They come with four channels, and they are compatible with anything that can take a PC cord, which unfortunately makes it more difficult to pair with flashes like the SB-700 or 430EX. They're currently running for $160 US each.

POCKETWIZARD FLEX

For those of you who grow money, or, you know, just have it for, like, burning purposes (it can get cold in the North), you should first consider donating to a charity. Clearly made it in life. But if you must buy the latest and greatest of flash equipment, this is what you should get. With Nikon and Canon compatibility only, these systems allow you to jump into a whole new world of high-speed sync beyond the usual 1/250th of a second sync speed, plus the ability to do remote TTL flash work (which is outside the scope of this book, but nonetheless a neat feature).

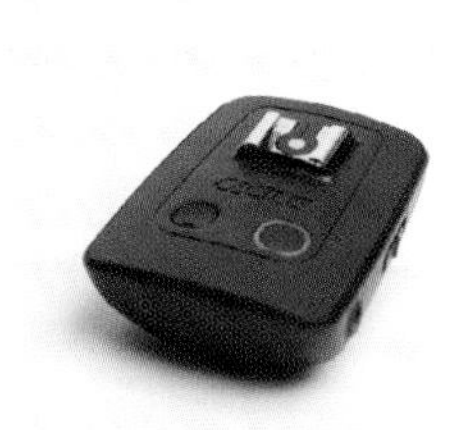

The Cactus V5 transceiver

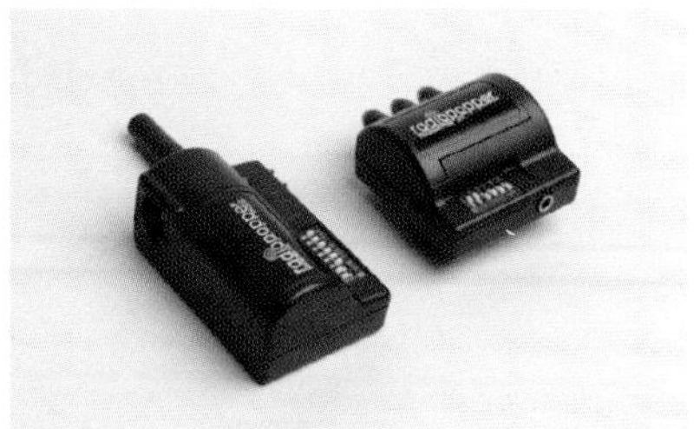

Radio Popper JrX units

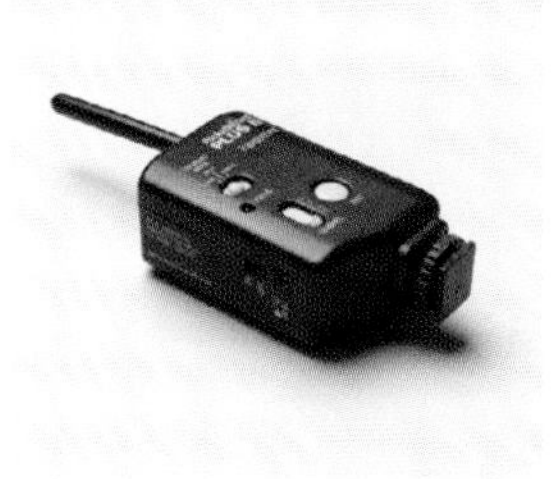

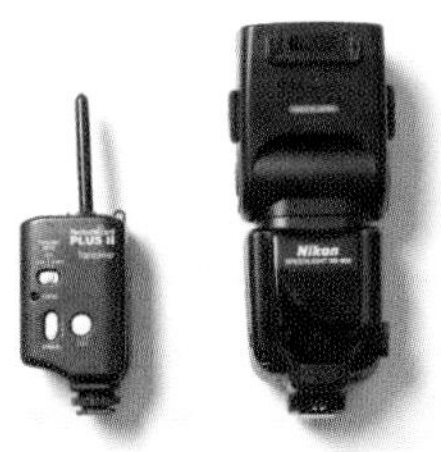

The PocketWizard Plus II, and shown next to a Nikon SB-900 for scale

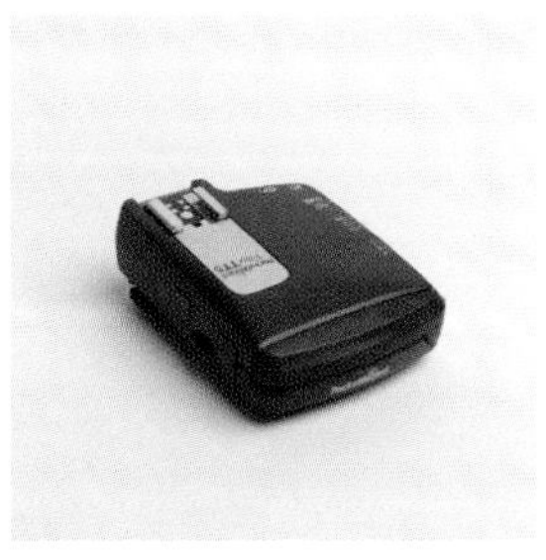

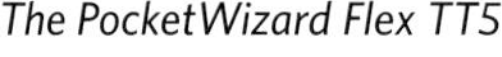

The PocketWizard Flex TT5

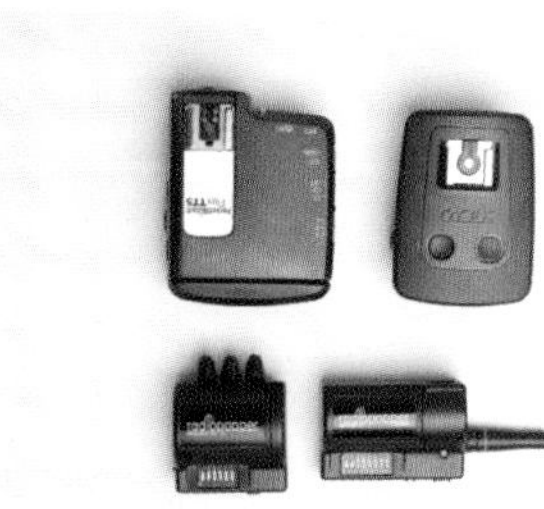

The PocketWizard Flex, Cactus V5, and Radio Popper units

LIGHT STANDS

Considering you've made your mind up on a flash and have the ability to trigger it remotely, you'll need a way to prop it up somewhere other than requiring a friend to hold it—not that forcing your friends to be human light stands is a bad idea. It's just that sometimes it's best to avoid treating your friends like objects, and you don't want to have that whole conversation, and it could get weird...but then later, after they finally agree to do it anyway, and they're not holding the flash right, and nobody is happy, and...yeah, it's a mess. You should just get some stands.

CALUMET 7' COMPACT STAND

Cheap, sturdy, does its job. Even fits in your standard school backpack. About $40 US. Do it.

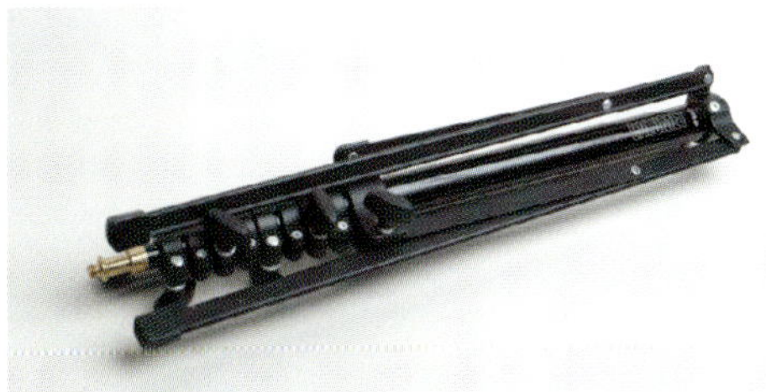

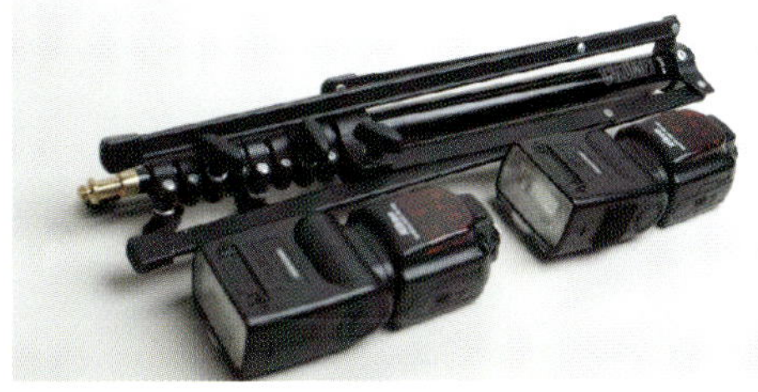

The Calumet 7' stand, shown with two SB-900 units for scale

MANFROTTO 6' NANO STAND

Perfect for street photography and traveling. Lightweight, sturdy, also fits in a backpack. Little bit more money. My personal favorite.

CALUMET 10' STAND

Because sometimes you need high lights. Ha ha ha. Get it?! I swear there is a joke in there somewhere. Okay, maybe not, but these are excellent for getting spotlights behind tall people or sticking in a corner at a wedding reception to spread light wide and far across large groups.

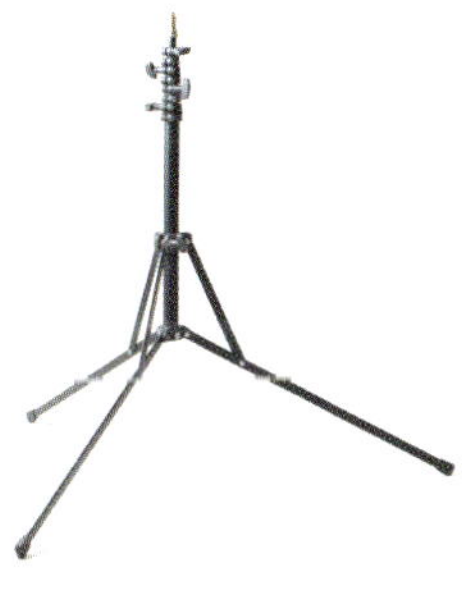

The Manfrotto 6' Nano stand

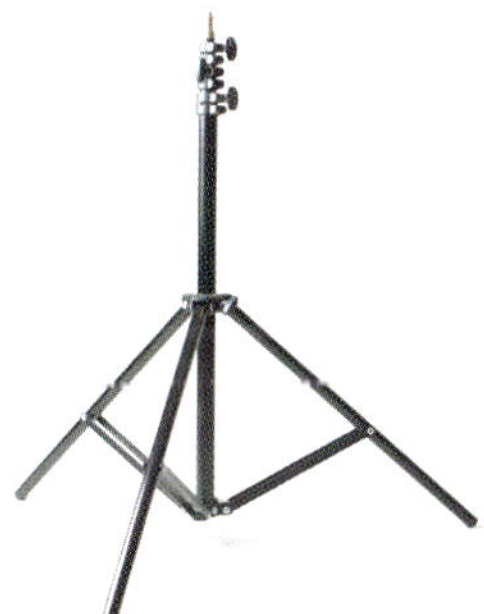

The Calumet 10' stand

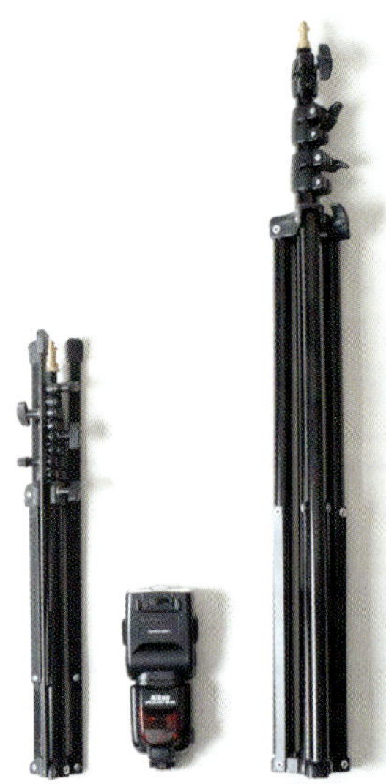

The Manfrotto 6' stand (left), an SB-900, and the Calumet 10' stand

MANFROTTO SUPER CLAMP

Don't leave home without it. You can clamp these guys on pretty much anything. Stop-sign poles, chain-link fences, regular fences, puppies, trees, you name it. They're also plenty useful for putting up in places where you normally wouldn't be able to stick a stand. I always put one in my bag—whether or not I use it—as they're quite the gem when the need arises.

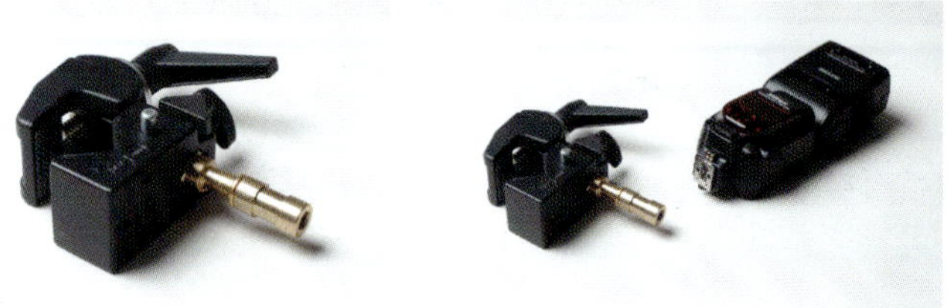

The Manfrotto Super Clamp

The Manfrotto Super Clamp, shown next to an SB-900 for scale

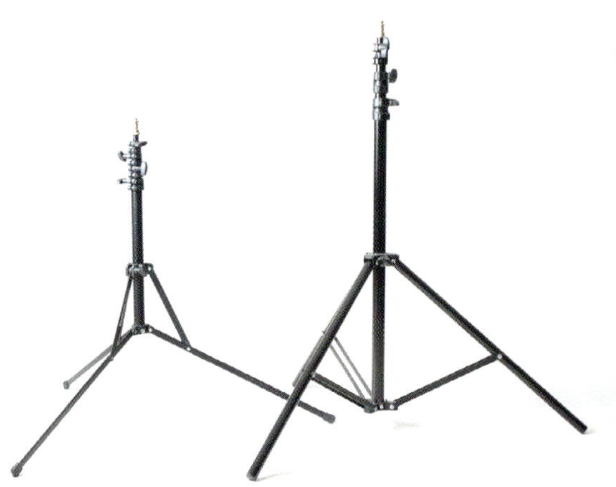

The Manfrotto 6' stand (left), the Calumet 10' stand (right)

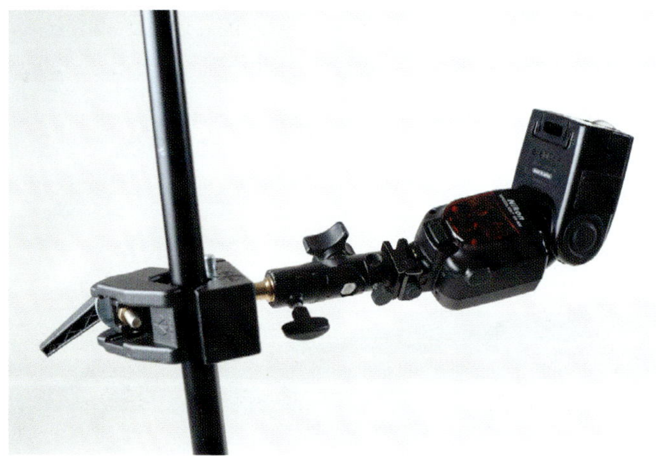

The Manfrotto Super Clamp in use

UMBRELLA ADAPTERS

These are perhaps one of the most crucial items to have, as they hold everything together, serving as the glue between the light stand, the flash, and its light modifier (umbrellas, softboxes, etc.). There are really only two types that I use.

CALUMET BASIC

These doodads (or doomoms, could you imagine? You're right, that doesn't make sense) are inexpensive, durable, and serve their purpose well. They swivel in one direction, mount to an umbrella shaft sans fuss, and can fit in your pocket, even for you hipsters in skinny jeans. They're also my personal favorite.

MANFROTTO SWIVEL

Because I feel the need to offer a second solution, if I had to pick anything beyond the first recommendation, the little Manfrotto swivels are nice. They provide less hassle on the shaft-tightening, and the swivel moves freely rather than the set-in-stone notches that the Calumet adapters have. But seriously, don't focus too much attention on seeking the perfect umbrella adapter. Any bells and whistles beyond "this thing holds a shaft and mounts a flash" is all fluff.

LASTOLITE TRIFLASH BRACKET

The TriFlash adapter is the real deal, once you're three speedlights in the hole. The main purpose of this amazing invention (aside from allowing you to place three lights on one adapter) is that you can now finally get softer light in bright environments, such as direct sunlight. Otherwise, for example, if you only have one light packed in a 50" softbox, it's unlikely you'll have enough power to beat the sun. But *three* at full power... yeah, do the math. Or not. But you get the point. You're now back in control and can worry less about Photoshopping blue skies to be blue.

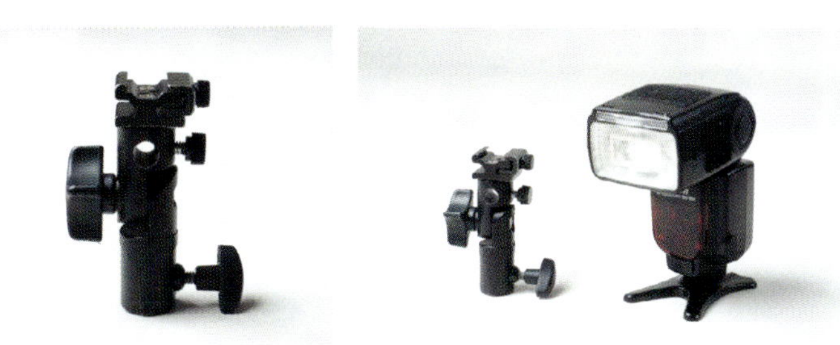

The Calumet umbrella adapter, and shown next to an SB-900 for scale

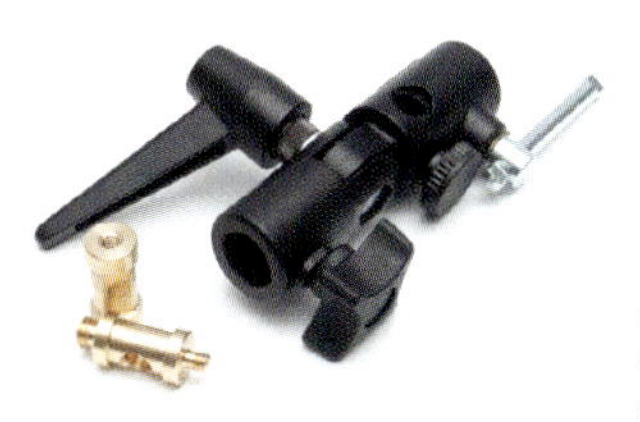

The Manfrotto swivel umbrella adapter

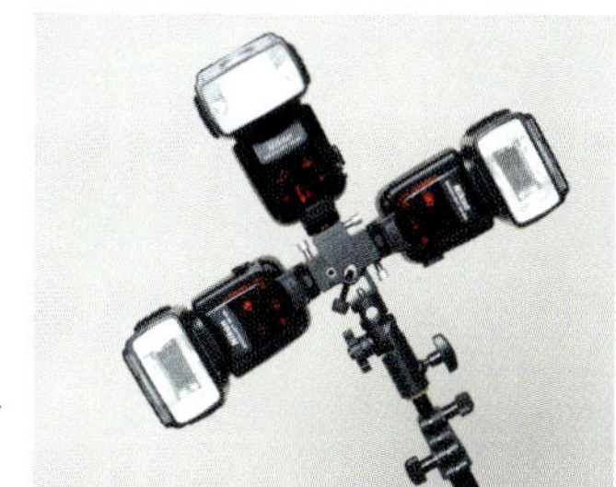

The Lastolite TriFlash bracket

LIGHT MODIFIERS

Admittedly, this part can get a little crazy. Here lies the most options—along with a slew of marketing to confuse buyers as much as they can as to why Company X's light modification system makes the best, most beautifully lit photos of all time. "Purchase now and get a free actress." As a matter of fact, my advice is to avoid anything with the word "system." Yeah. That sounds like a safe bet. Nevertheless, here are a few that I've found useful for one purpose or another.

43" COMPACT UMBRELLA

This staple umbrella is simply a must. Do yourself a favor and buy two or three to start, even if you only have one flash. They're the perfect single portrait-sized umbrellas, providing sufficiently even, soft, round lighting, and their lightweight, compact size easily allows you to pack a few of them into your bag. Beware, these fall like milk, so don't cry when you watch one spill to the ground (Seriously, you gotta admit that one was pretty original.) Okay, point being, they can bend and get wonky when the wind takes control. Luckily, however, they're cheap—almost always under $20 US.

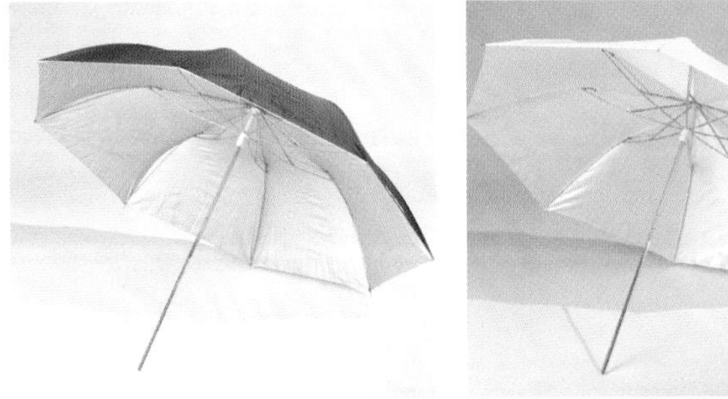

The 43" umbrella, shown as both a reflective (left) and a shoot-through (right) umbrella

45" UMBRELLA

I can't entirely explain what it is about the extra two inches, but something magical happens. The light is softer, and curves come out rounder. Note that this umbrella will not fit in a regular backpack. However, it collapses down much nicer when focusing light onto a human face. Take special note when seeing a collapsed umbrella in various setup shots throughout the book. This umbrella is my personal favorite.

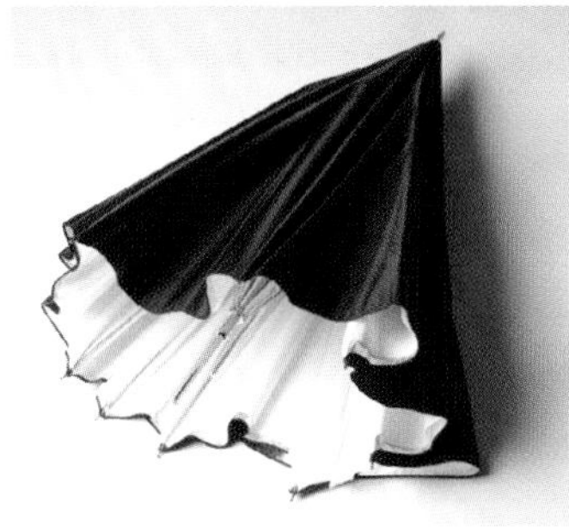

The 45" umbrella, collapsed down

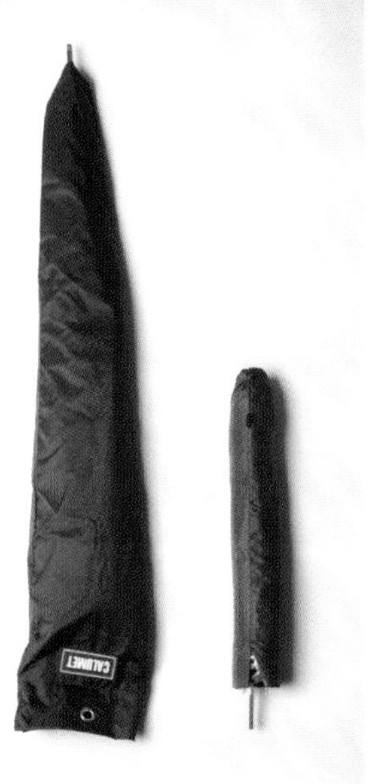

The 45" umbrella, all packed up (left), next to the 43" umbrella (right)

60" UMBRELLA

The biggest umbrella you'll want/need. Without question, scientifically speaking, for softer light you need bigger apparent light sources. This umbrella is the go-to umbrella for soft, beautiful, fashionably well-rounded light. Also useful for lighting multiple people.

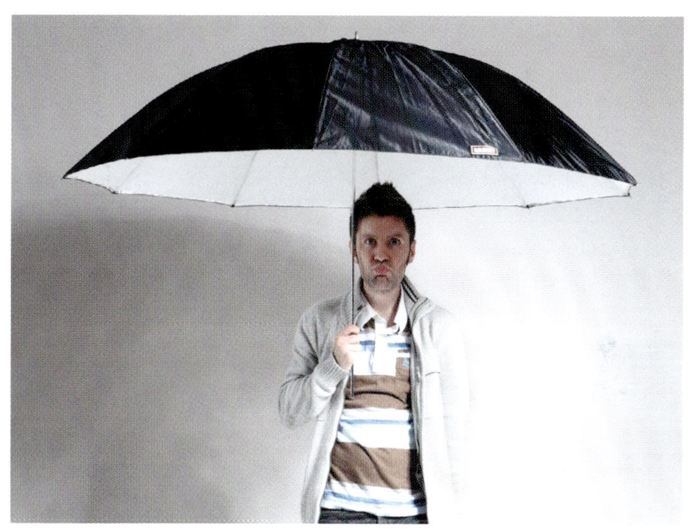

The 60" umbrella

REFLECTORS

The silver reflector is for all those times you need just a smidgen extra of light, and not cause a catastrophic light spill all over a room. I'll often use this massive silver-dollar lookin' thing to fill in what would otherwise be a complete light falloff into the shadow of darkness. That's not to say a complete fade to black couldn't get edgy, sexy, or mysterious—but sometimes it's nice to know the second half of someone's face still has a human shape.

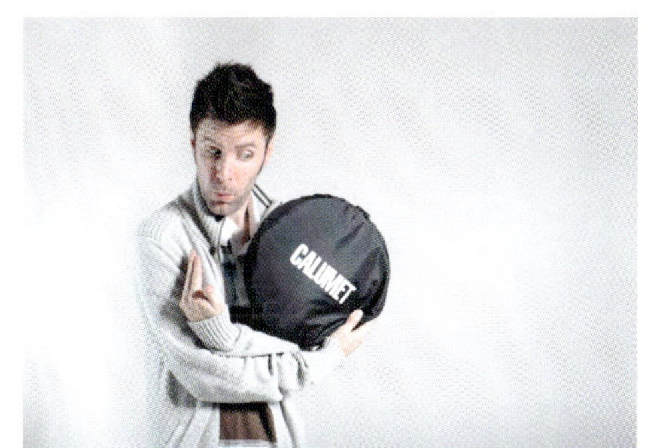

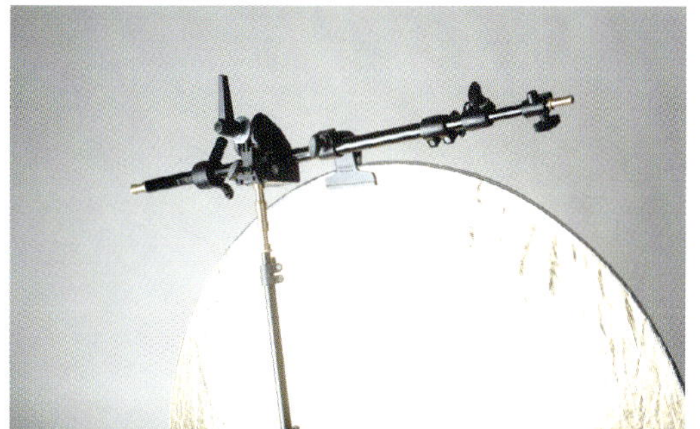

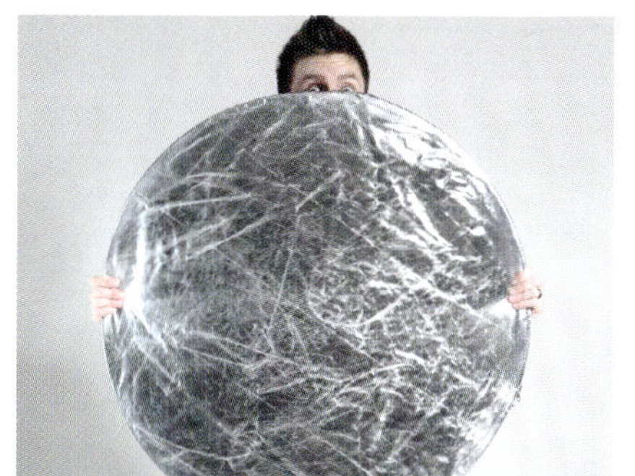

A Calumet 42" reflector, shown packed up, mounted, and expanded

28" WESTCOTT SOFTBOX

This one is a beauty. It's great for traveling, and it contains an umbrella shaft, which allows you to pair it with your speedlight, unlike most other softboxes that require mounting "systems" (see, I told you, avoid "systems"). As an aside, some of my best work came as a product of the 28" softbox. Excellent for single-person half-body portraits.

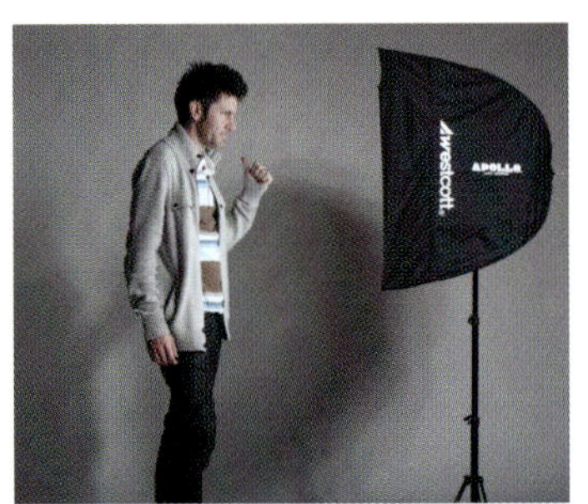

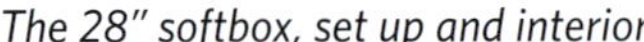

The 28" softbox, set up and interior

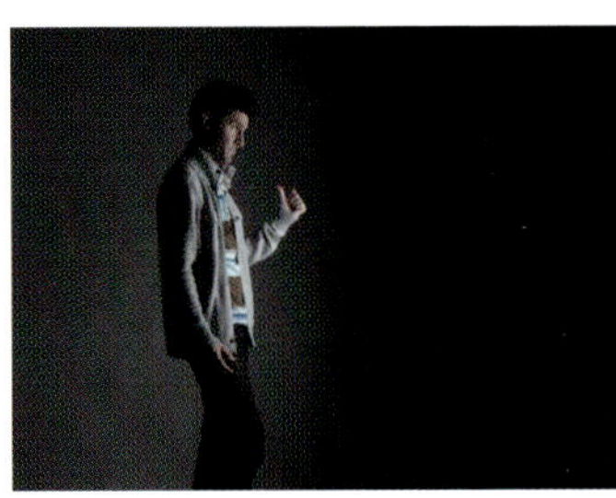

The 28" softbox's directional light

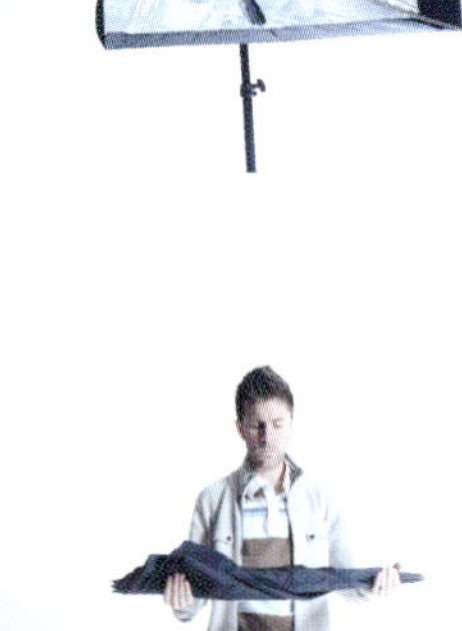

The 28" softbox, packed up

50" WESTCOTT SOFTBOX

Useful starter fact: I can fit inside one of these. No joke. It would make for a nice mini-fort if I were still a child. Unfortunately, the cost will probably make you think twice before you retrofit this piece of lighting equipment as a base for setting up camp. Nevertheless, on the brighter side (yes, the puns don't stop!), the 50" big mama is truly one of the most fun softboxes to conjure up scenes with. Using this modifier allows you to achieve large, soft, and directional lighting that would otherwise spread far and wide with an umbrella.

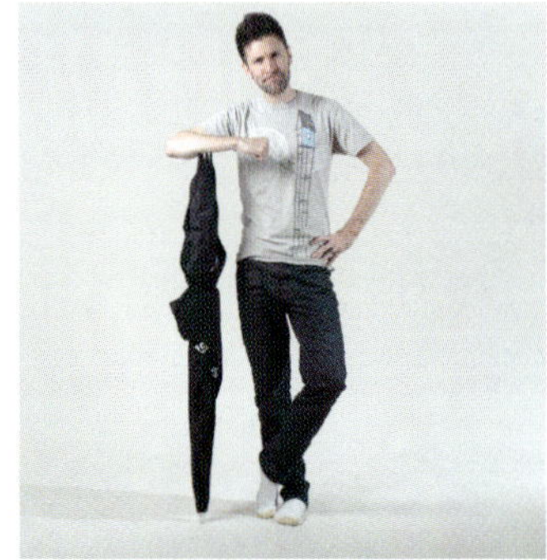

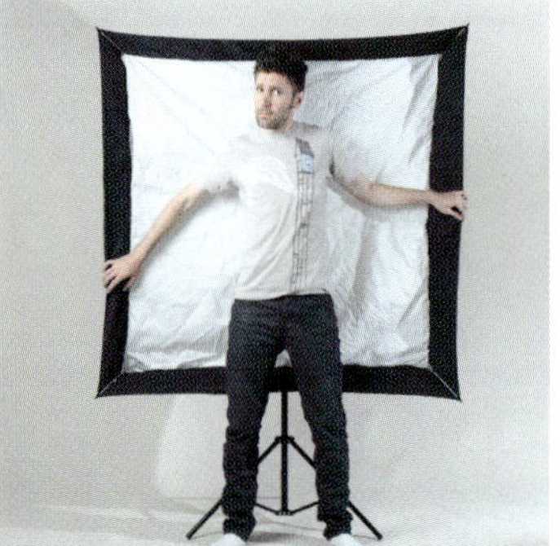

The 50" Westcott softbox, shown when not in use, and when set up

HONL 8" SOFTBOX

The 8" softbox is a pretty sweet deal, and it can fit in your Trapper Keeper. It doesn't slide through your umbrella adapter shaft like most other light modifiers, but rather it sticks right onto your speedlight with some extra (provided) Velcro. In technical terms, it's the first light modifier that's a step away from not having one at all (bare bulb). Another benefit of the 8" softbox is that you can take it outside in the windy winds and not worry about getting owned by the Mary Poppins effect.

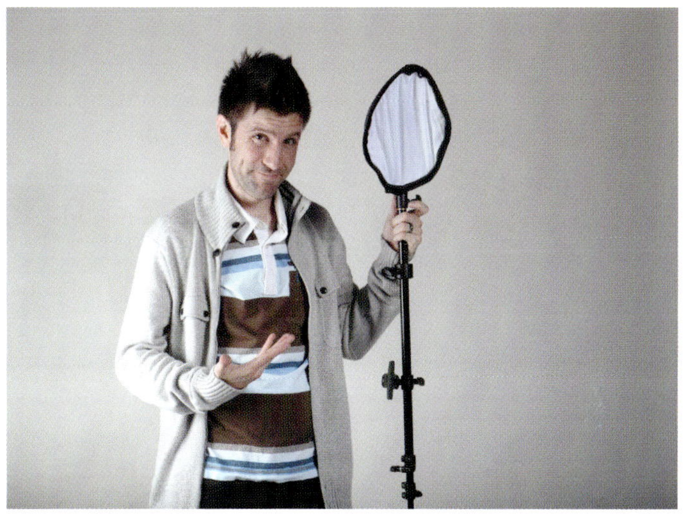

The Honl Traveller8 softbox

GRID SPOTS

Honestly, there's a bit too much in the snoot, gobo, and grid scene. With that in mind, there's only one that I've ever bothered using, the Honl 1/8" Speed Grid. Basically, it's useful for putting a tightly focused spotlight on an area. More than usually, it's for creating backlight on a wall behind a person or for creating rim light to hit the sides of people. And, of course, the anti-use of the grid spot would be setting it directly in front of your subject as a main (key) light. Don't get me wrong; people do it. I'm just not a fan, artistically speaking.

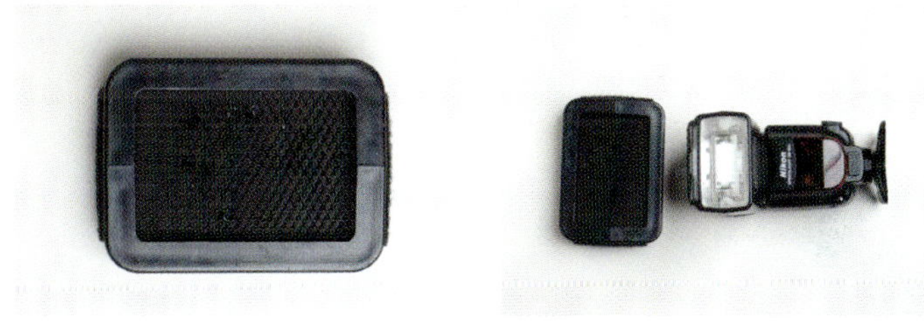

The Honl 1/8" Speed Grid, and shown next to a Nikon SB-900 for scale

BUYING ADVICE

Without a doubt, all of this can seem like a bottomless pit that you can drop your money into when taking a jump into buying all this "stuff." However, consider this: If you started with the basics, which includes a flash, stand, adapter, umbrella, and a pair of triggers, you can walk away with a $400 solution. Then think for a moment how much your next lens or camera might cost you. $500? $1,000? $2,500? More? Bring justice to your photography bag and invest in lights first! After all, the camera you have is probably fine, and that all-purpose lens currently mounted to your camera is doing a great job. So get your bargain-hunting skills on, and chase after the light into your heavenly future. And any more cheesy one-liners I write into this book won't help anyone.

two! Understanding Light Travel

Admittedly, one of the most boring subjects in photography is the inverse square law. Matter of fact, it shouldn't even be a thing. Most people don't even know it's a thing, but it's a thing. So deal with it. And with that in mind, before you begin scratching your head and yelling out, "The inverse-jigga-whu?" and "Who put science in my art?!"...just hold on a sec.

Learning the inverse square law is a lot like riding a bike. No. Scratch that. Riding a bike is easy. Matter of fact, if you can't ride a bike, put this book down and learn that instead. So really, it's more like learning how to drive a car. It takes some time, concentration, and getting used to. Then, before you know it, you're not thinking about driving; you're just moving forward, next to other cars, slightly altering your direction from left to right, all while playing your favorite music and chatting with your friends.

Therefore, you do not need to memorize the physics of future time-travel to begin taking pictures, or even to become a professional. But for anyone with an SLR who truly wants to master all the variables in an exposure, you should at least know about the "inverse square law" and have a good sense of how it works. And, of course, the main reason to know about this law (if you haven't figured it out already) is for when you make the dive into flash photography.

So, if you're one of those who claim, "I don't shoot with flash, I only use available light," then have fun on your little pedestal making up excuses on why you pretend not to be interested in flash photography. Sure, your brand-new top-of-the-line Canon or Nikon with a 50mm f/1.4 lens is going to destroy the darkness with stunning images at ISO 3200, but we are talking about well-lit professional studio portraiture/magazine quality photography that utilizes flash to create amazingly sharp, colorful, vibrant, beautifully lit photos. Not to mention, your flashes are "always available"—use them to your advantage.

Alright, now that we have that out of the way, let's look at some basics that we might already know.

SHUTTER SPEED, APERTURE, AND ISO SENSITIVITY

SHUTTER SPEED

By now, everyone knows that the longer the shutter speed, the more light you let in. Inversely, the faster the shutter, the less light you let in. And, of course, stops of light (in terms of shutter speed) work in factors of two. That means if you double a shutter speed of 1/100, it becomes 1/50. That is "one stop of light" brighter. Inversely, if you cut it in half from 1/100 to 1/200, you have made your exposure "one stop darker."

Great, let's move on.

APERTURE

We should all have our f-stops memorized. If not, it's a simple scale where we can double our numbers, starting at f/1, and each time we double, we will increase by two stops of light. Therefore:

1 → 2 → 4 → 8 → 16 → 32

To calculate our increments in between those two-stop jumps, we simply multiply each stop by the magic number 1.4 (which is, coincidentally, the rounded number of the square root of 2 [which is roughly 1.414]). This makes our first stop easy: 1 x 1.4 = 1.4! We can now fill in our gaps accordingly!

1.0 → 1.4 → 2 → 2.8 → 4 → 5.6 → 8 → 11 → 16 → 22 → 32

We now have an aperture scale displaying full one-stop increments. Just for kicks, let's have a brief look at what a classic 1/3-stop aperture scale looks like (since many of you will be working with these numbers on your SLR):

...1.4 → 1.6 → 1.8 → 2.0 → 2.2 → 2.5 → 2.8...

Okay, I get the aperture numbers. Remind me of the exposure relationship?

Let's say we had a correct exposure of 1/125 at *f*/8. Your model sitting there patiently is waiting for their beautiful portrait to be taken. You (the photographer) have made a design decision to go for a more shallow depth of field. So you drop your aperture to *f*/4. That's two stops of light brighter: *f*/8 → *f*/5.6 → *f*/4. So to compensate, you speed up your shutter by two stops: 1/125 → 1/250 → 1/500. Easy peezy, makes sense, been there done that.

ISO SPEED

We all know that our lowest ISO produces our cleanest files. Our light stops will look fairly similar and our ISO scale usually looks something like this:

100 → 200 → 400 → 800 → 1600

Some of the latest cameras go up to crazy ISOs like 25,600, which is four stops brighter than ISO 1600!

Jumping quickly back to our example, if we were originally at ISO 400 and needed to drop two stops of light, we could have simply gone from ISO 400 → 200 → 100.

OKAY, NOW WHAT ABOUT THIS FLASH THING?

Flashes have stops of light, too! Like shutter speed, these stops of light are measured in half increments. This is what we call the *flash power*, or rather, how much light it spits out. Our scale looks like this:

1/1 → 1/2 → 1/4 → 1/8 → 1/16...

From left to right, we say *full power*, *half power*, *quarter power*, etc. Some flashes can let out light as dim as 1/128 (the SB-800/900 and the Canon 580EX II can do this).

One of the main things you should consider when buying a flash is to look at how powerful it is. Meaning, "How bright will this be at full power compared to this other flash at full power?" We can tell how powerful they are by looking at the flash Guide Number (GN). This number is extremely important to know when buying a flash. Almost nearly as important as knowing how many millimeters your lens is. For example, you wouldn't go out and buy a 200mm lens without knowing it's, well, 200mm! Right?

WHAT IS A GUIDE NUMBER?

In simple mathematical terms, it is the aperture multiplied by distance, in which your flash can properly expose a subject at a given distance (aperture and distance). The standard Guide Numbers you should be looking for are measured at ISO 100 (film speed), at the 35mm head position, at full 1/1 power.

Ummm...wha?

Let's take a basic Nikon flash, for example. The SB-700 has a GN of 92. To make our math easier, we'll round it off to 100. Let's take a look at our diagram to see what this means. We have a flash and a subject. They are 20 feet apart in distance.

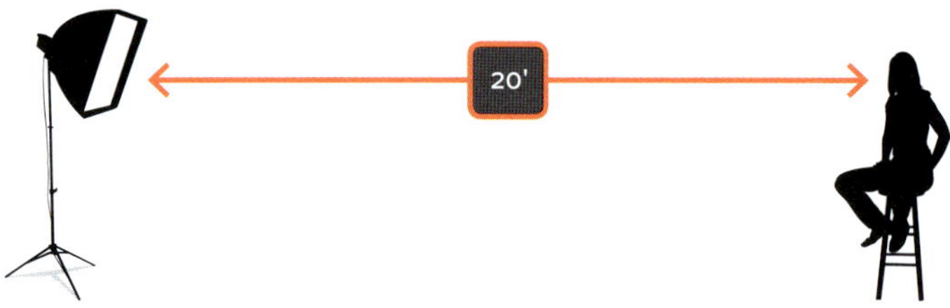

To properly expose our subject, we would need an aperture of *f*/5. Why? Because *f*/5 × 20' = 100 GN.

Now what happens if we move our subject 20' further away:

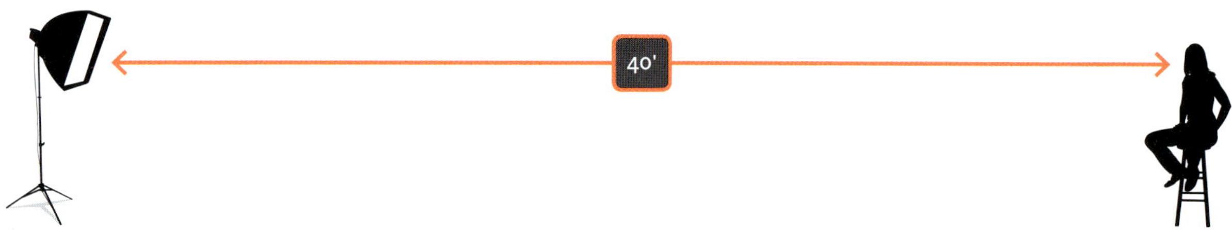

To compensate for this additional distance, we would need to let in more light! This means we'll have to open up our aperture to *f*/2.5: *f*/2.5 × 40' = 100 GN.

If we kept our aperture at *f*/5, we would underexpose our subject. Likewise, if we opened up our aperture too much—for example, to *f*/1.4—we would overexpose our subject. Got it?

OKAY, I'M READY FOR THAT INVERSE SQUARE THINGY

Well, no better time than now. The inverse square law states:

The intensity of light radiating from a point source is inversely proportional to the square of the distance from the source.

Therefore, an object twice as far away receives only one quarter the amount of light. Or if it's twice as close, then it's four times as bright. Each of these is a difference of two stops.

This is confusing, I know. I'm not a math major and I didn't fully understand it the first time, either.... (I guess because I'm not a math major, nor a philosophy major for that matter.) But luckily, and coincidentally, we already know a little about this already with our aperture scale. Know this:

Light has "depth" in the same way that our focal plane does.

By now you know that the closer you get to an object, the shallower your depth of field looks, which allows us to conclude that all the objects behind your subject "quickly fall out of focus." This same exact rule applies to light. (Thank heavens!) Let's look at a simple example, and we'll use the numbers on our aperture scale to make it easy.

In this illustration, we added a background:

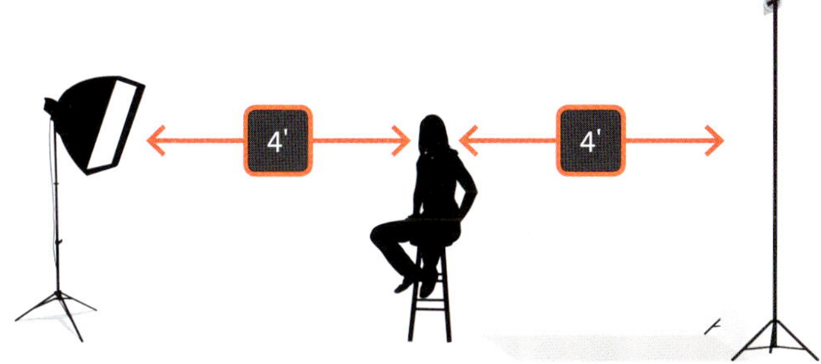

Let's assume these settings:

- ISO 100
- *f*/4
- Flash is at 1/4 power

It is safe to assume that our background is two stops underexposed: 4' → 5.6' → 8'. Now what if we moved our subject two feet closer toward the flash?

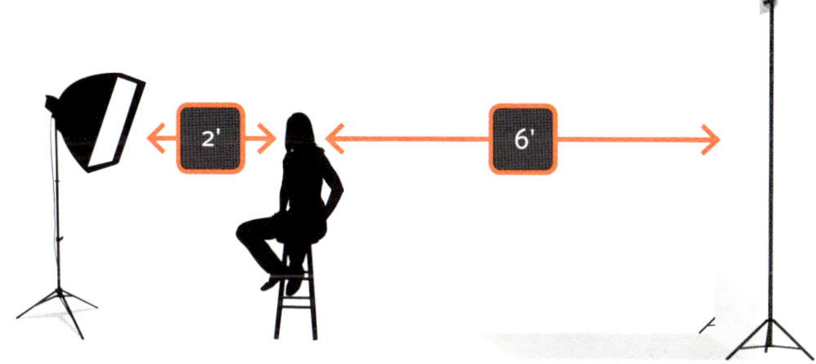

Since we just moved our subject "twice as close" we made it two stops brighter! Therefore, to make up for this overexposure, we need to do one of two things:

- Dial down the flash two stops: 1/4 → 1/8 → 1/16, or
- Close down the aperture: f/4 → f/5.6 → f/8

Each will keep your subject properly exposed, but it's an artistic decision for you to make if you want to keep your shallow depth of field (the first option), or remove more ambient light and get a slightly sharper image (the second option). Also, pay close attention that due to the inverse square law, our background is now four stops underexposed: 8' → 5.6' → 4' → 2.8' → 2'.

RIGHT ON. SO NOW WHAT?

So you learned to drive a car, now all you need to do is go on a road trip. Take what you know, run a few red lights, make mistakes, try it again, get it right. Plus, there is no such thing as *right*. So just do what looks good. After a while you'll be driving your camera in full manual alongside a dozen speedlights, not even knowing you're shifting gears.

Thus, the best place to start is to go with your gut and adjust from there. It's pretty rare that you walk into a new environment and automatically think, "Oh yeah...*f*/5.6 at ISO 400 with my two lights at eighth power with quarter CTO gels." If you're that good, then perhaps it's time to step back and focus on the art of photography and just try random new settings you would have never thought of. But in the meantime, you know you picked up this book to learn some new stuff—so let's go with that for now. And with that, go forth and light the way... or be a shining star...or come up with a better closer than this. Anything that makes this final sentence less awkward. Anything. I believe in you.

three! This Is Strobist® Info

You've now arrived at the part of the book where you can skip to any page you want. With that in mind, use each photo as a guide to provide means to your own ends. So get out there, take some pictures, rock the lights and...*oh my gosh I sound like every other photographer giving advice!*

Oh well, I tried. Good luck, and may the schwartz be with you.

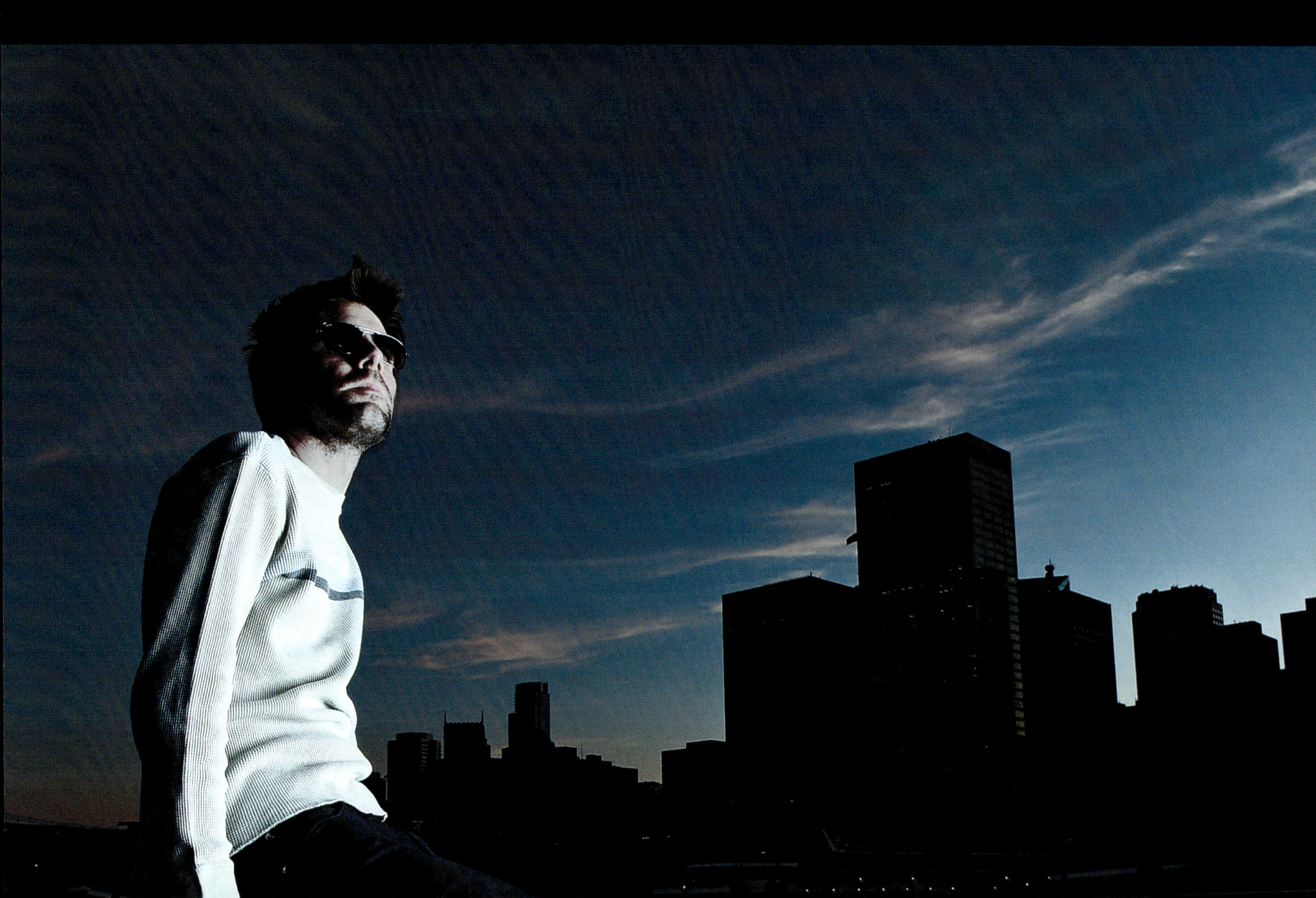

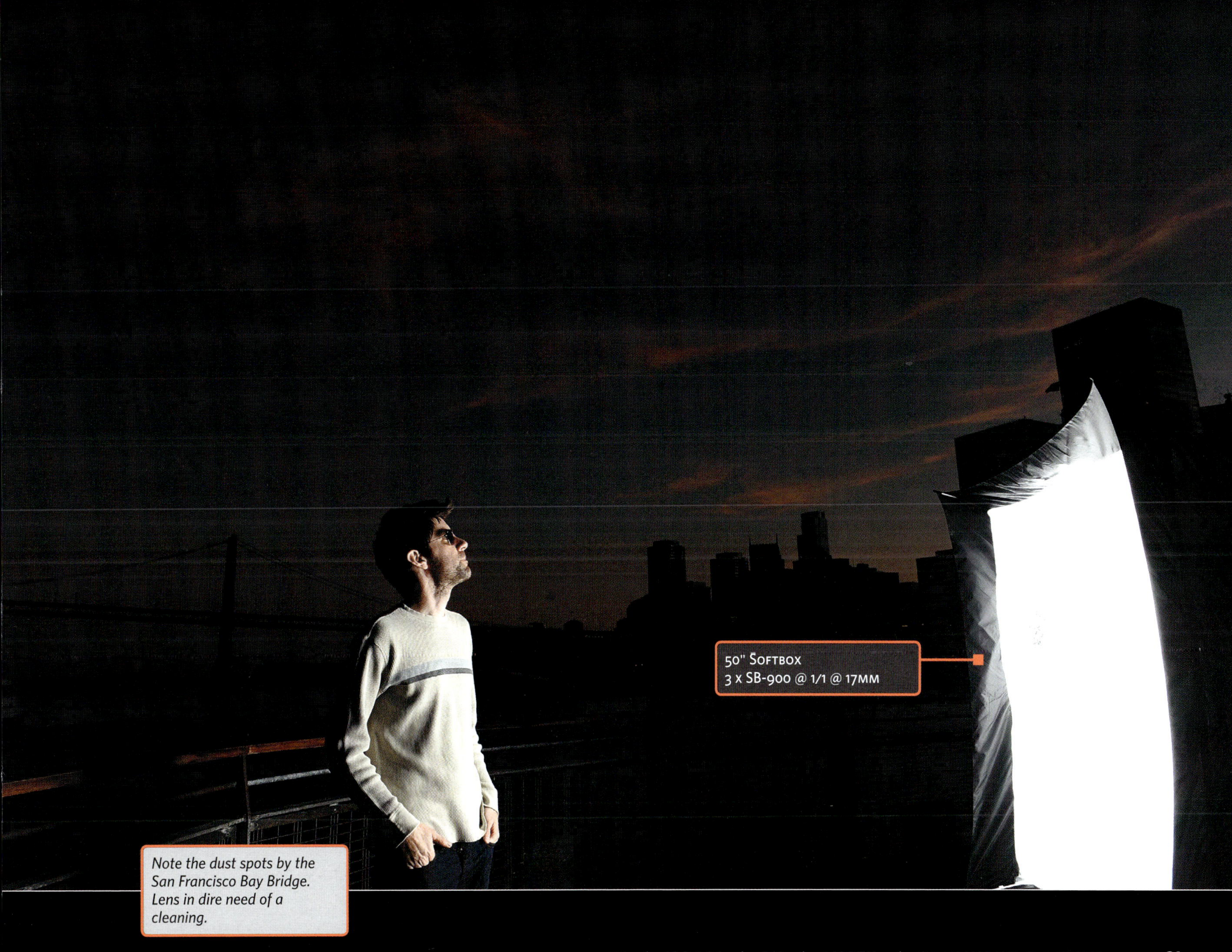

Note the dust spots by the San Francisco Bay Bridge. Lens in dire need of a cleaning.

D3 | ISO 200 | F/8 | 1/80TH | 24-70MM F/2.8 @ 24MM

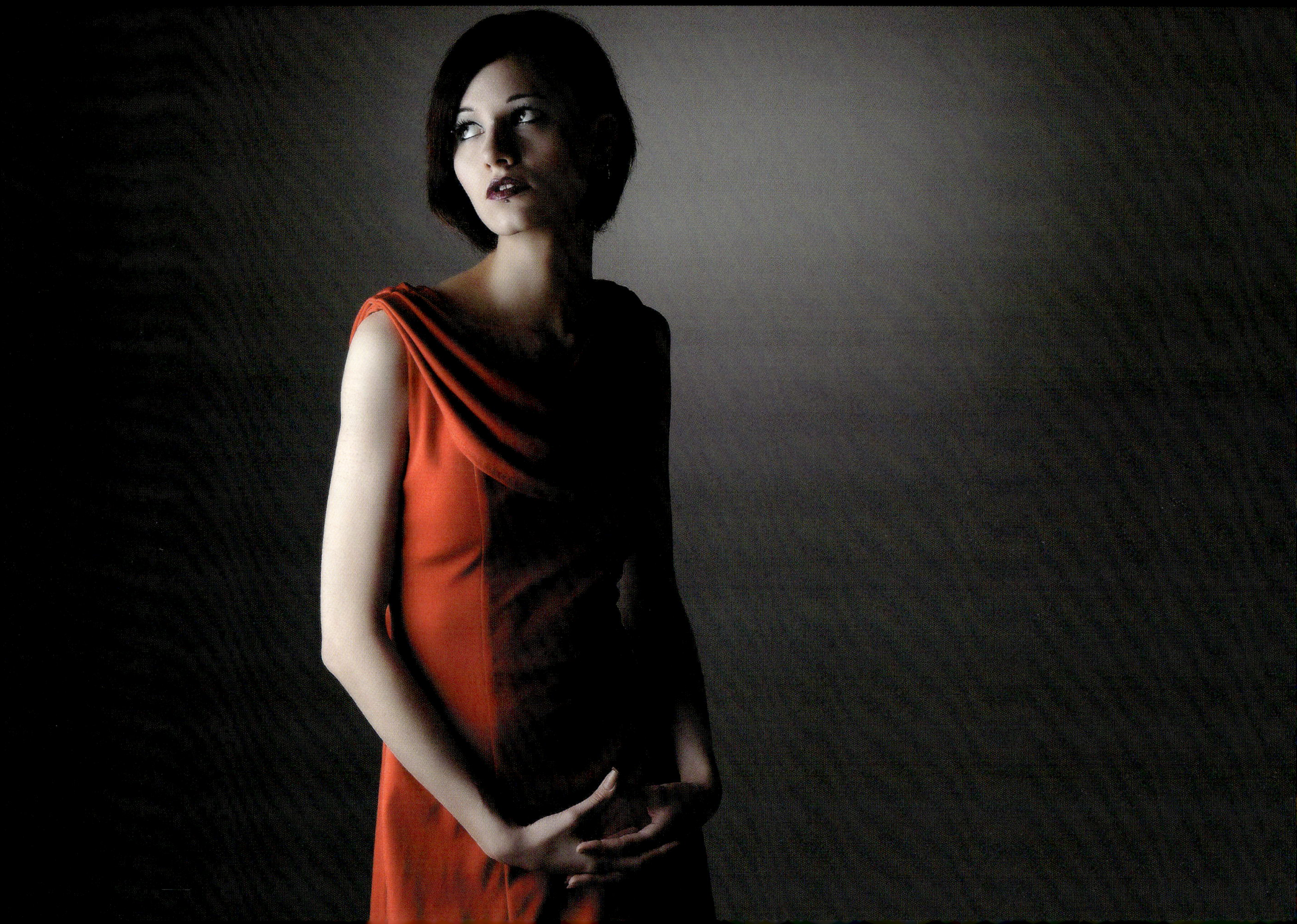

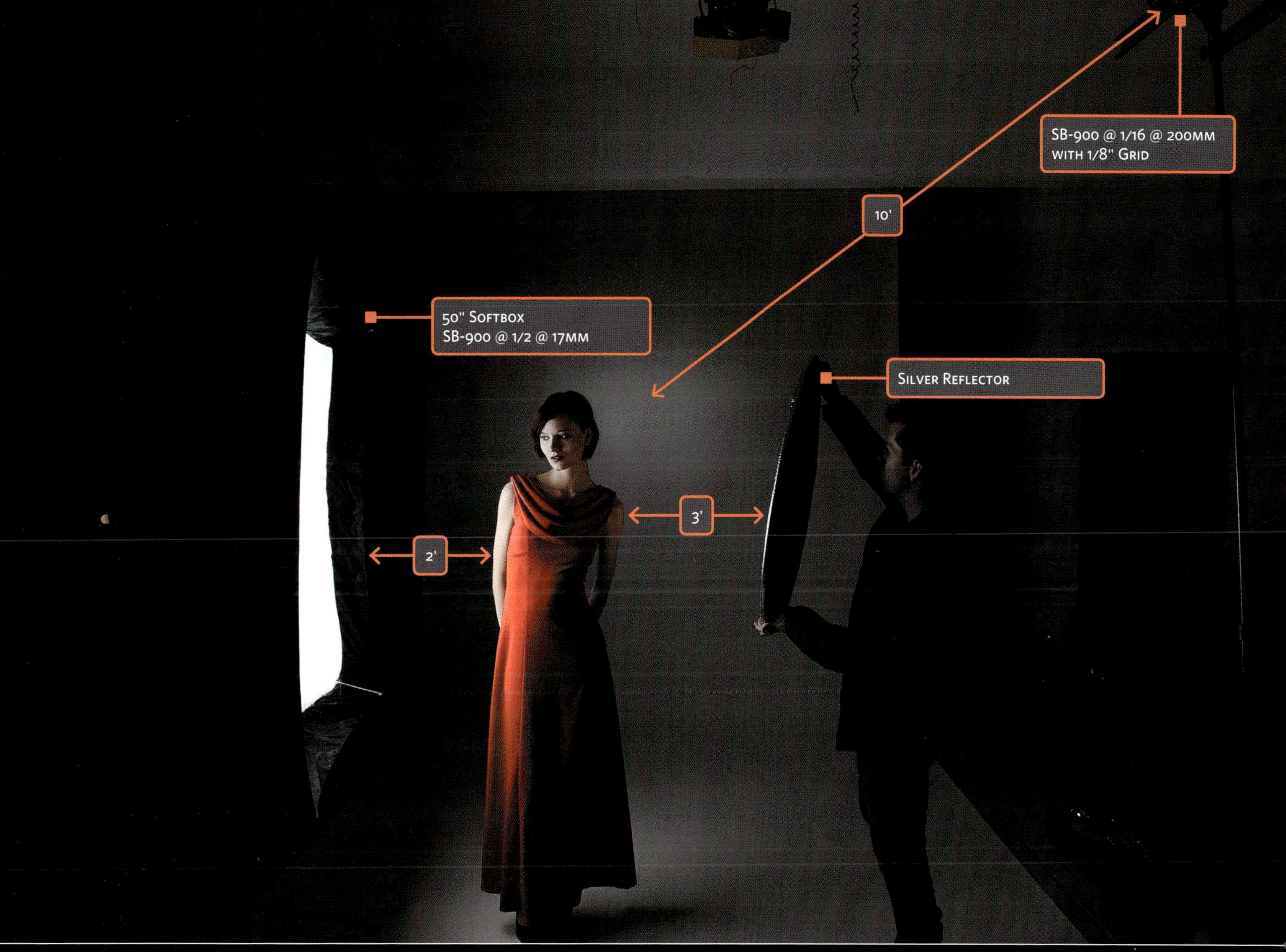

D3 | ISO 250 | F/7.1 | 1/250TH | 24-70MM F/2.8 @ 70MM

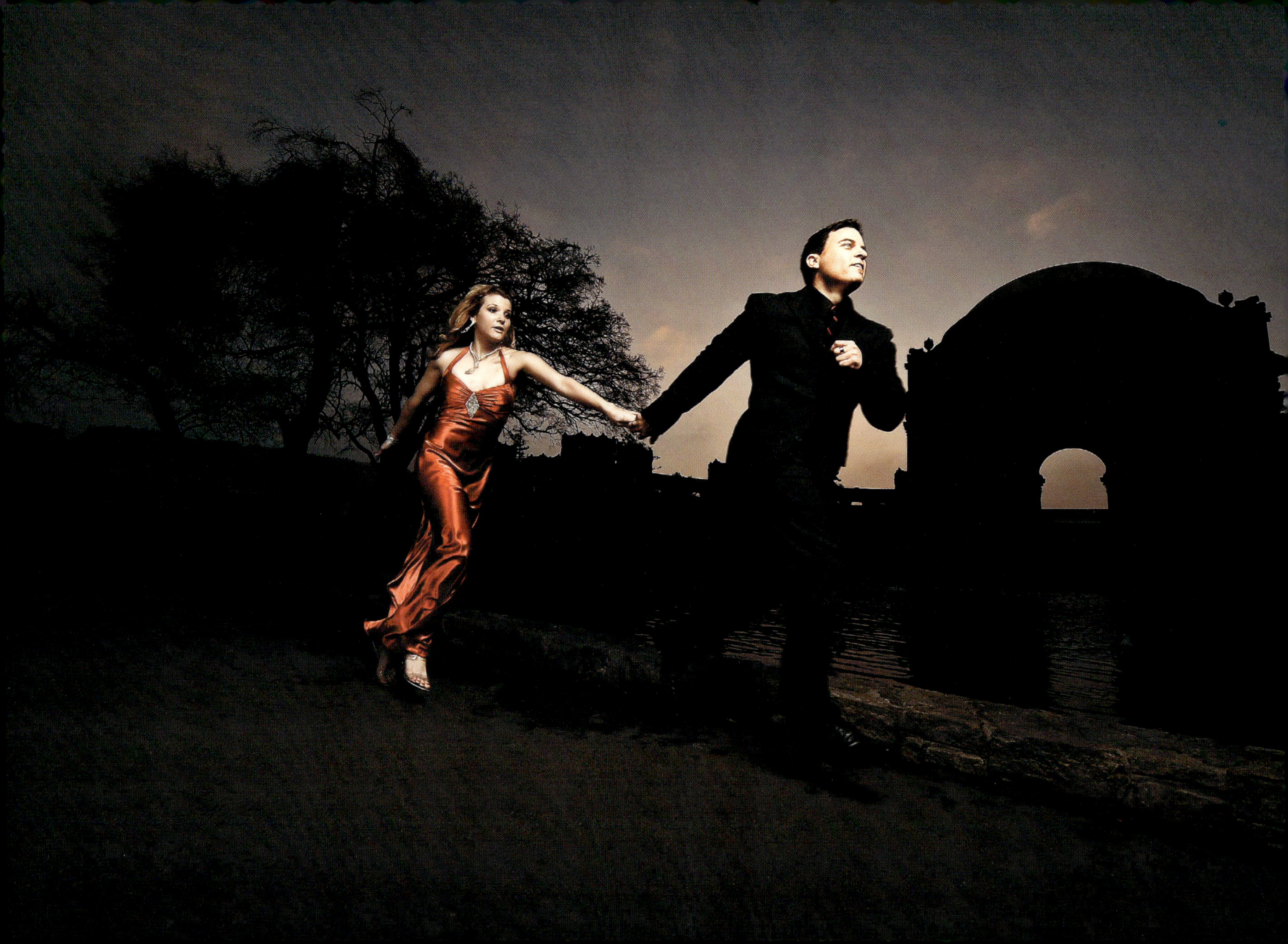

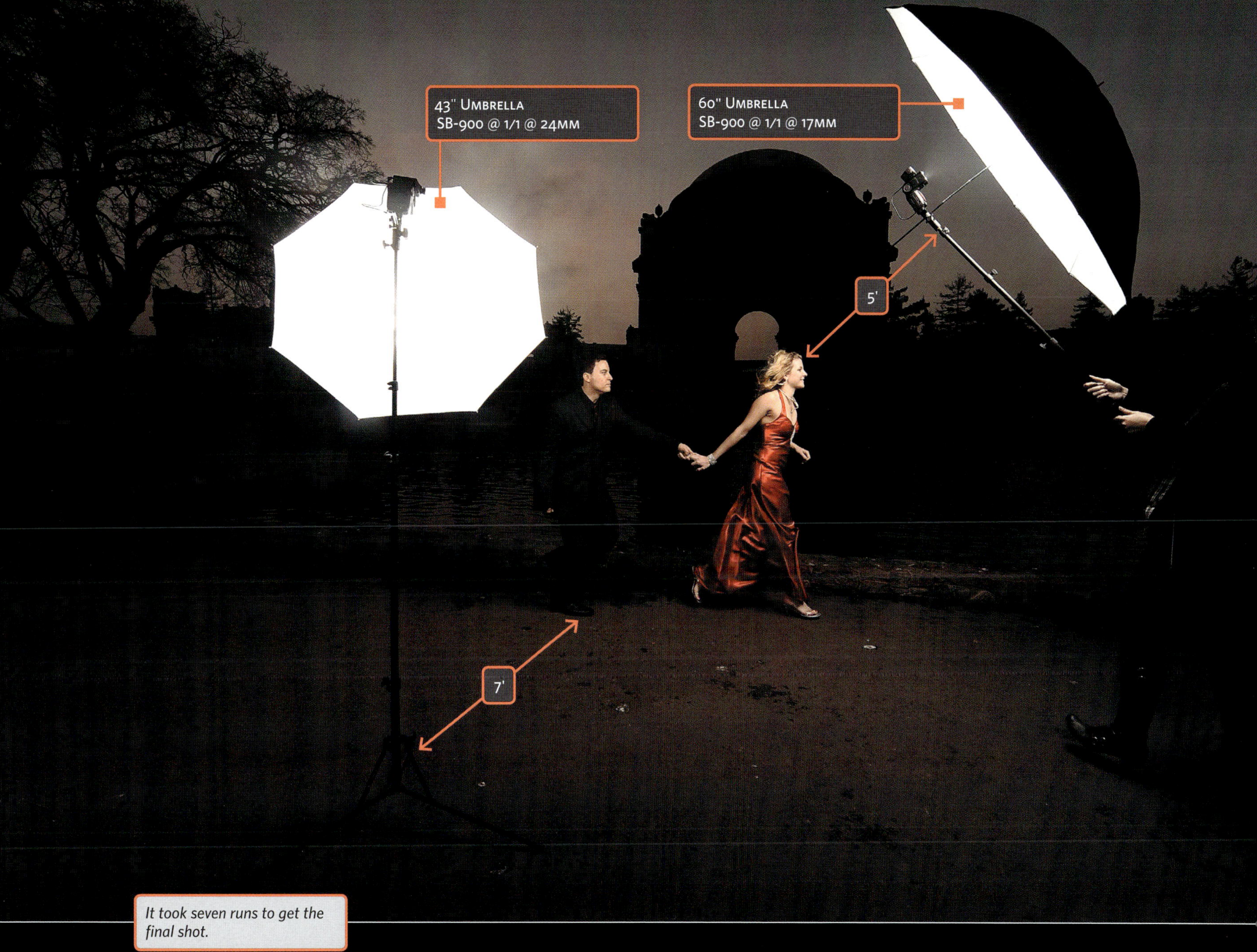

It took seven runs to get the final shot.

D3 | ISO 100 | F/6.3 | 1/250TH | 14-24MM F/2.8 @ 14MM

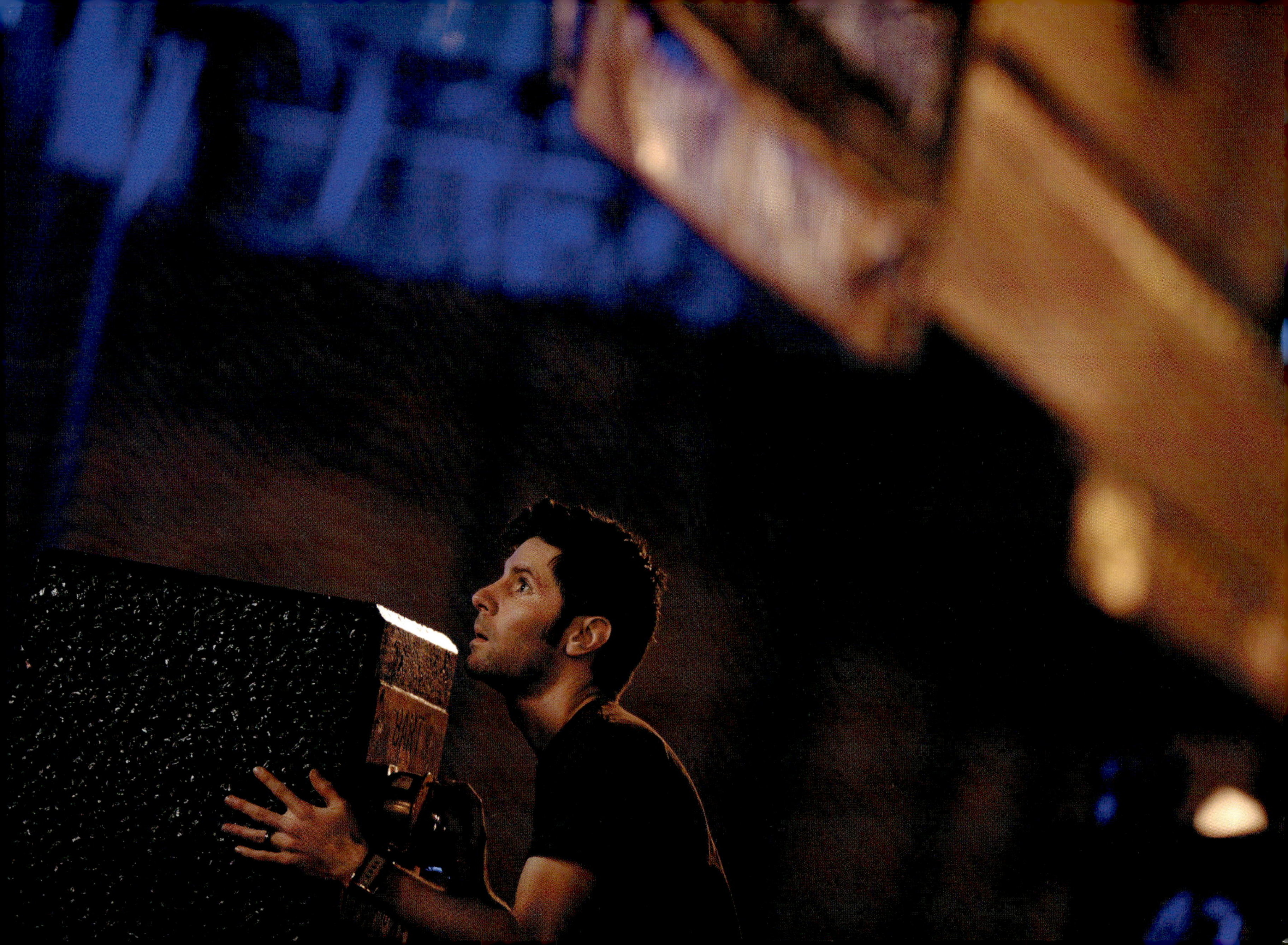

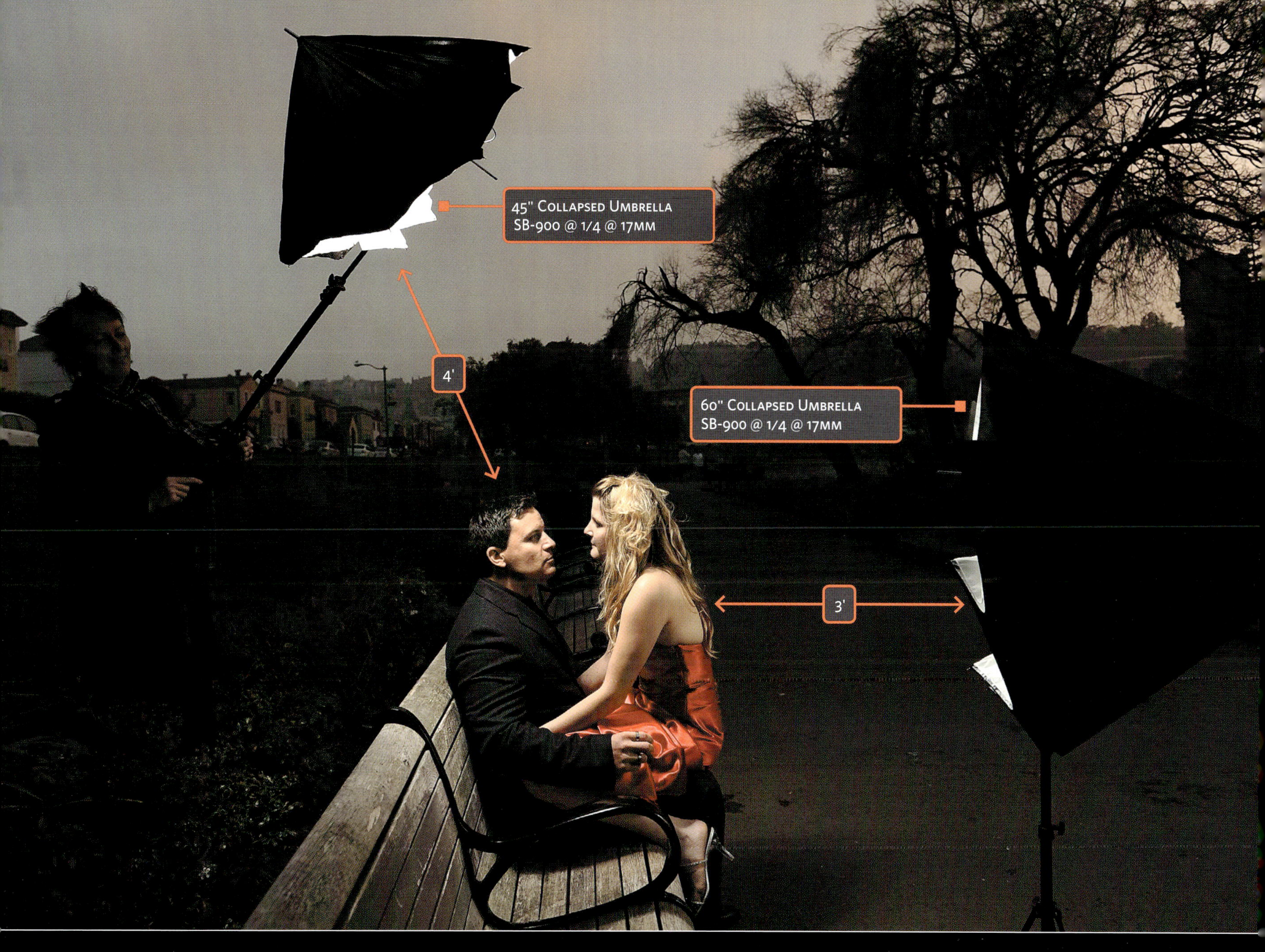

D3 | ISO 100 | F/3.5 | 1/250TH | 85MM F/1.4 @ 85MM

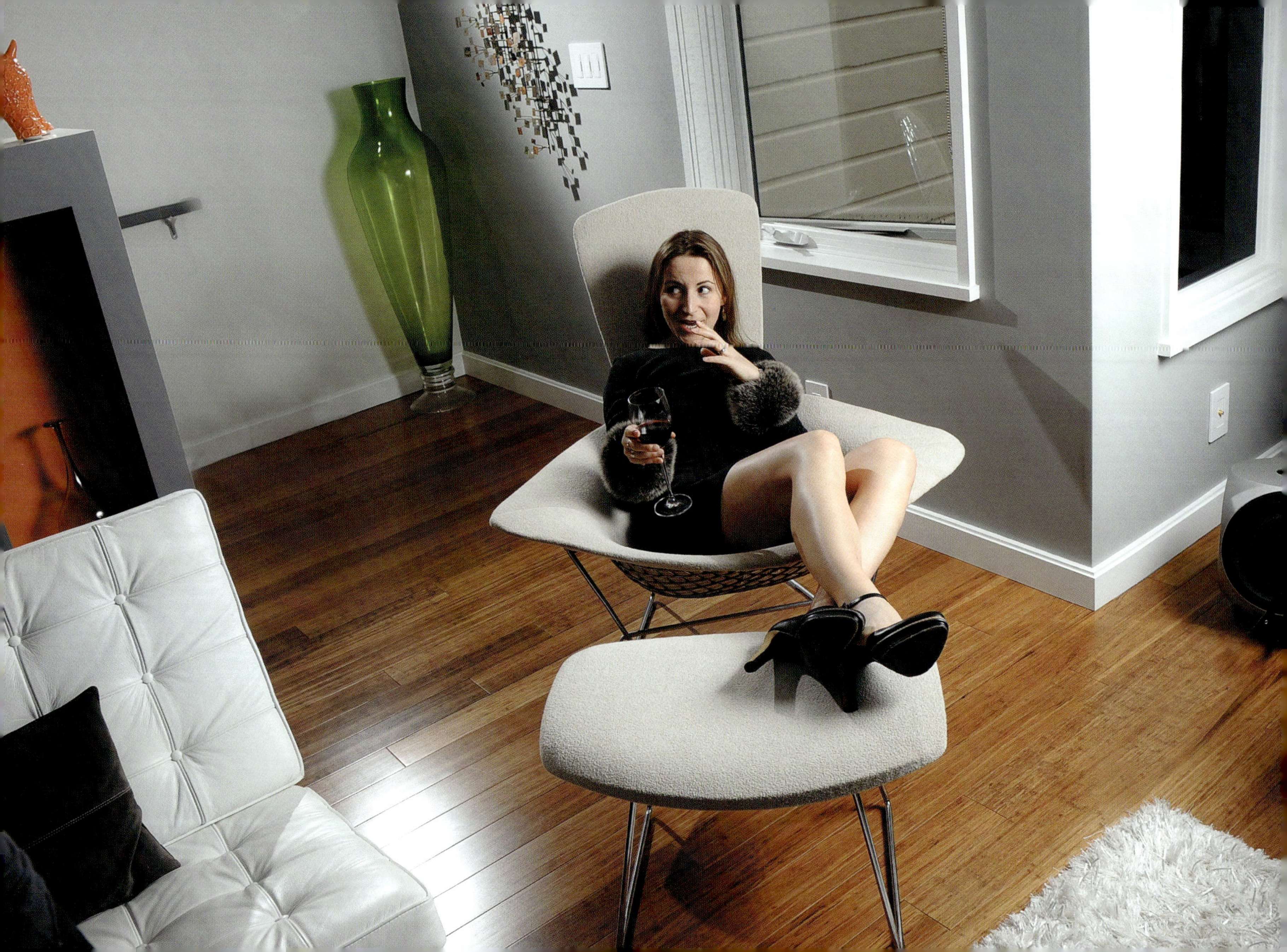

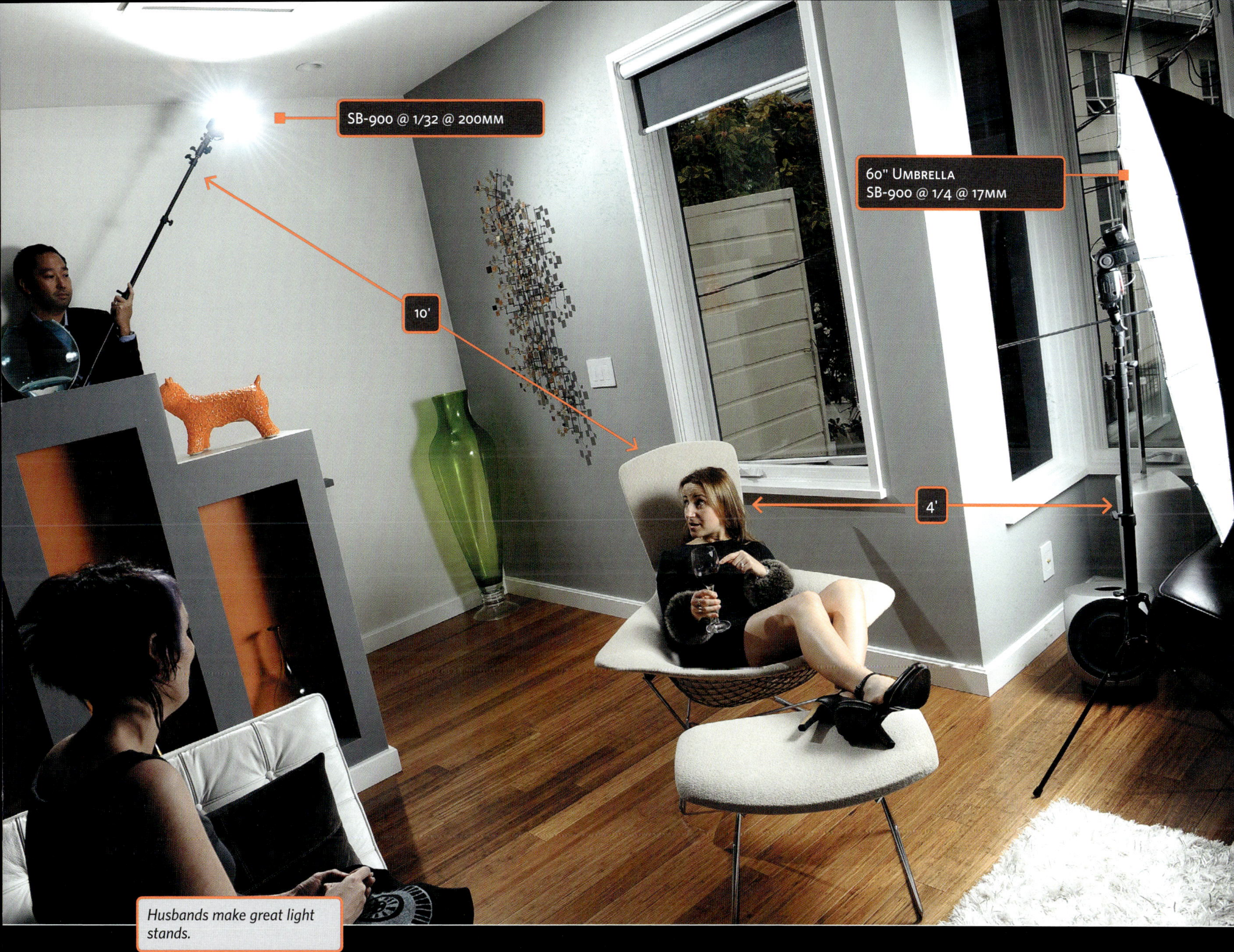

Husbands make great light stands.

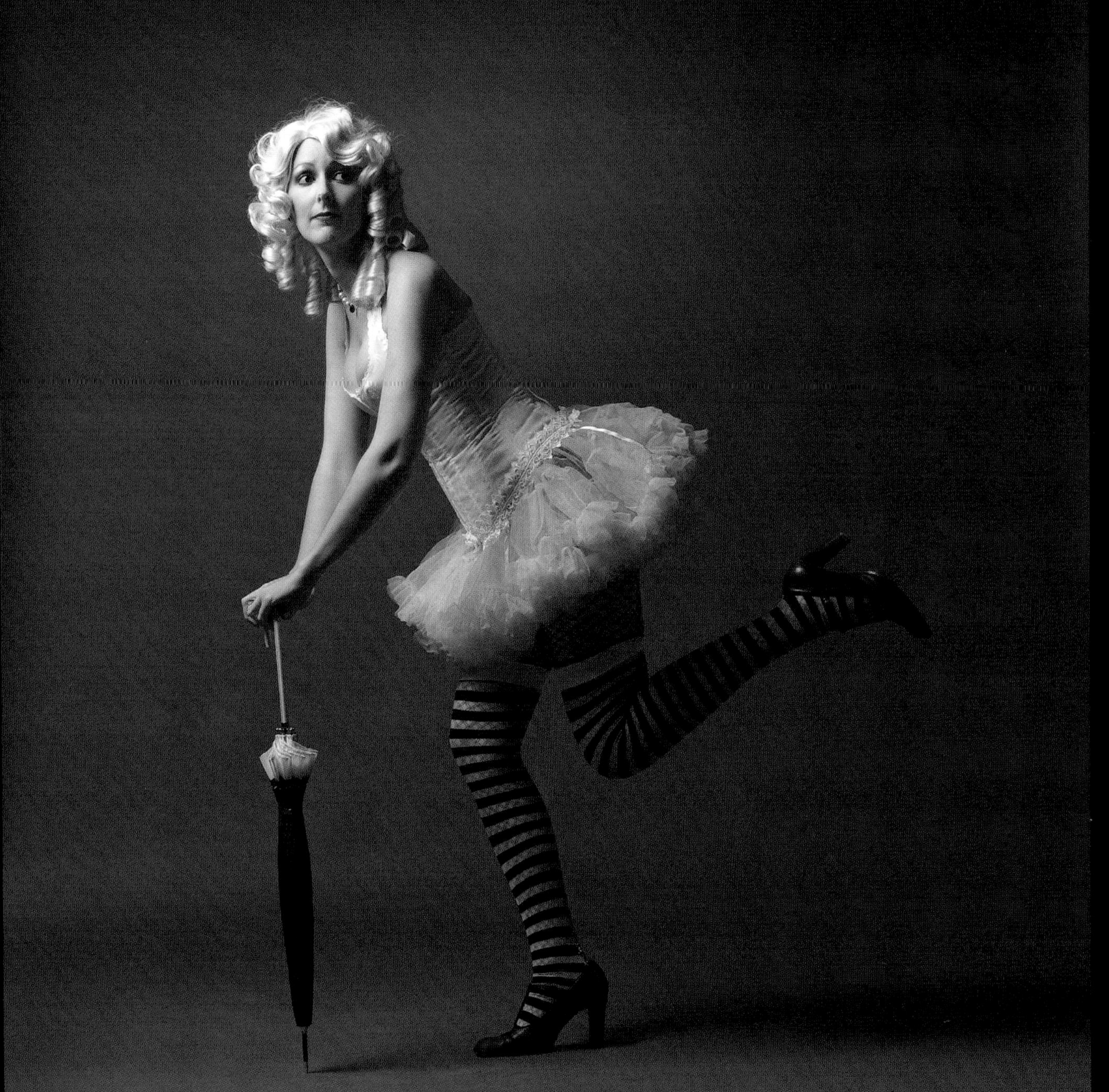

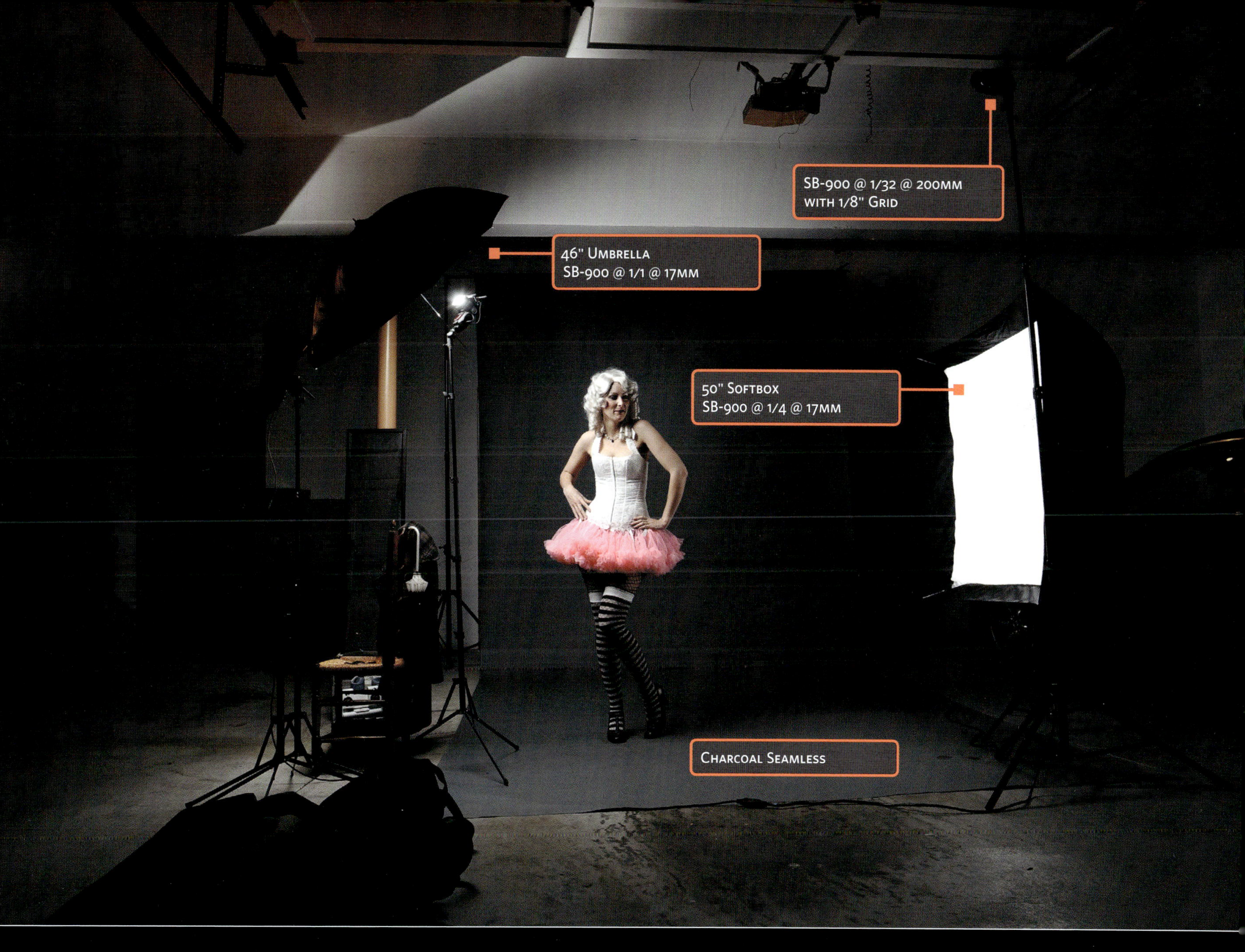

D3 | ISO 250 | F/7.1 | 1/100TH | 24-70MM F/2.8 @ 70MM

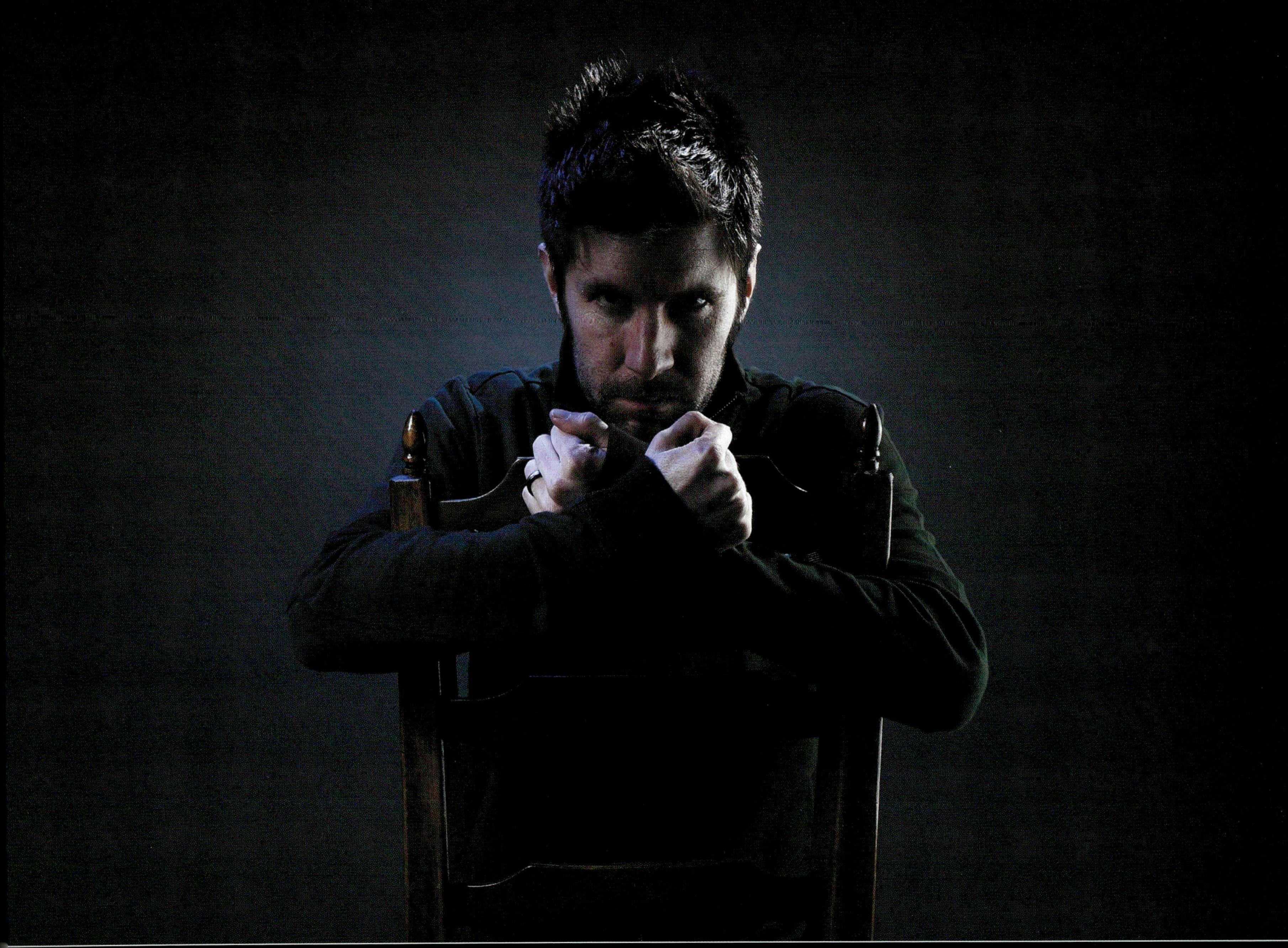

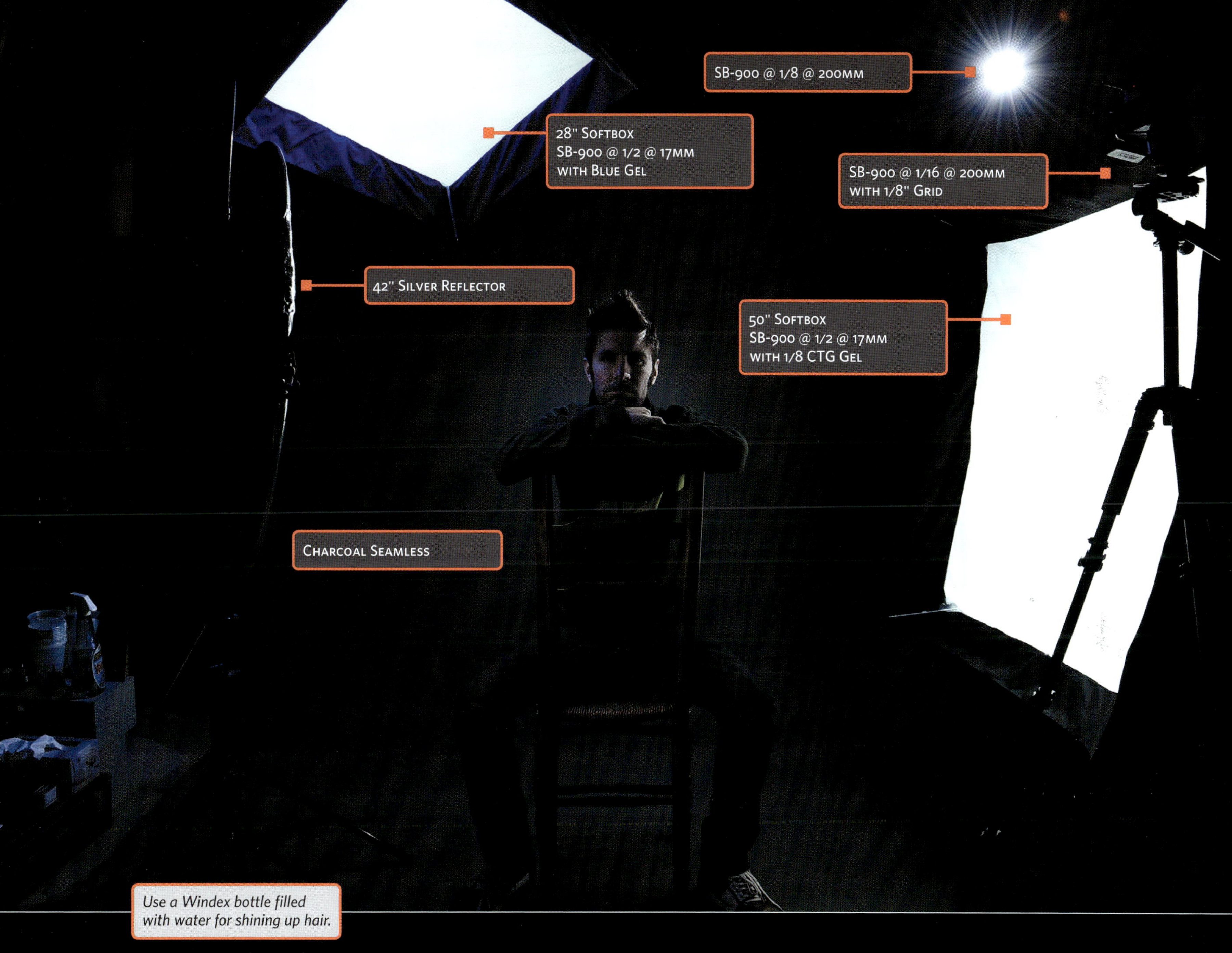

Use a Windex bottle filled with water for shining up hair.

D3 | ISO 200 | F/8 | 1/200TH | 24-70MM F/2.8 @ 70MM

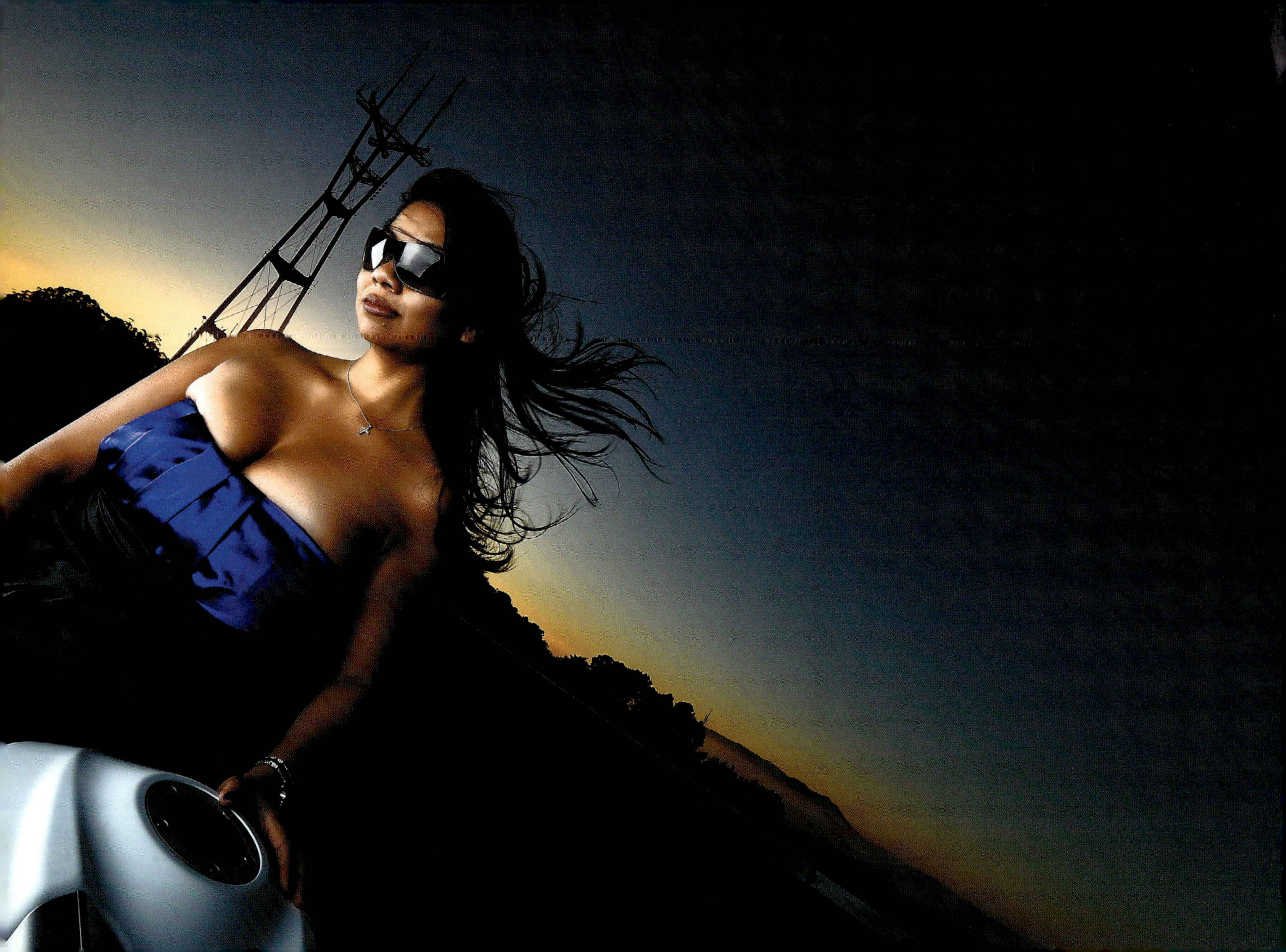

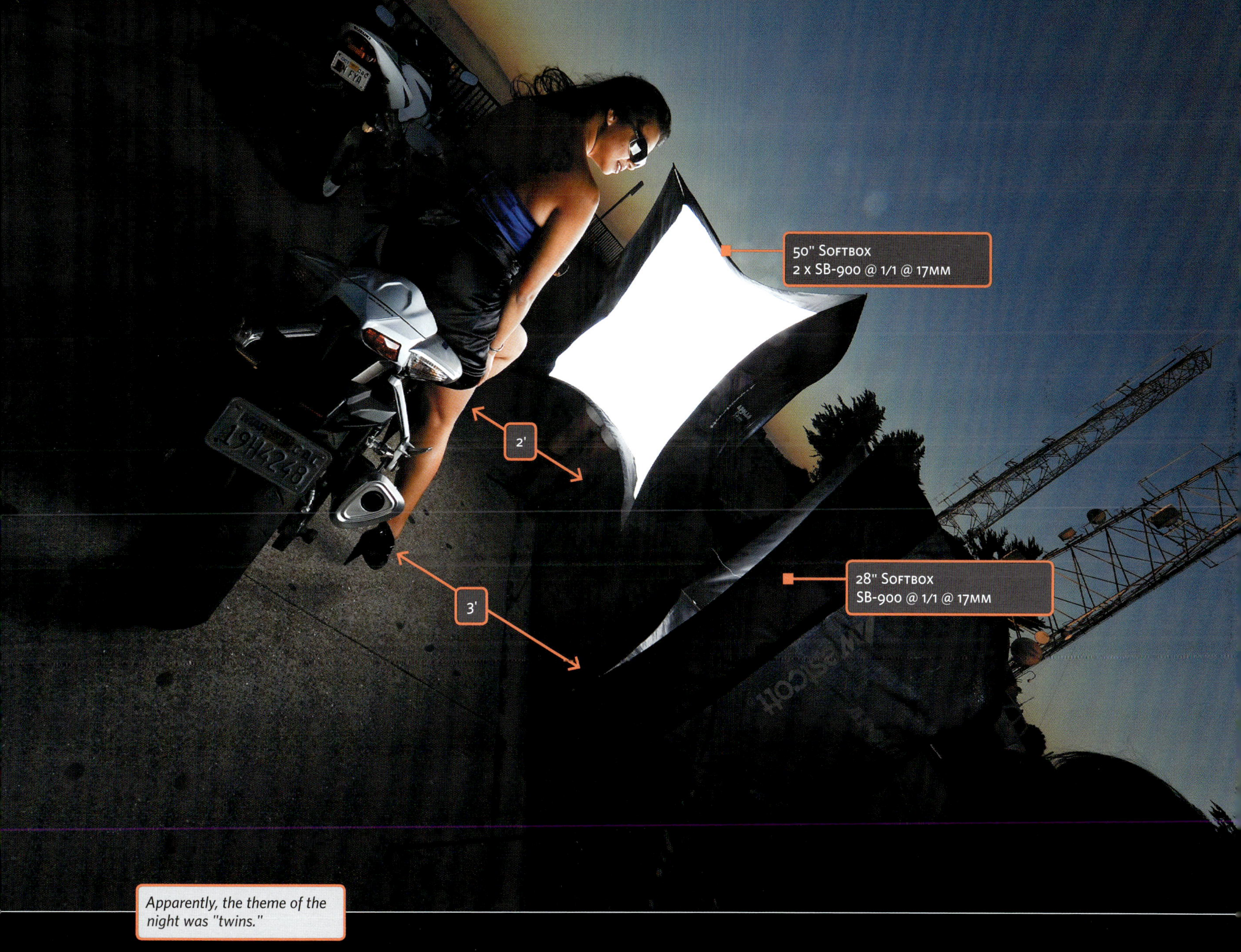

Apparently, the theme of the night was "twins."

D3 | ISO 200 | F/11 | 1/250TH | 14-24MM F/2.8 @ 16MM

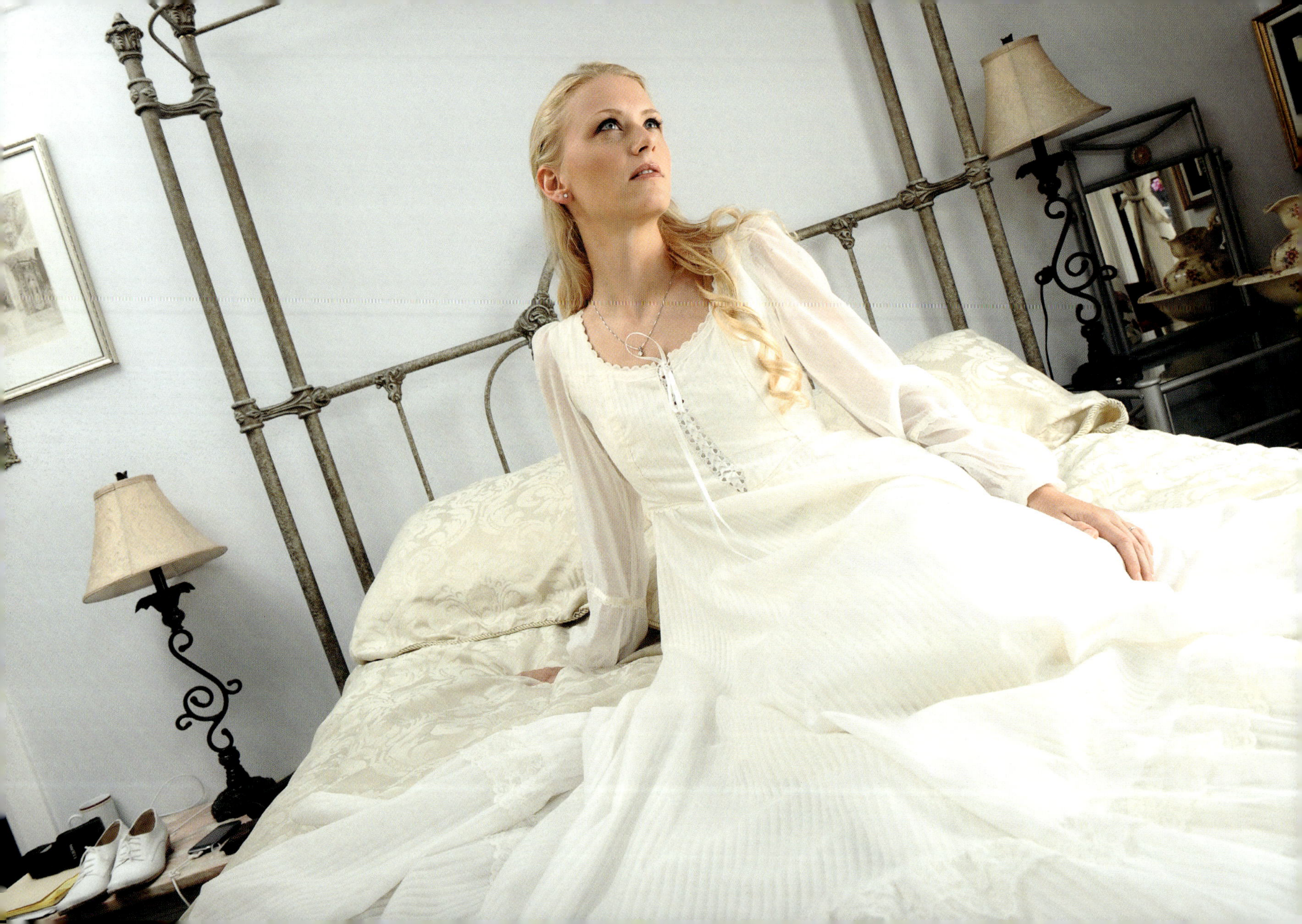

SB-900 @ 1/2 @ 17mm
Bounced to Ceiling
43" Reflective Umbrella
SB-900 @ 1/2 @ 24mm
50" Softbox
SB-900 @ 1/1 @ 17mm
28" Gold Reflector

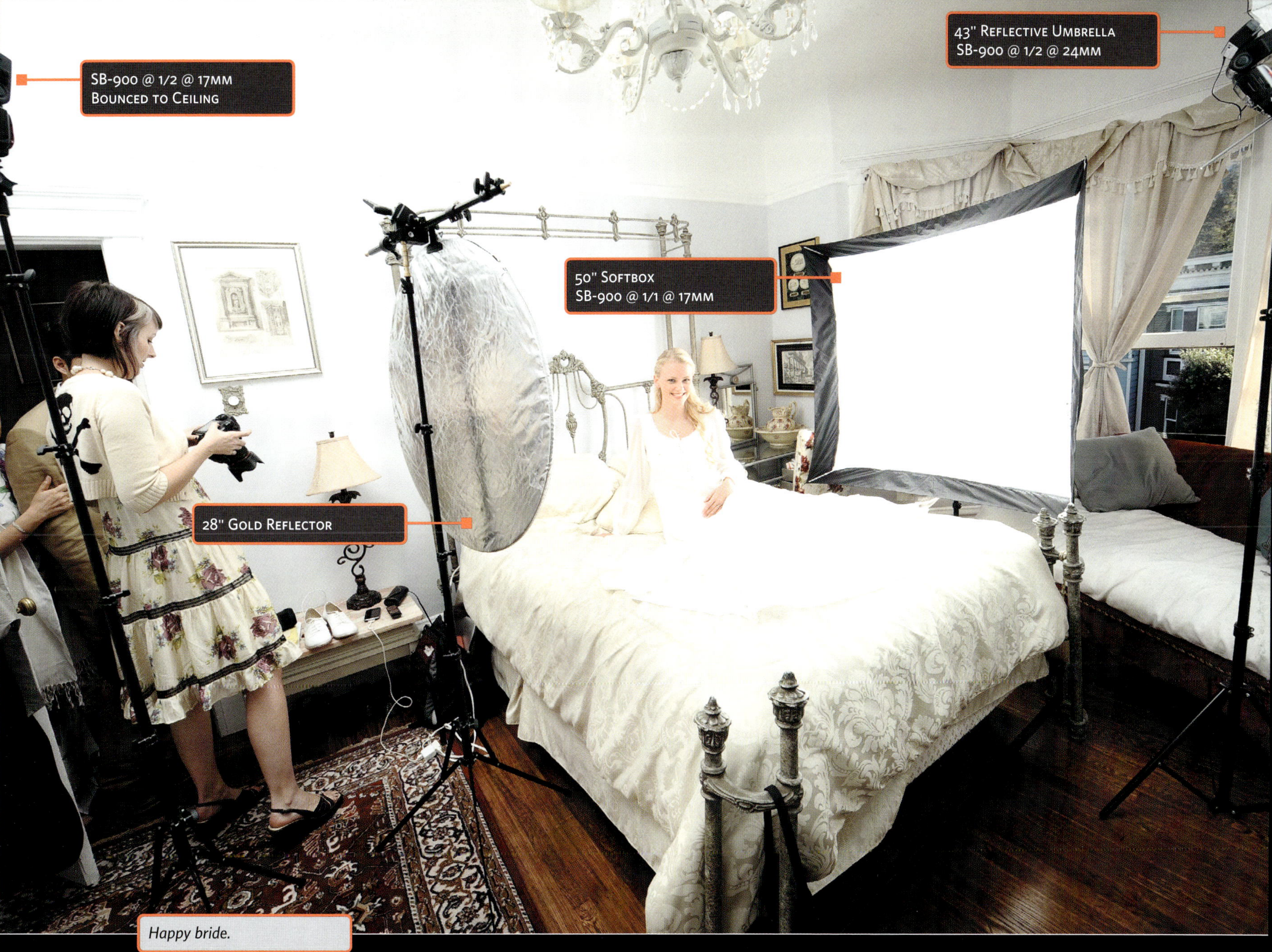

Happy bride.

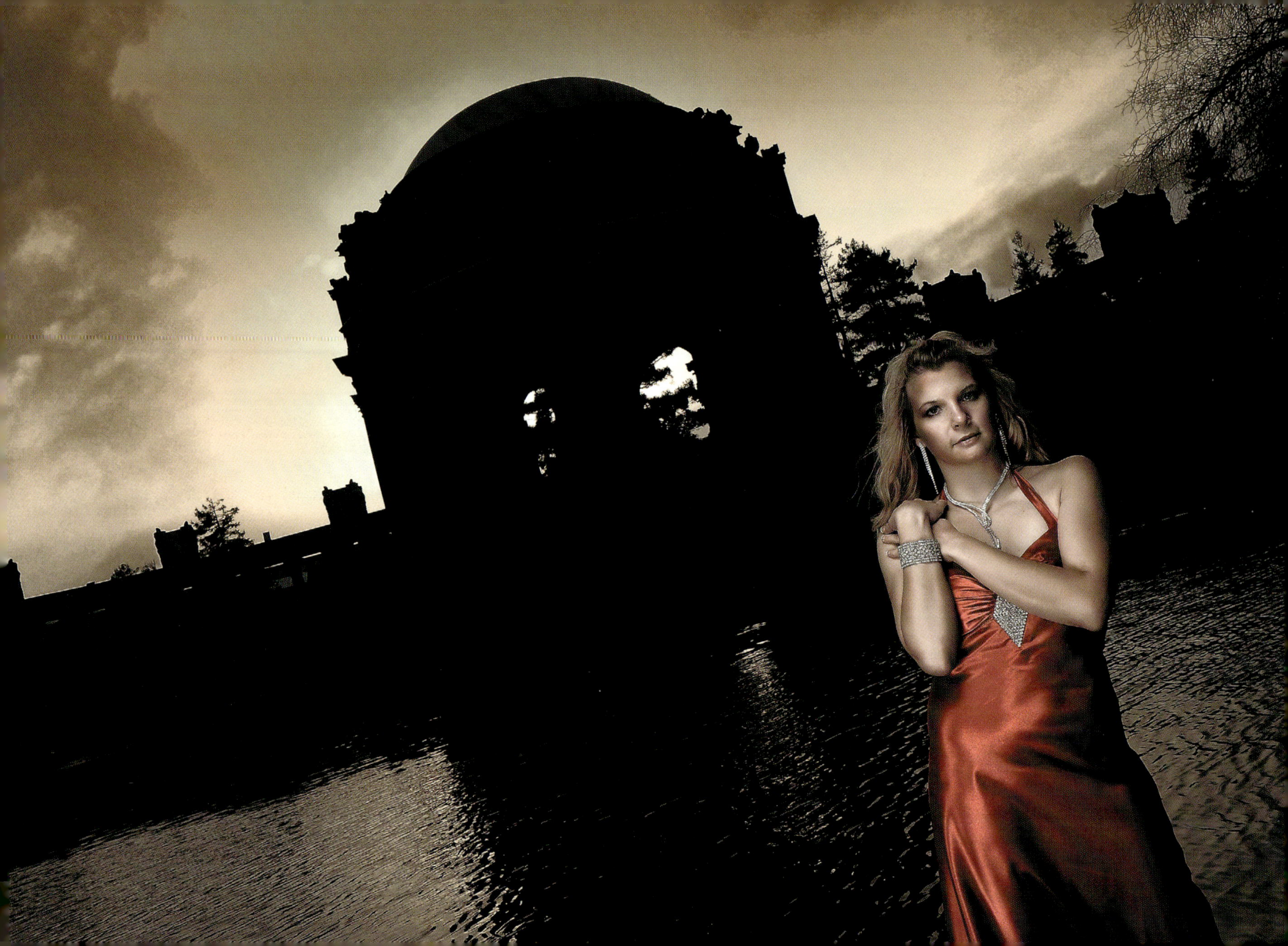

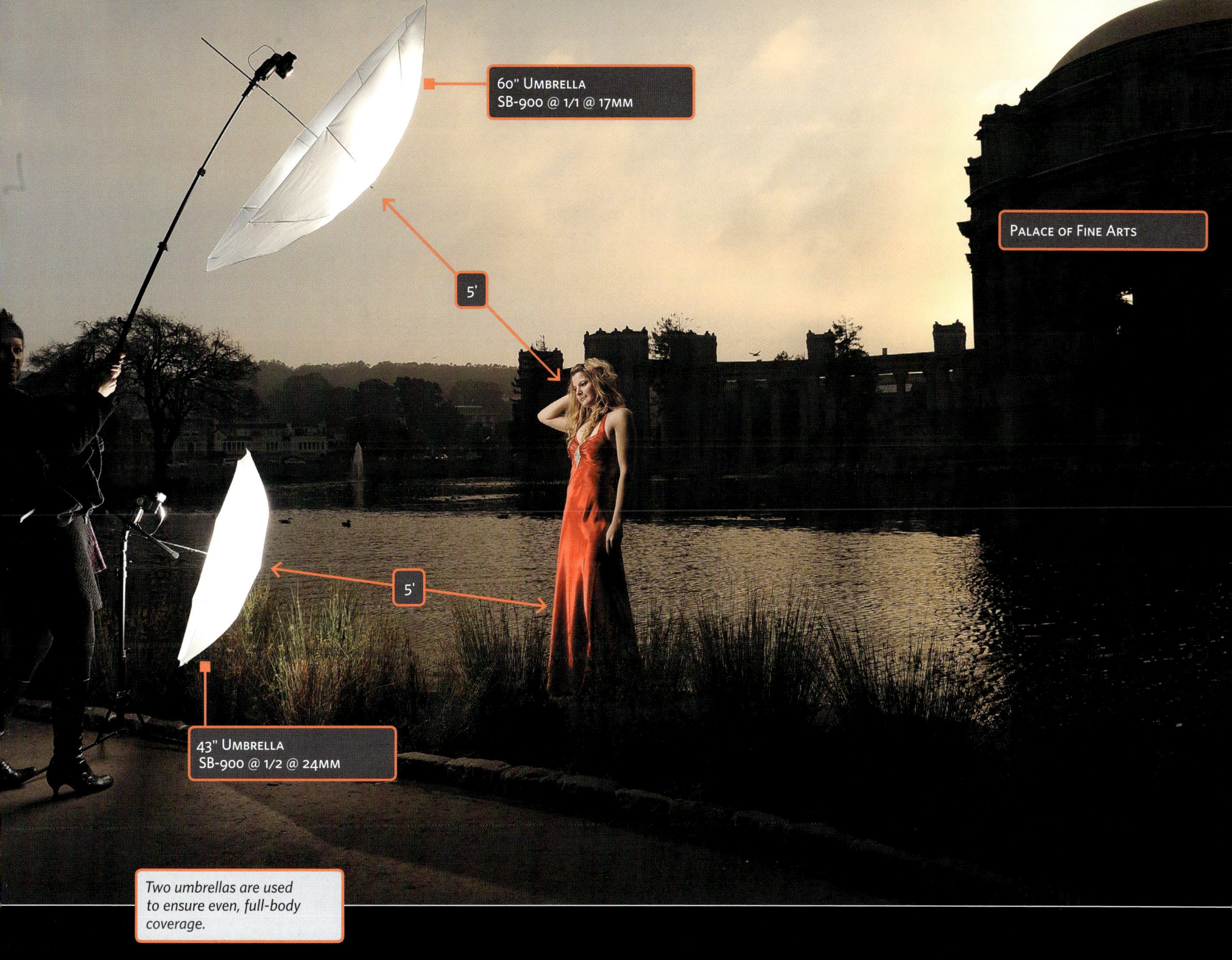

Two umbrellas are used to ensure even, full-body coverage.

D3 | ISO 200 | F/10 | 1/200TH | 24-70MM F/2.8 @ 31MM

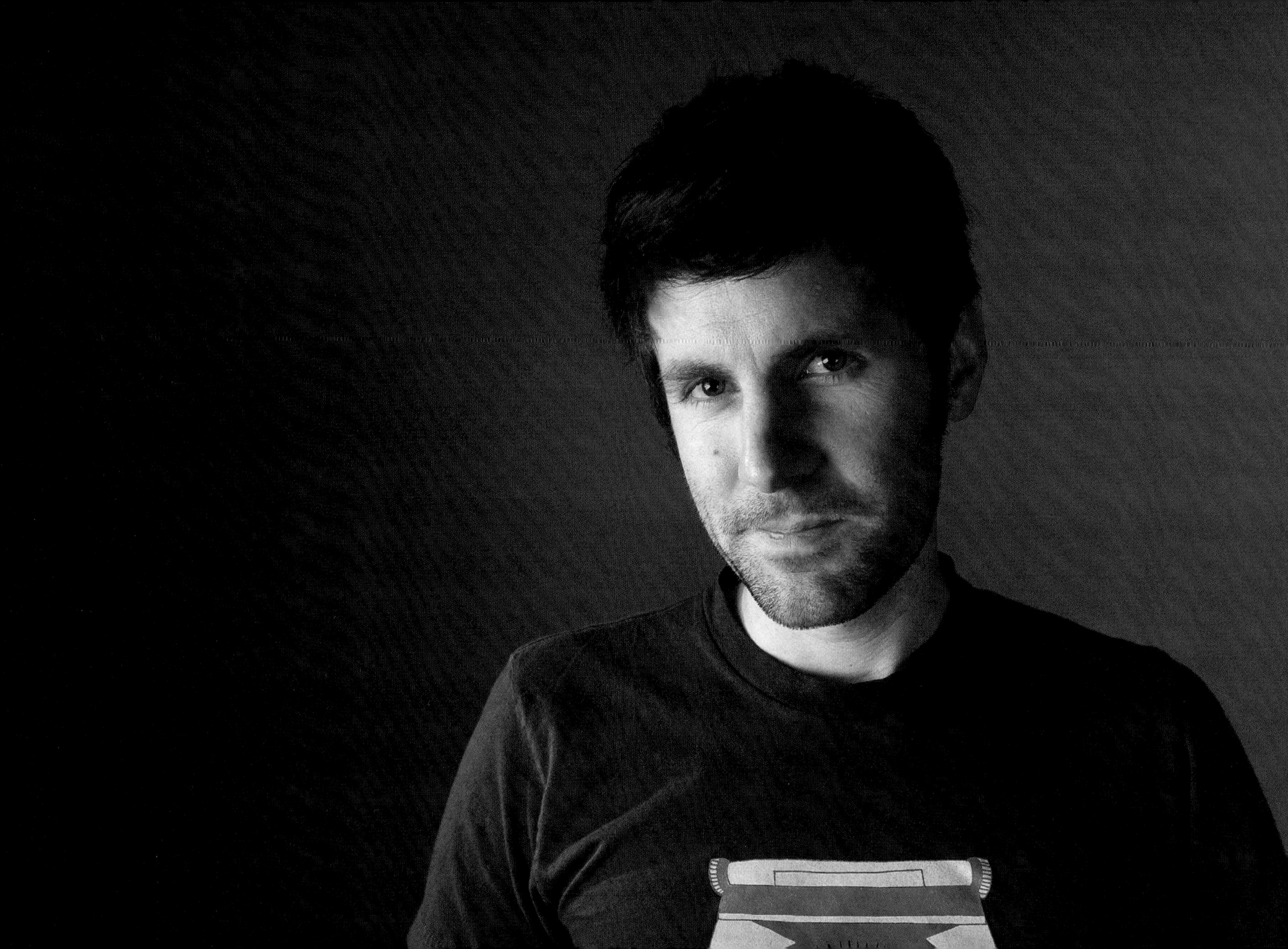

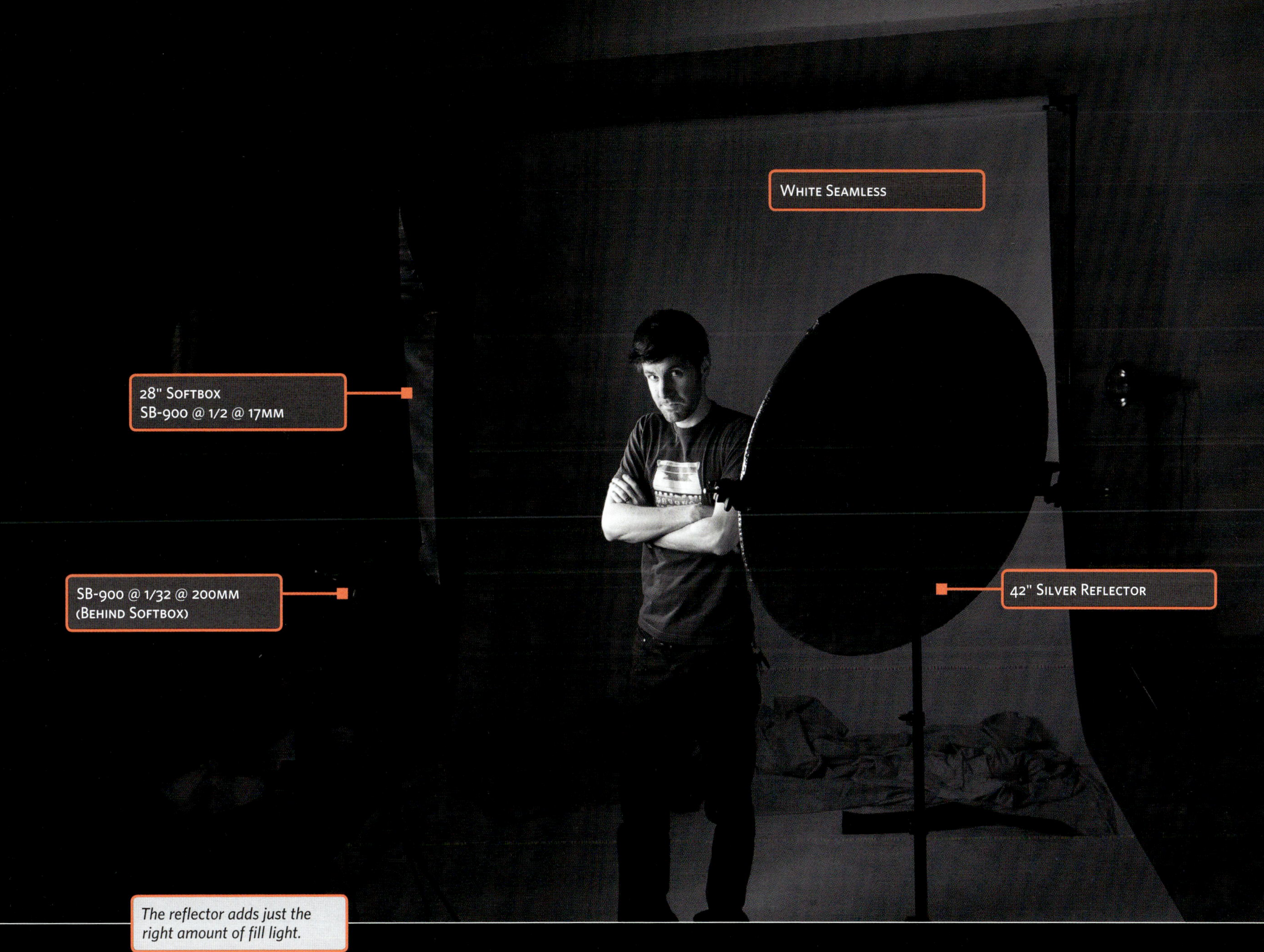

The reflector adds just the right amount of fill light.

D3 | ISO 200 | F/6.3 | 1/250TH | 24-70MM F/2.8 @ 48MM

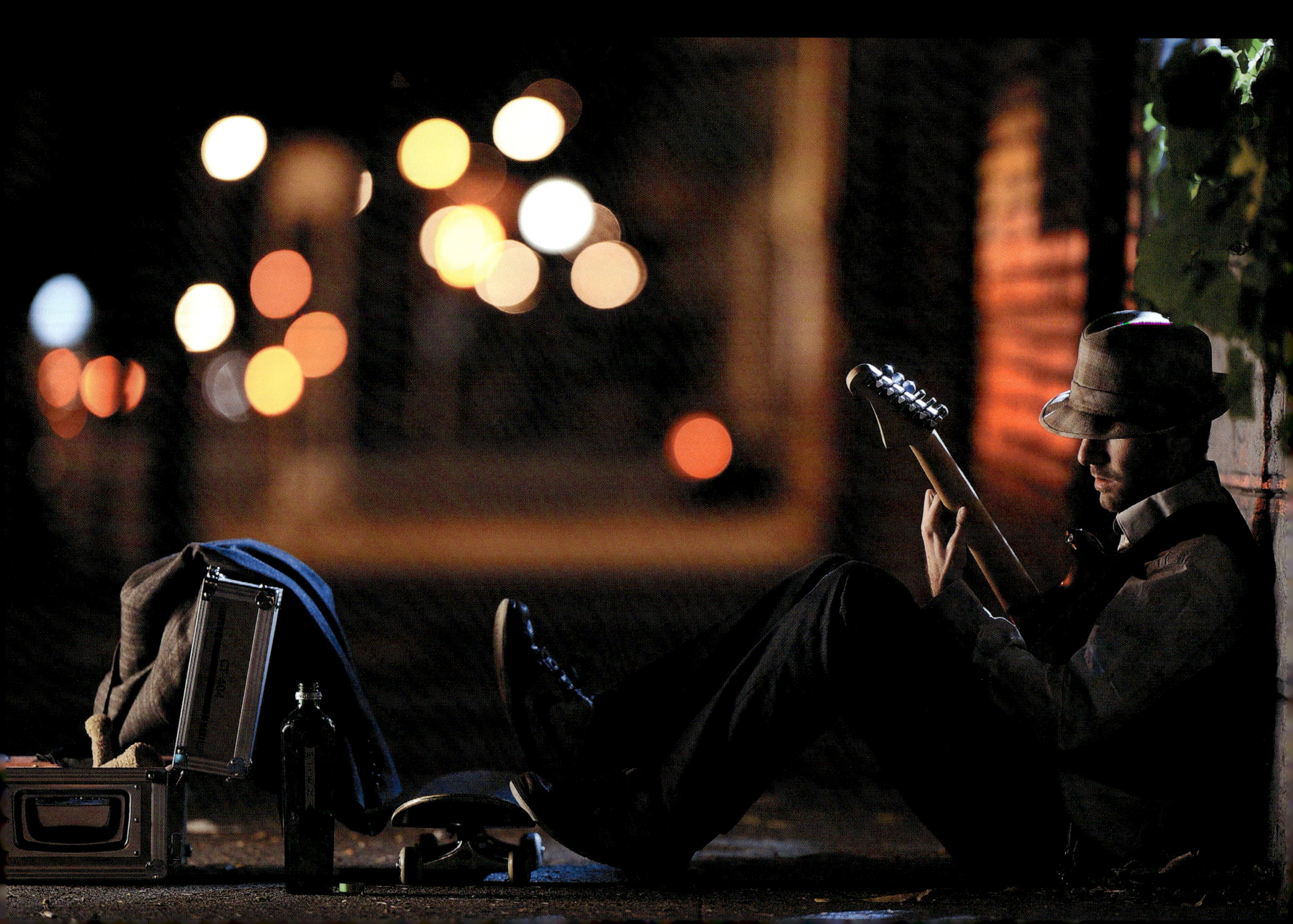

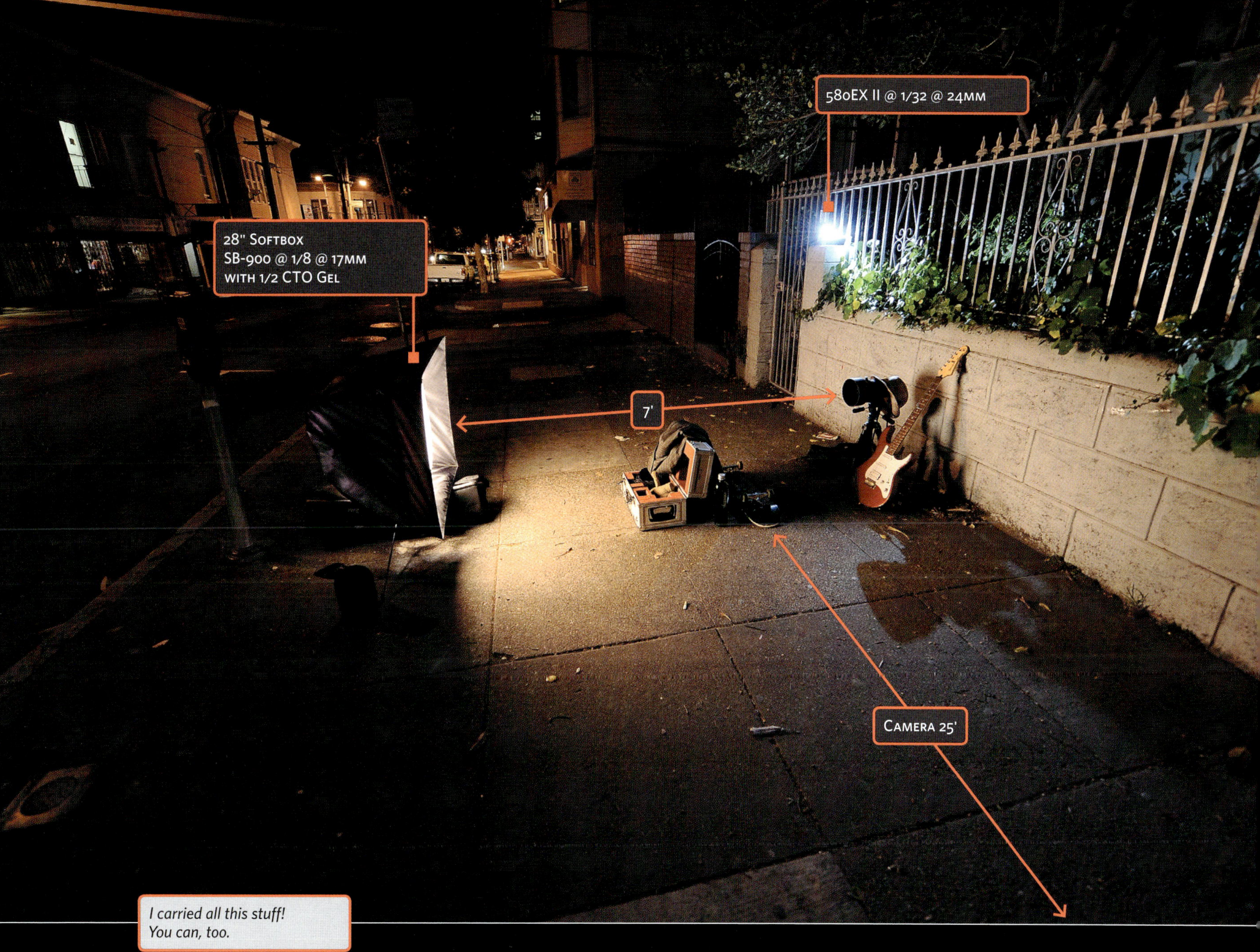

I carried all this stuff!
You can, too.

D700 | ISO 500 | F/2 | 1/25TH | 200MM F/2 @ 200MM

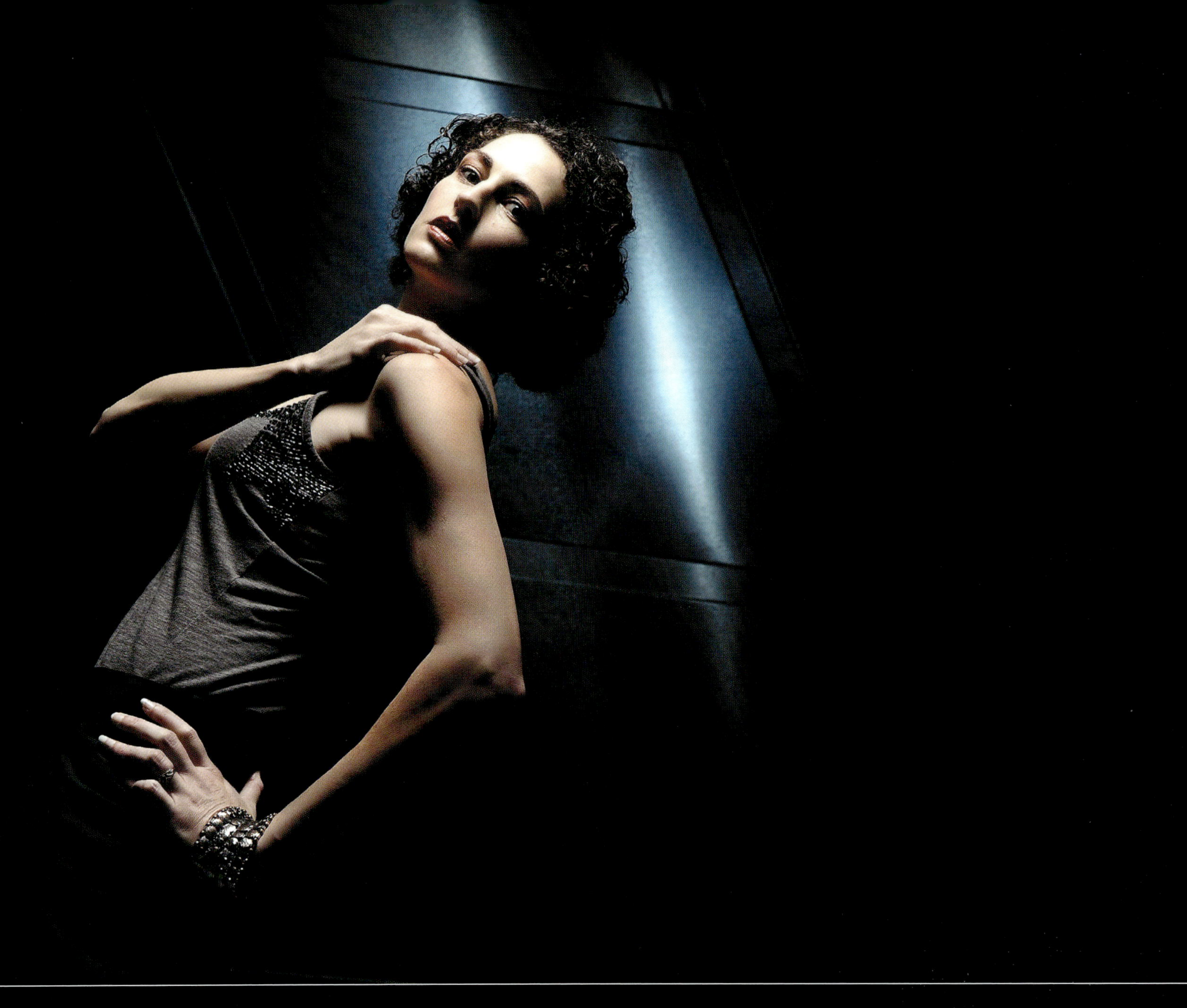

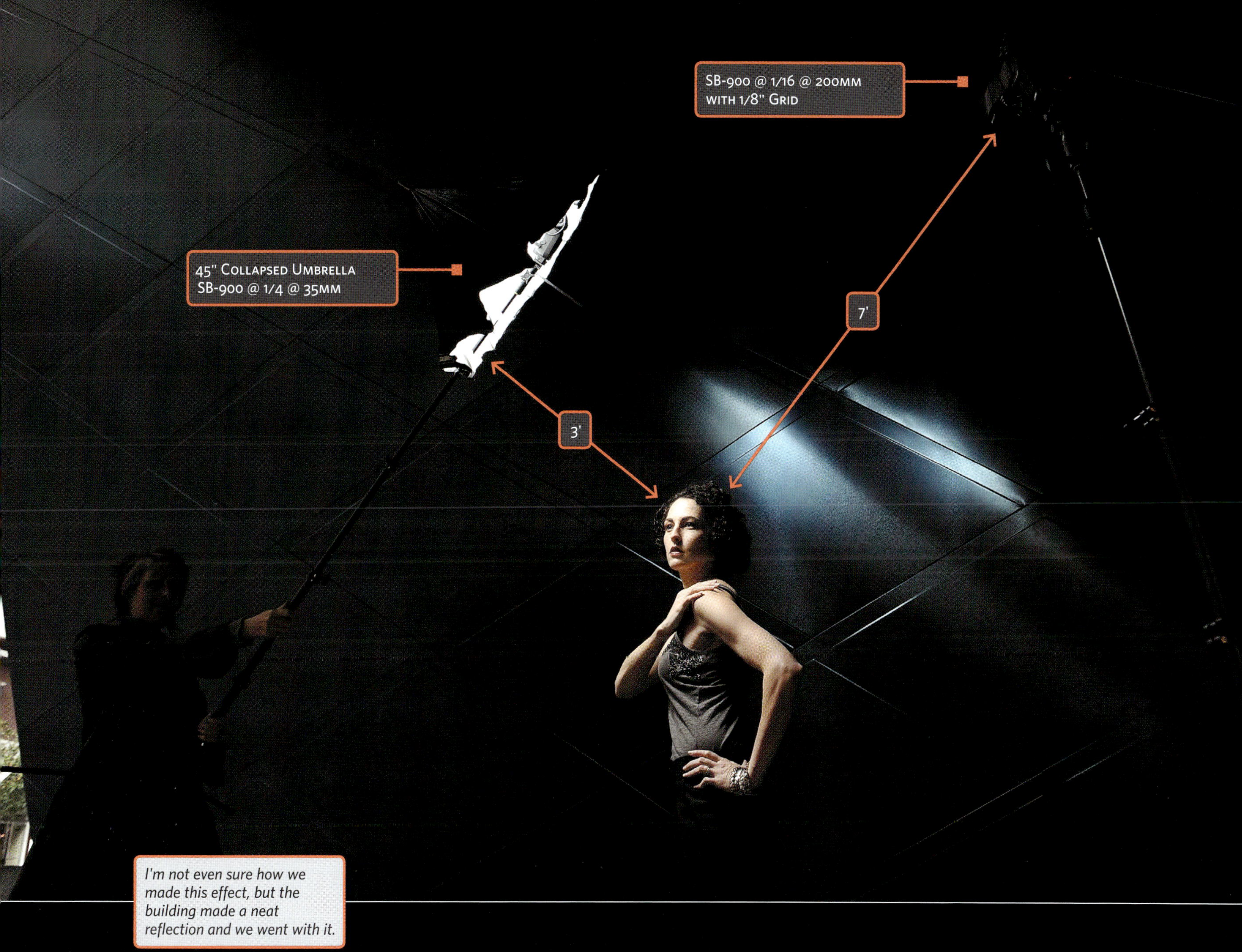

I'm not even sure how we made this effect, but the building made a neat reflection and we went with it.

D3 | ISO 200 | F/5 | 1/100TH | 24-70MM F/2.8 @ 42MM

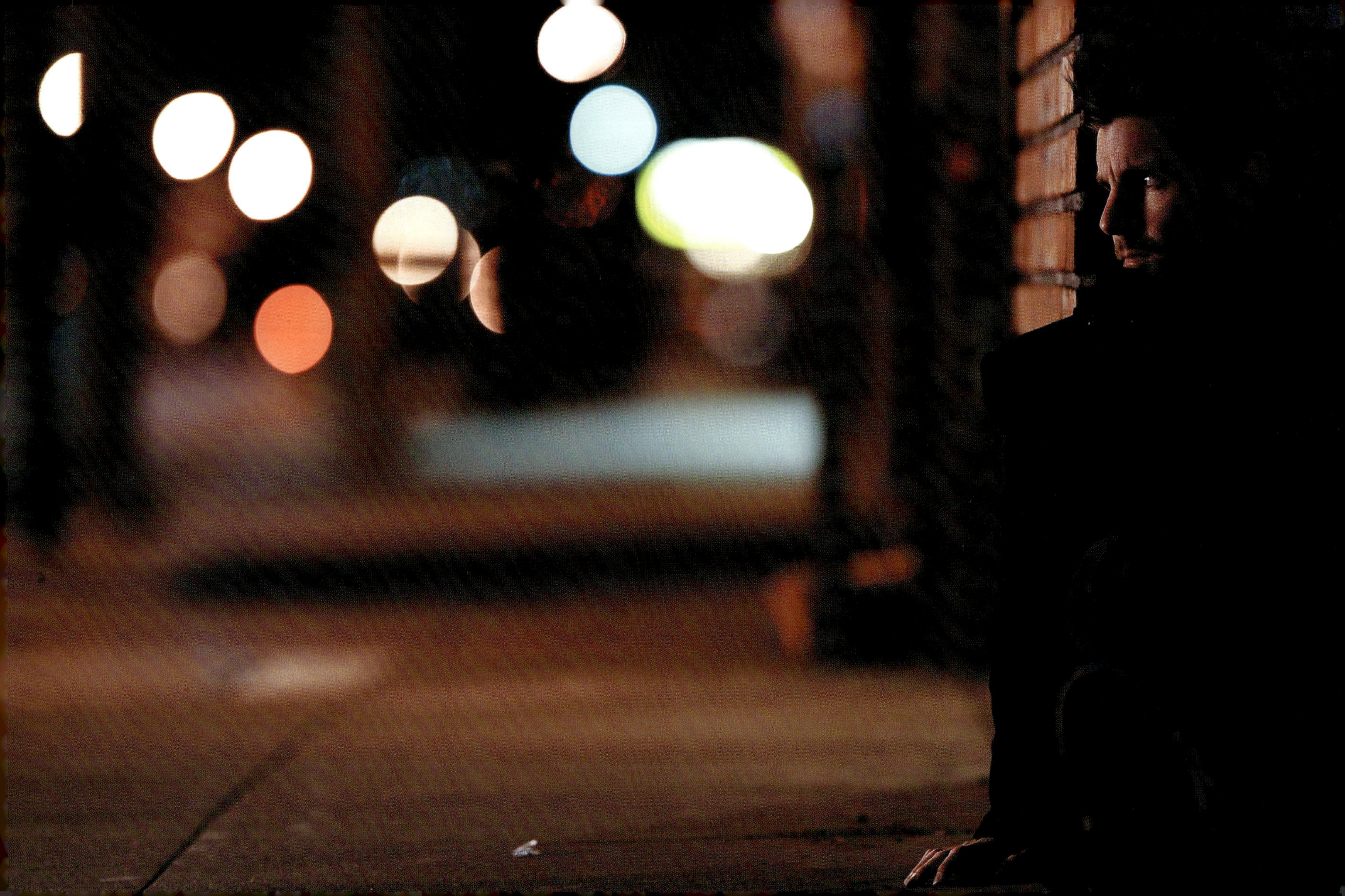

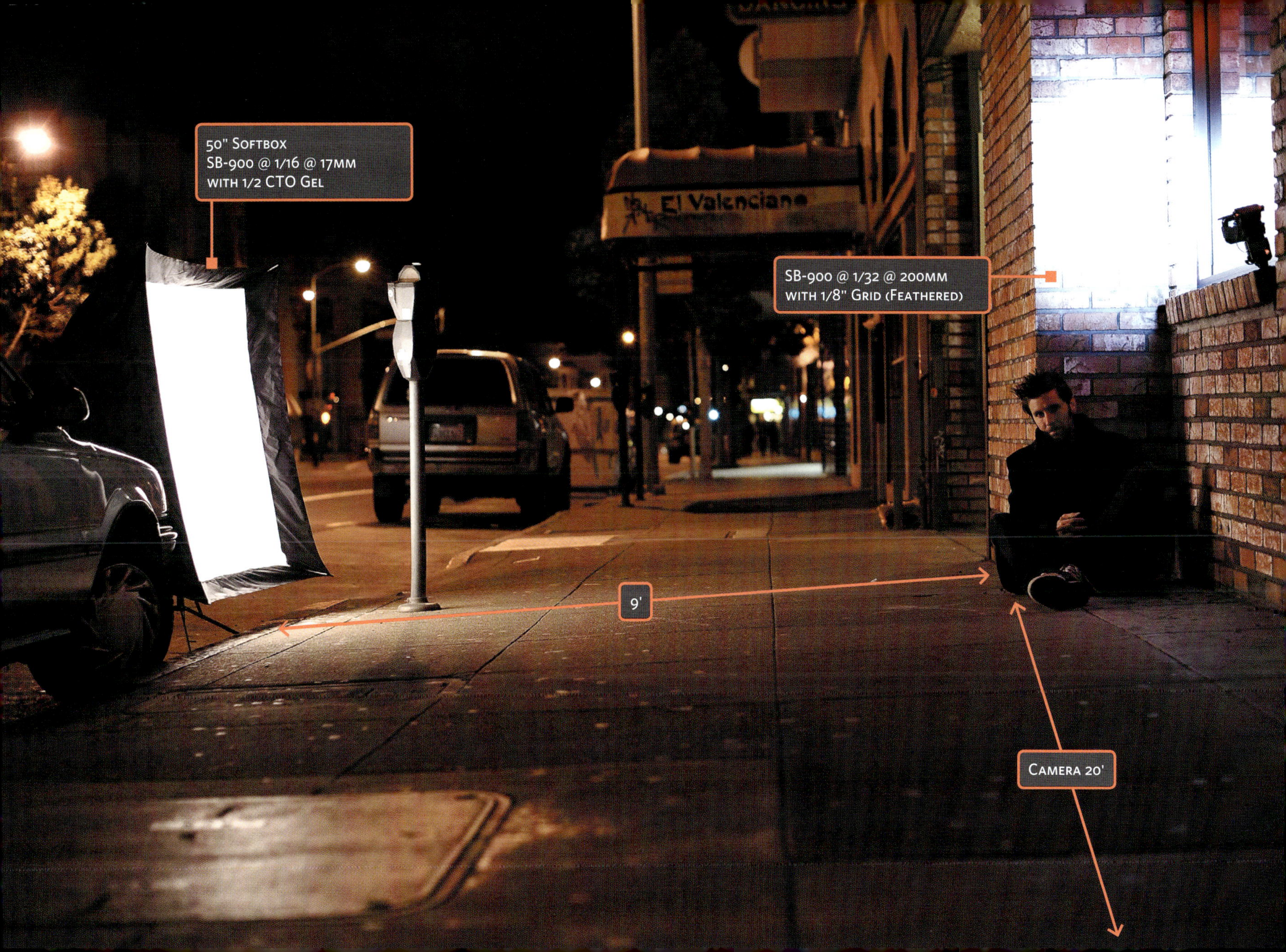

50" Softbox
SB-900 @ 1/16 @ 17mm
with 1/2 CTO Gel
SB-900 @ 1/32 @ 200mm
with 1/8" Grid (Feathered)
9'
Camera 20'
El Valenciano

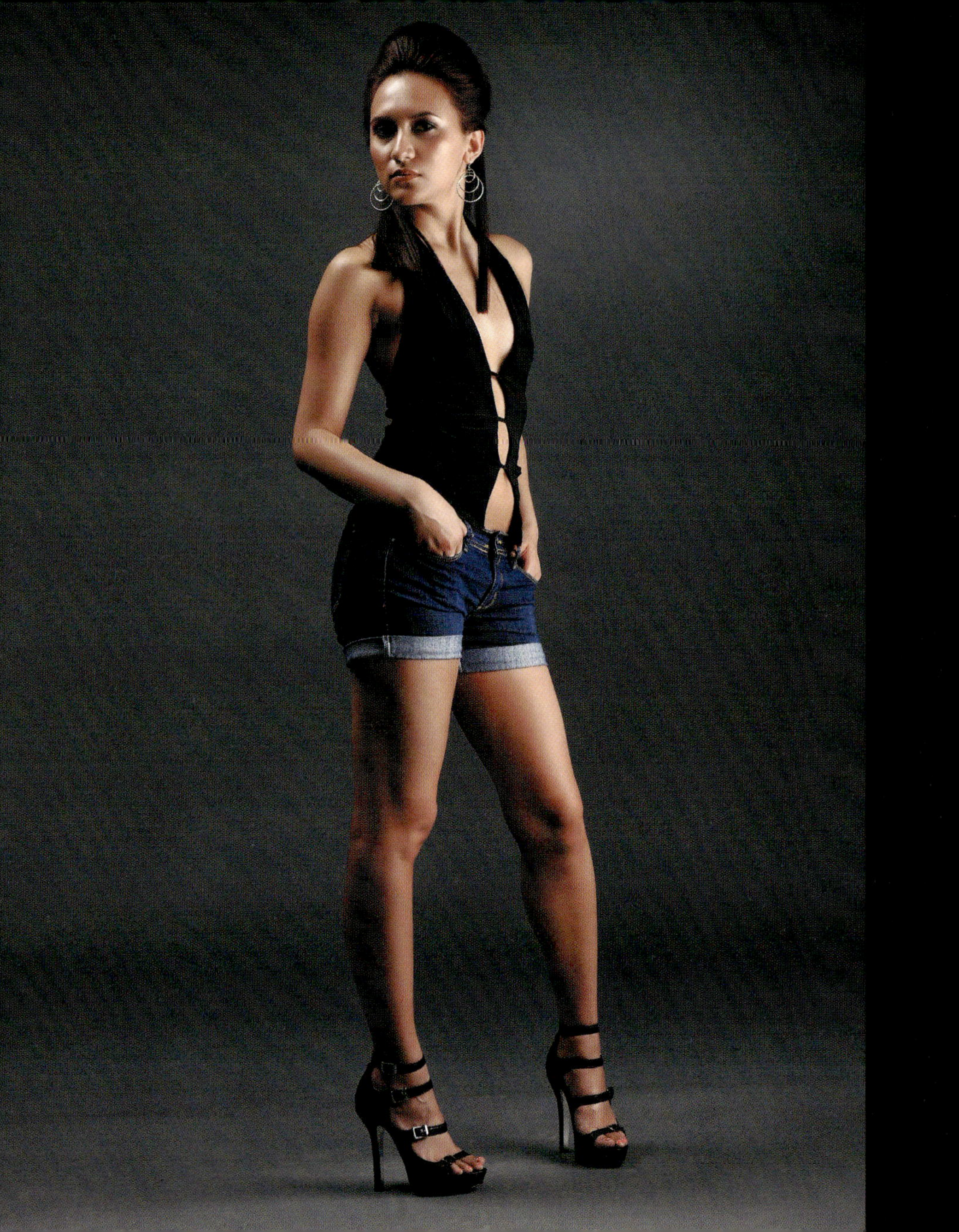

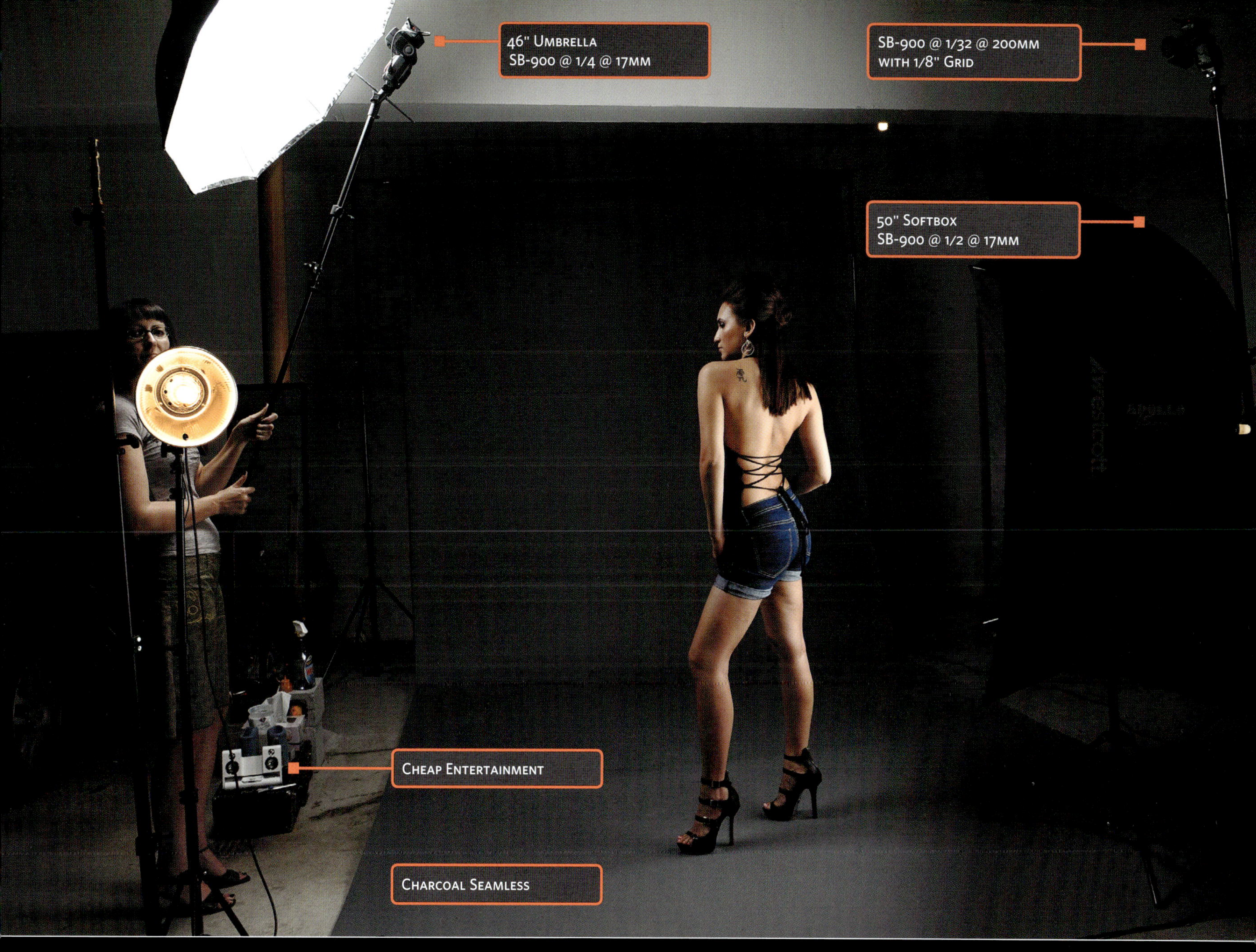

D3 | ISO 320 | F/6.3 | 1/250TH | 24-70MM F/2.8 @ 70MM

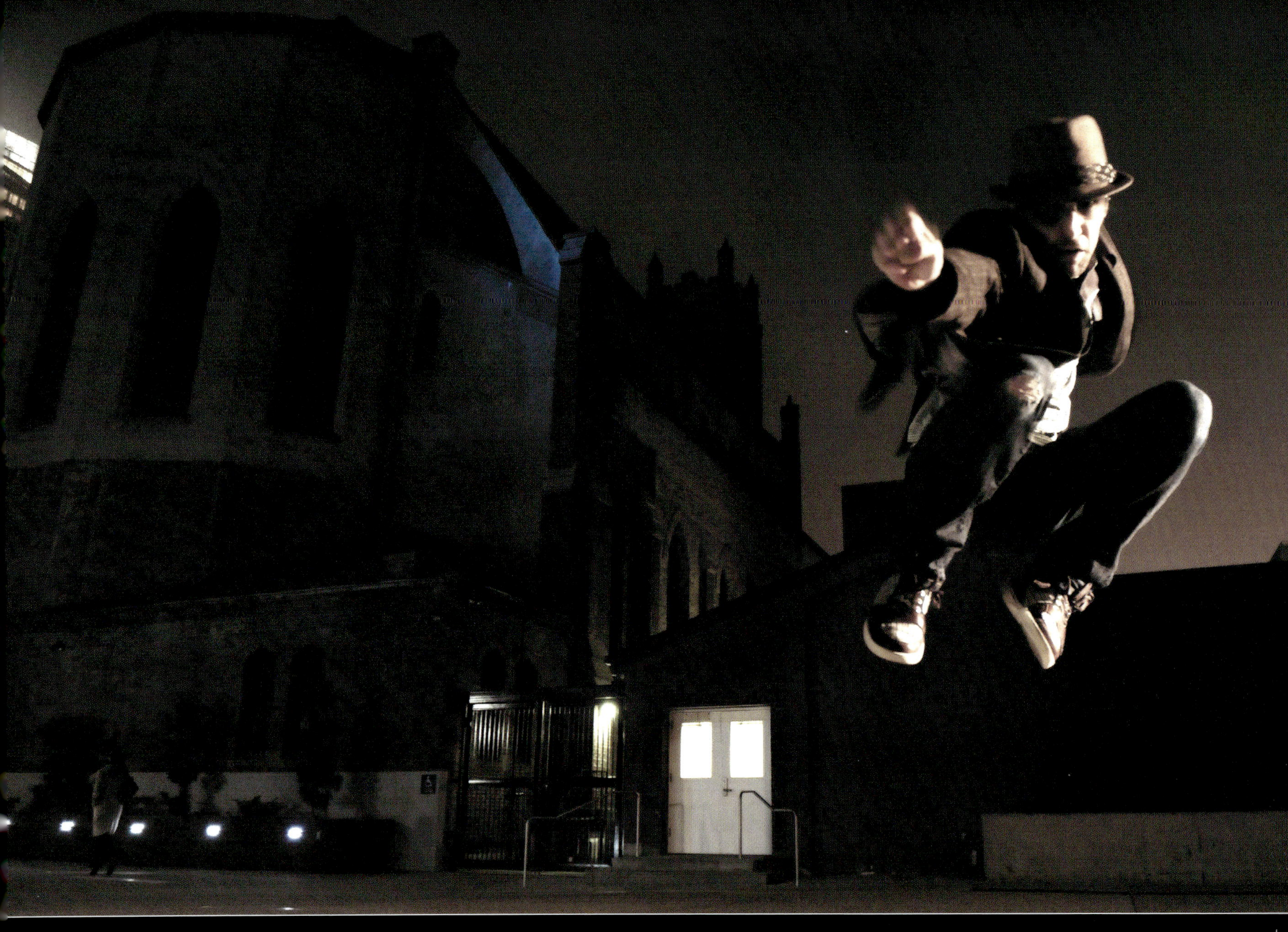

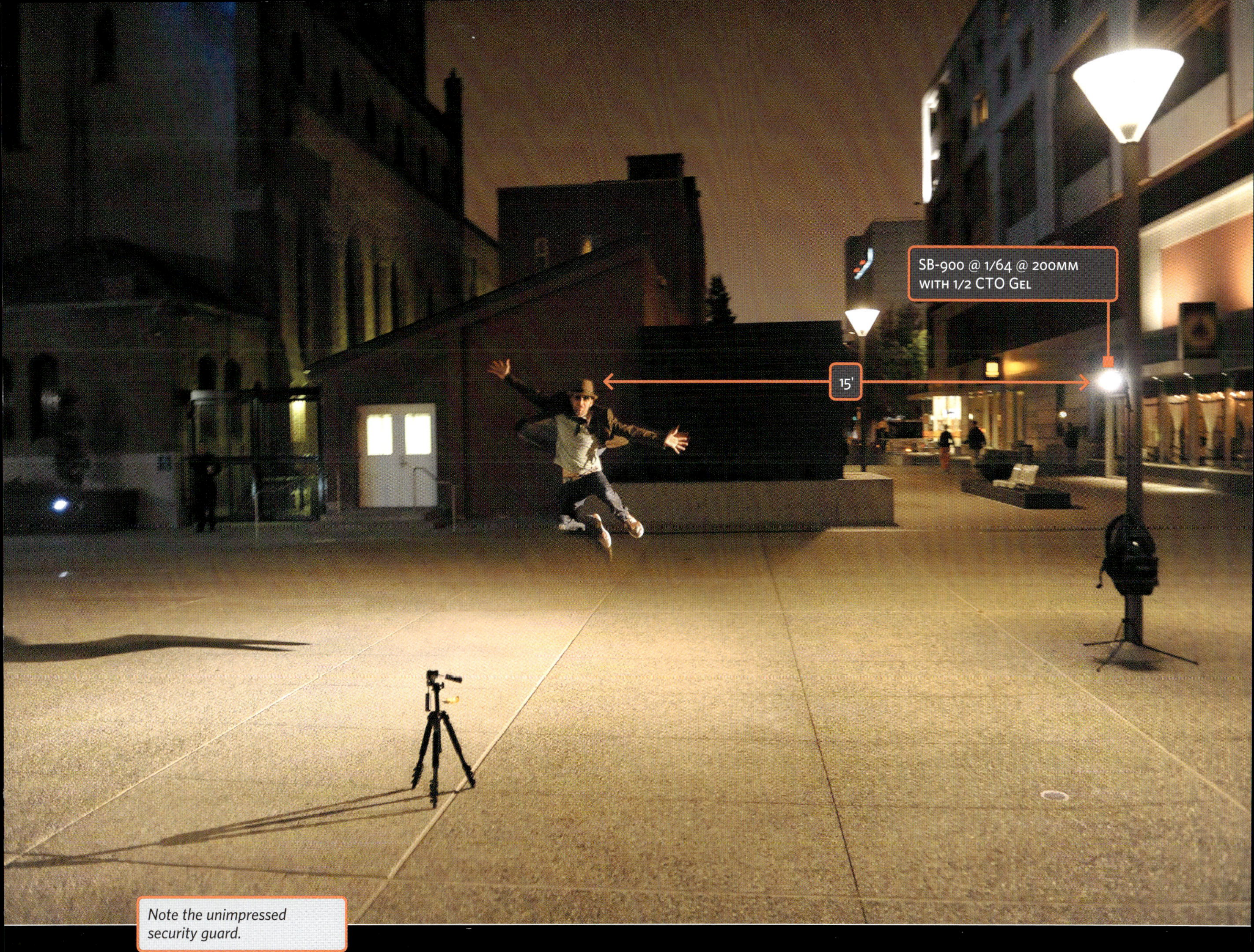

Note the unimpressed security guard.

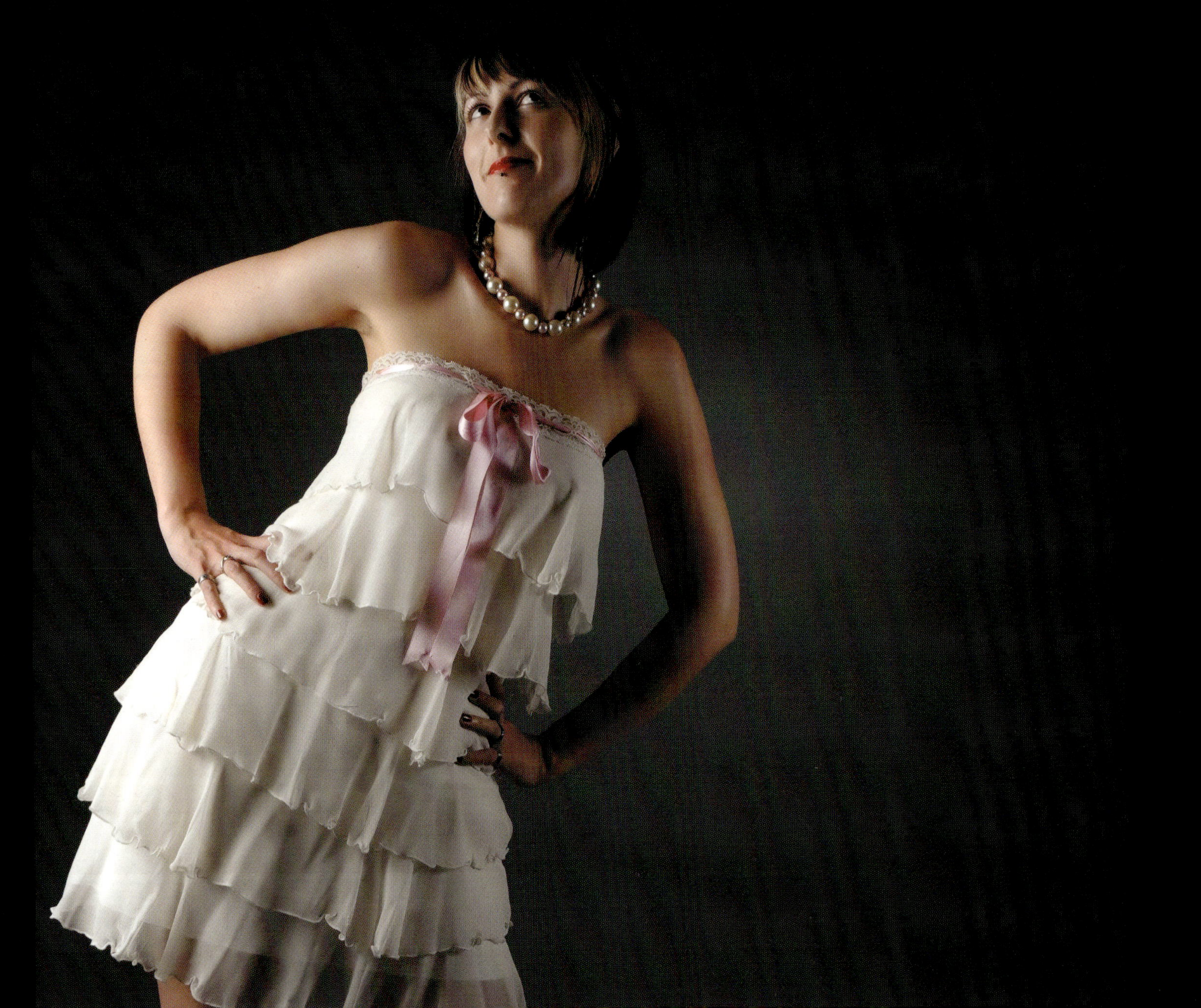

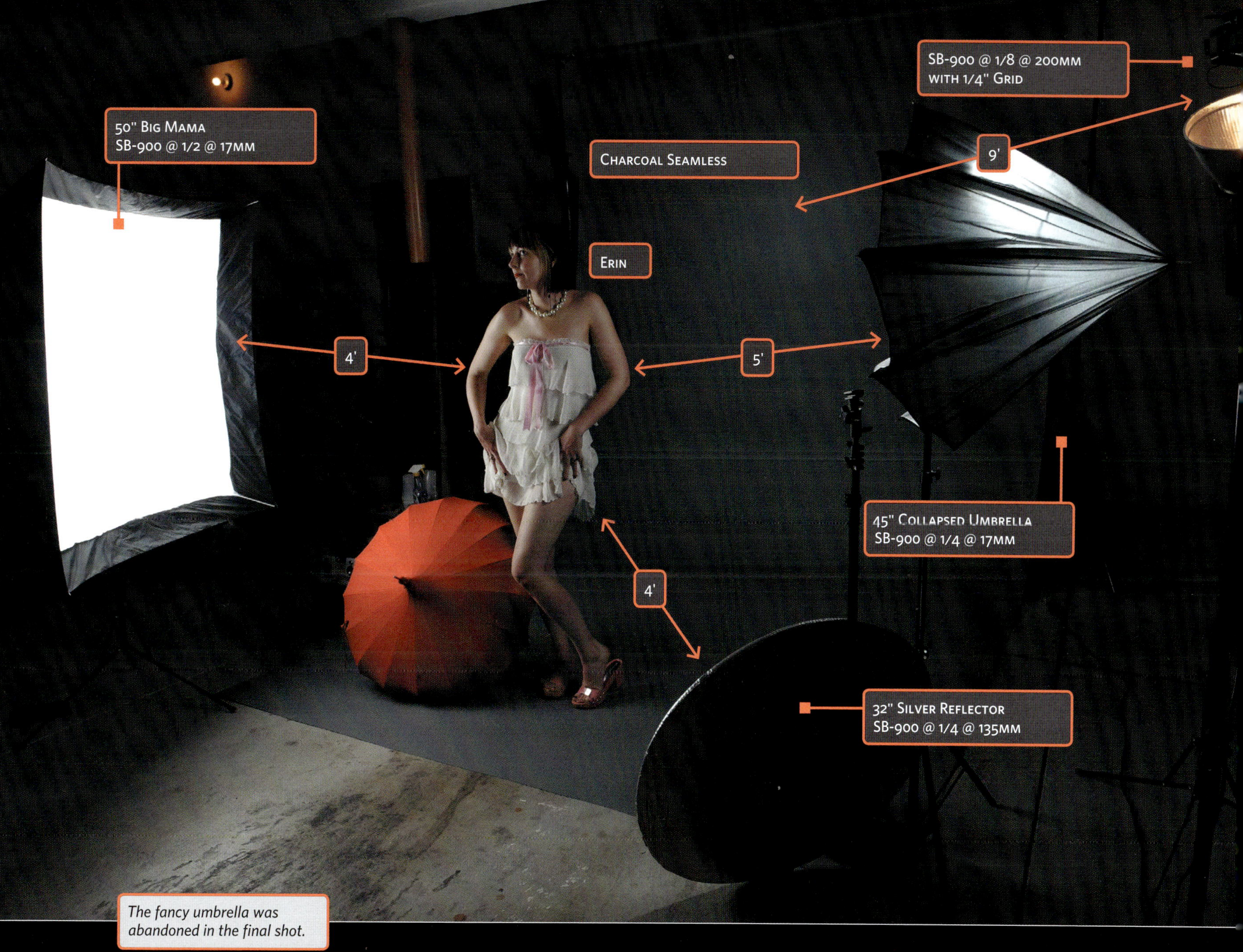

The fancy umbrella was abandoned in the final shot.

D3 | ISO 200 | F/6.3 | 1/125TH | 24-70MM F/2.8 @ 48MM

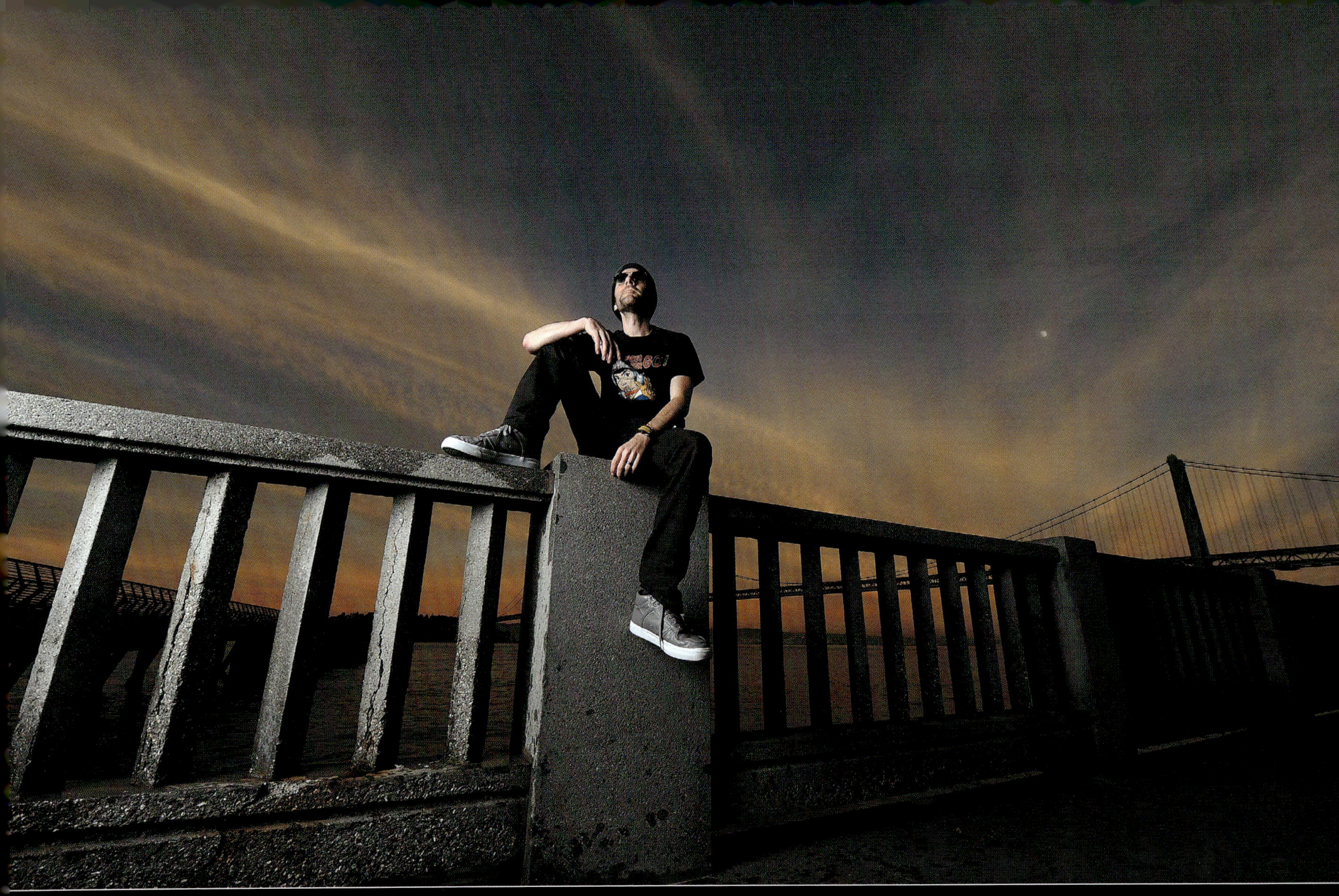

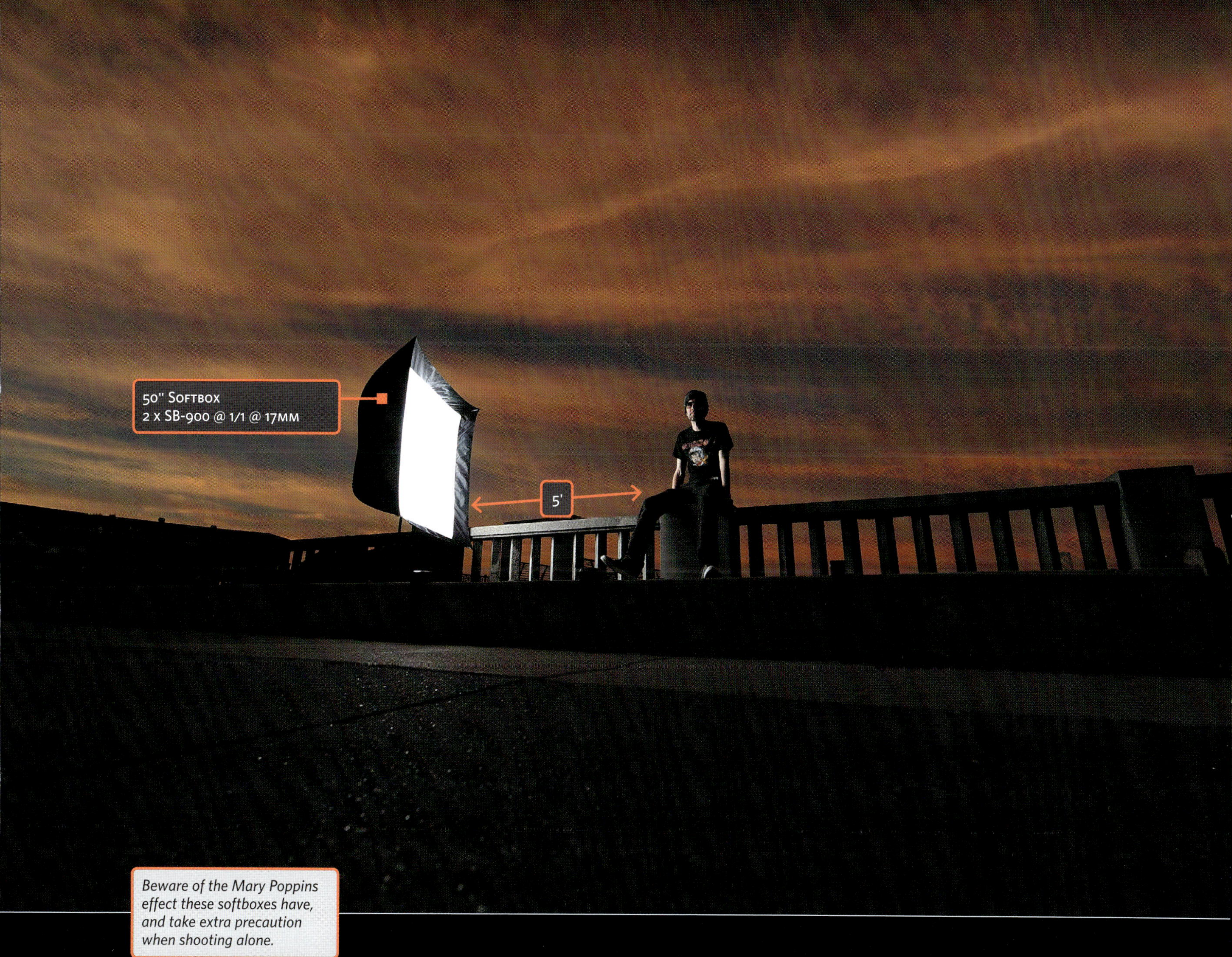

Beware of the Mary Poppins effect these softboxes have, and take extra precaution when shooting alone.

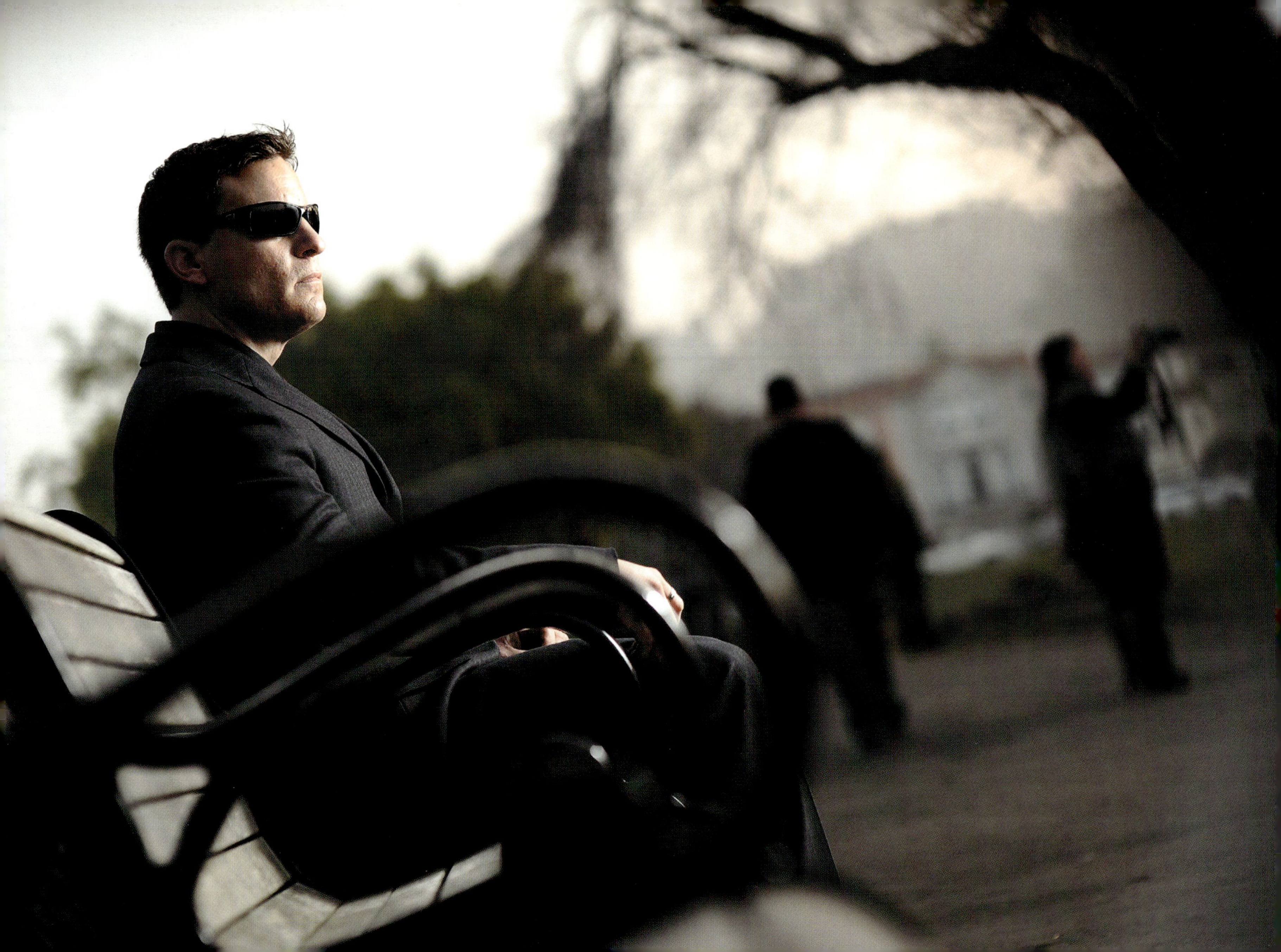

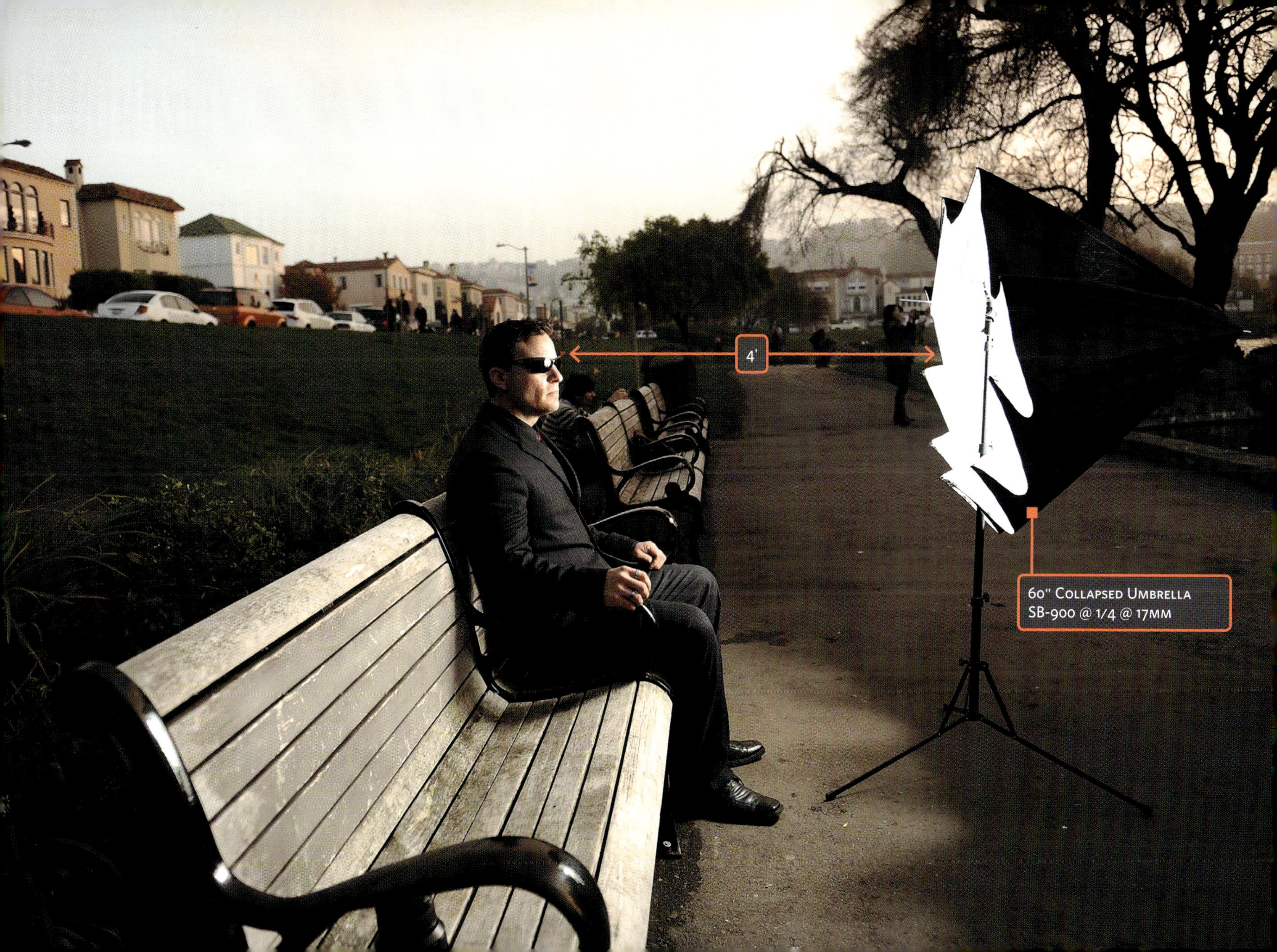
4'
60" Collapsed Umbrella
SB-900 @ 1/4 @ 17mm

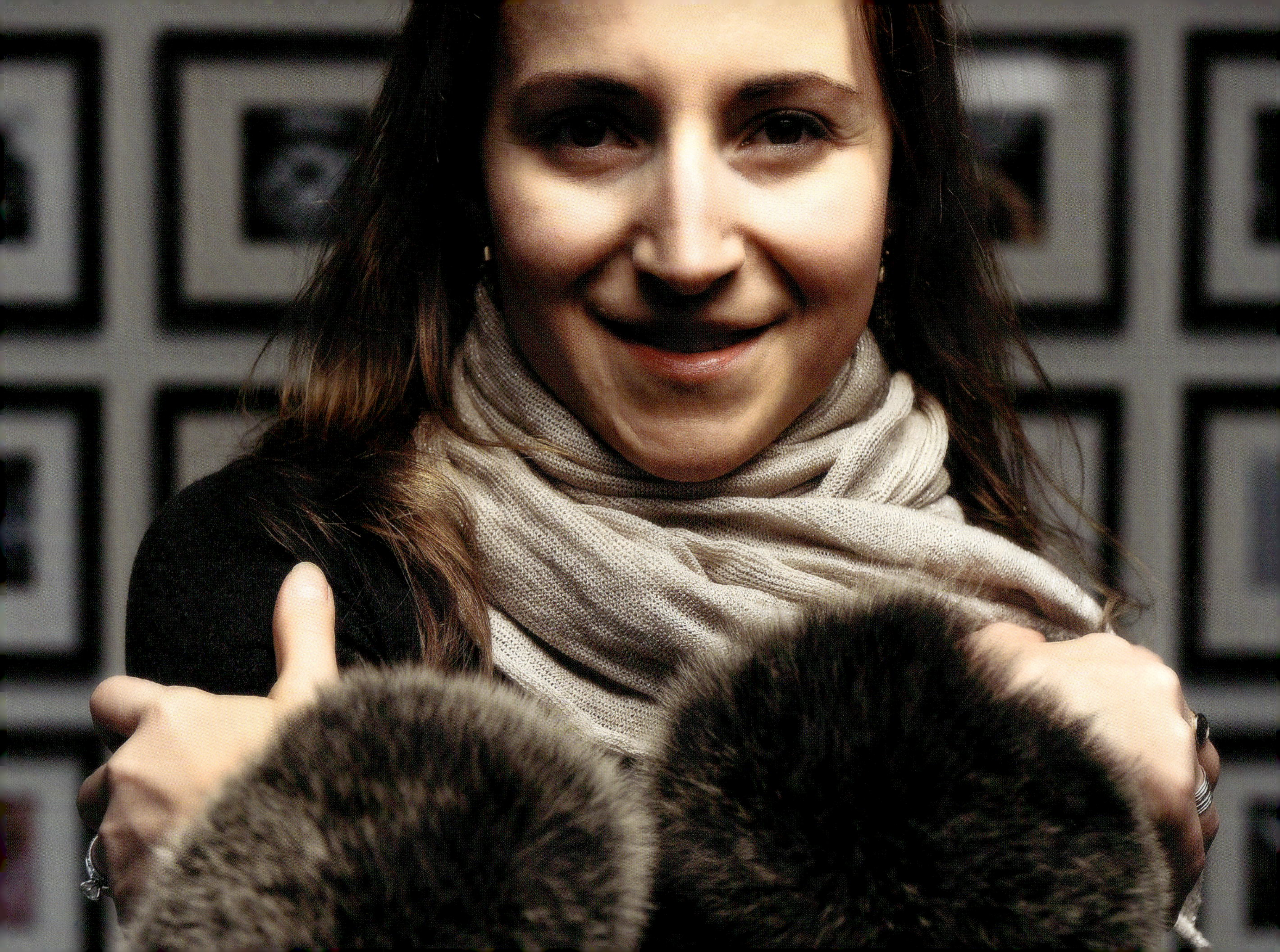

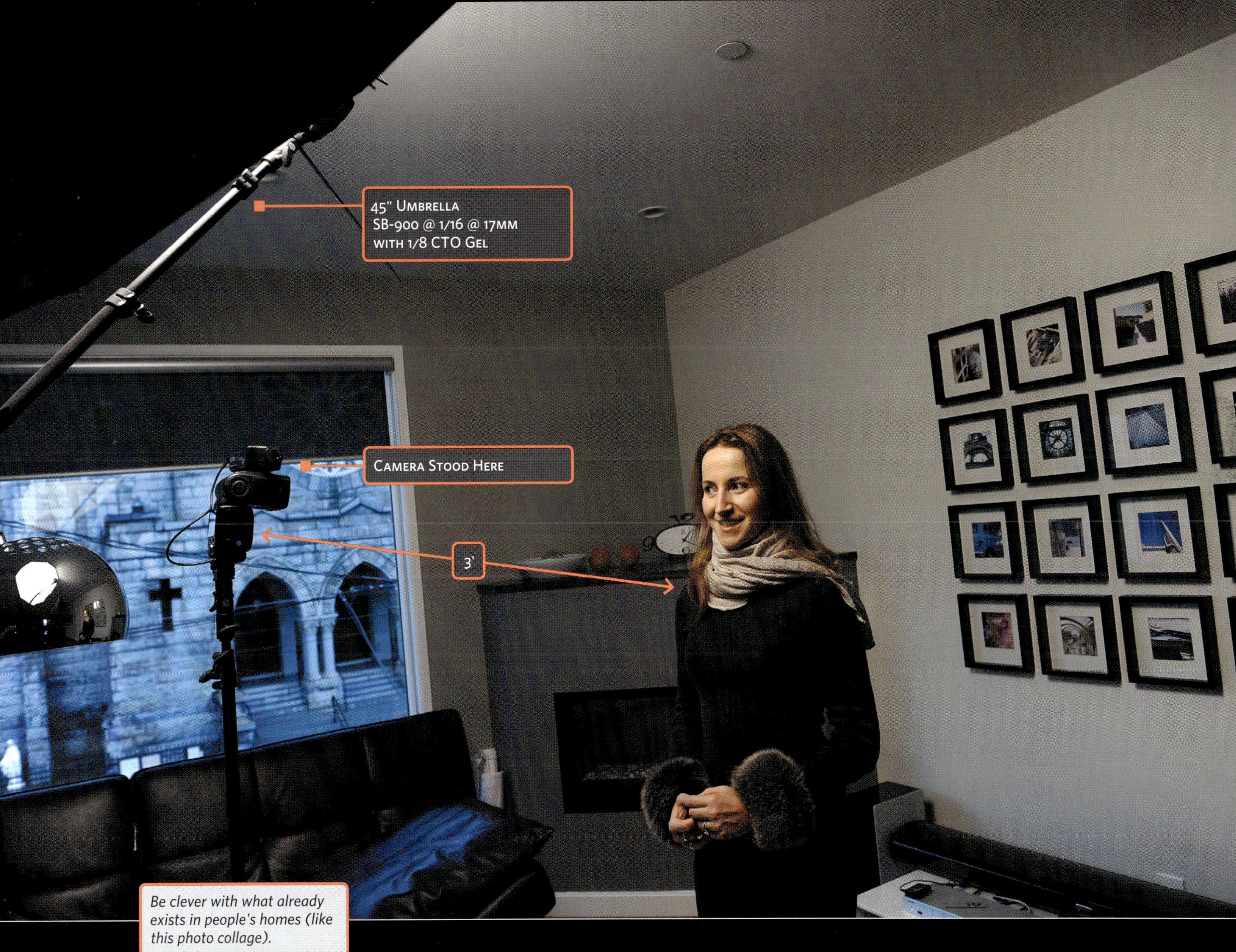

Be clever with what already exists in people's homes (like this photo collage).

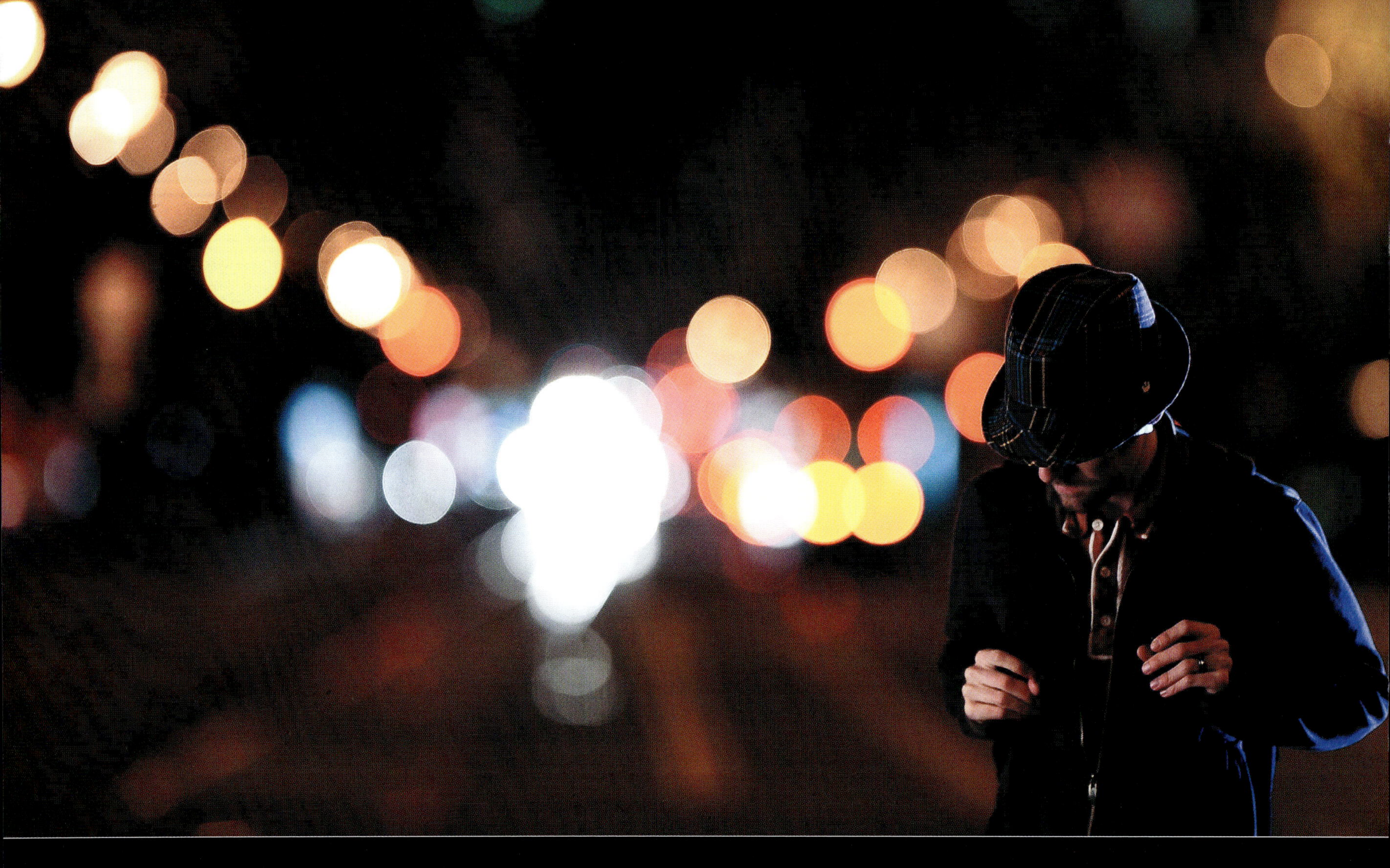

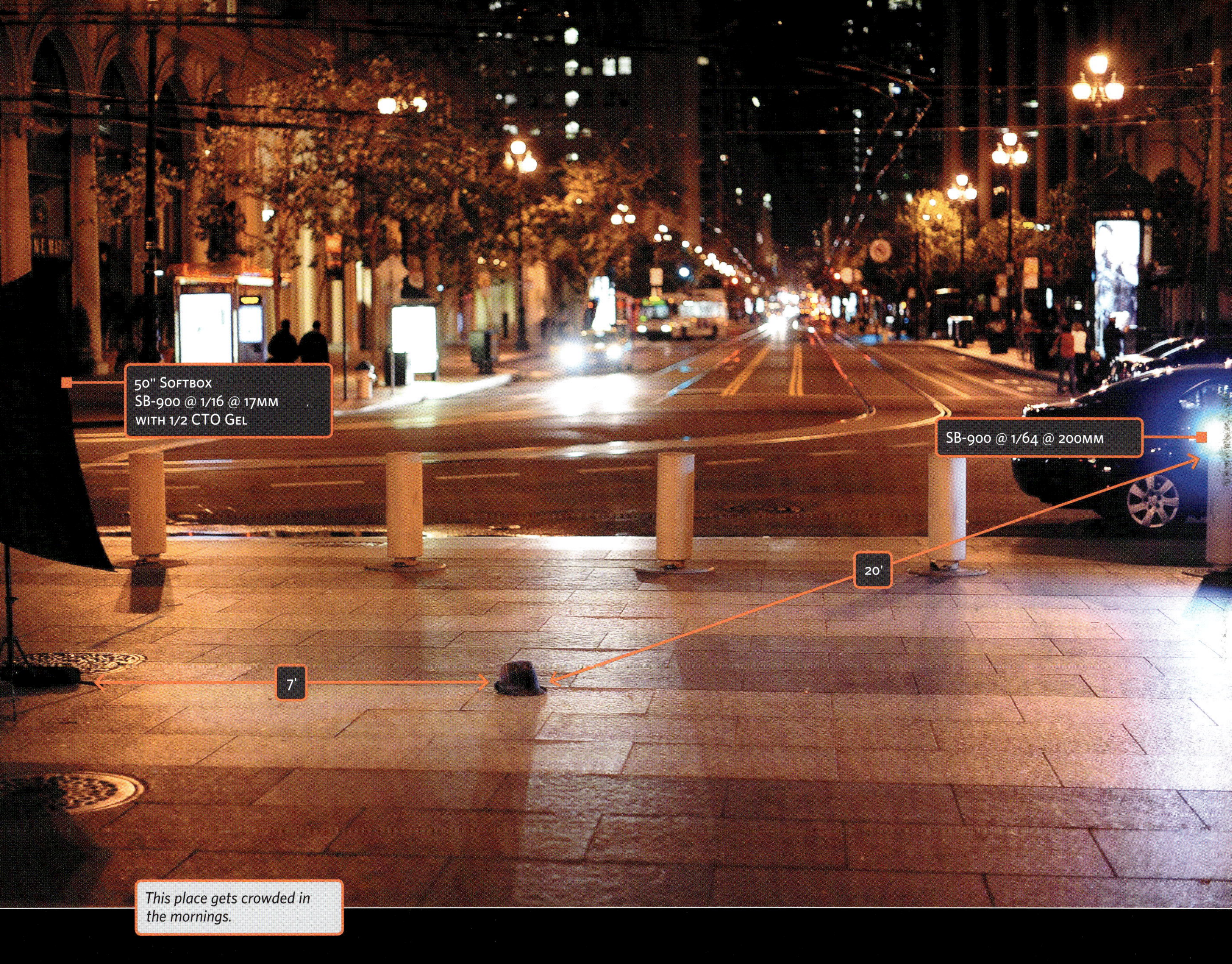

This place gets crowded in the mornings.

D3 | ISO 640 | F/2 | 1/30th | 200mm F/2 @ 200mm

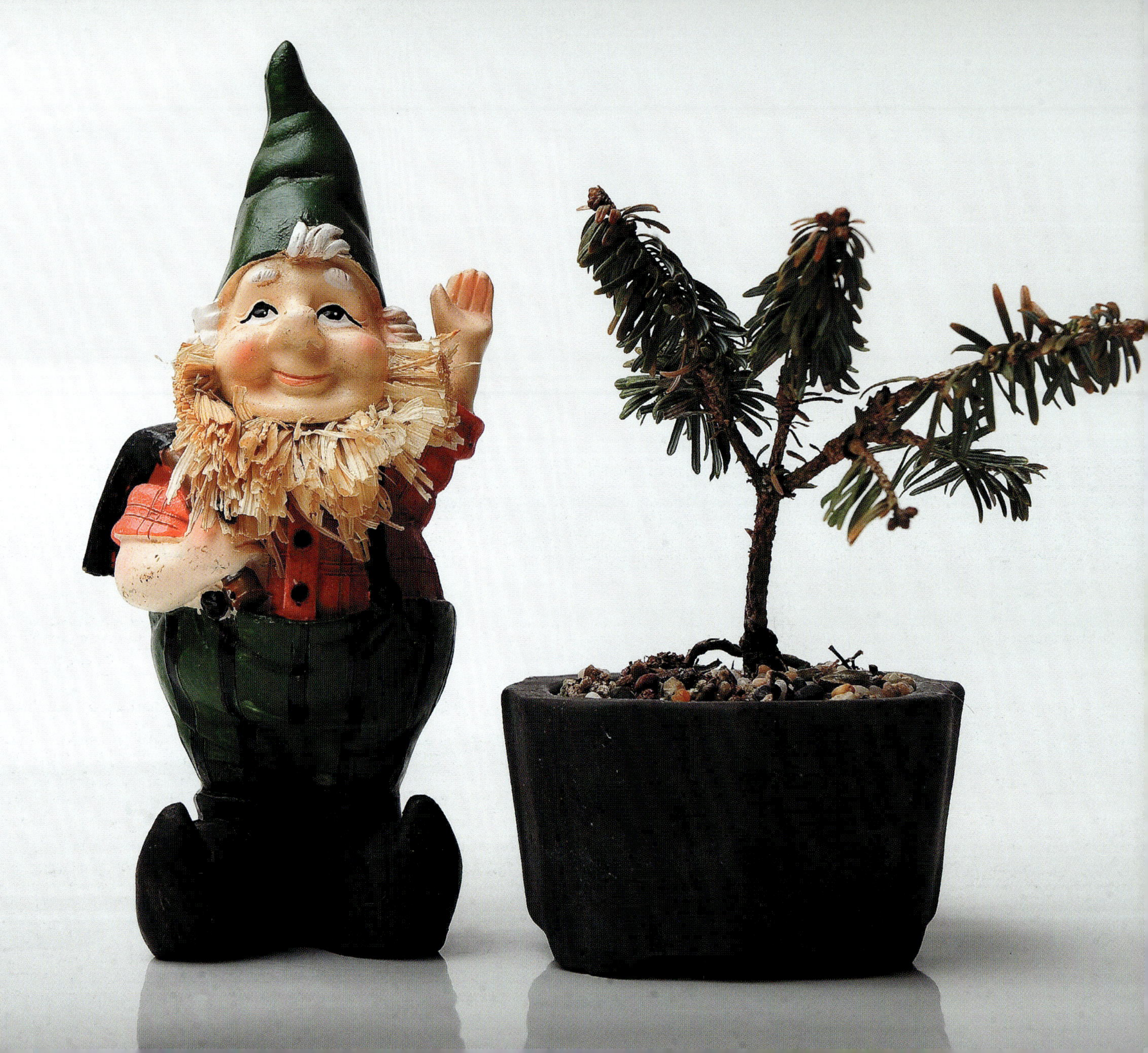

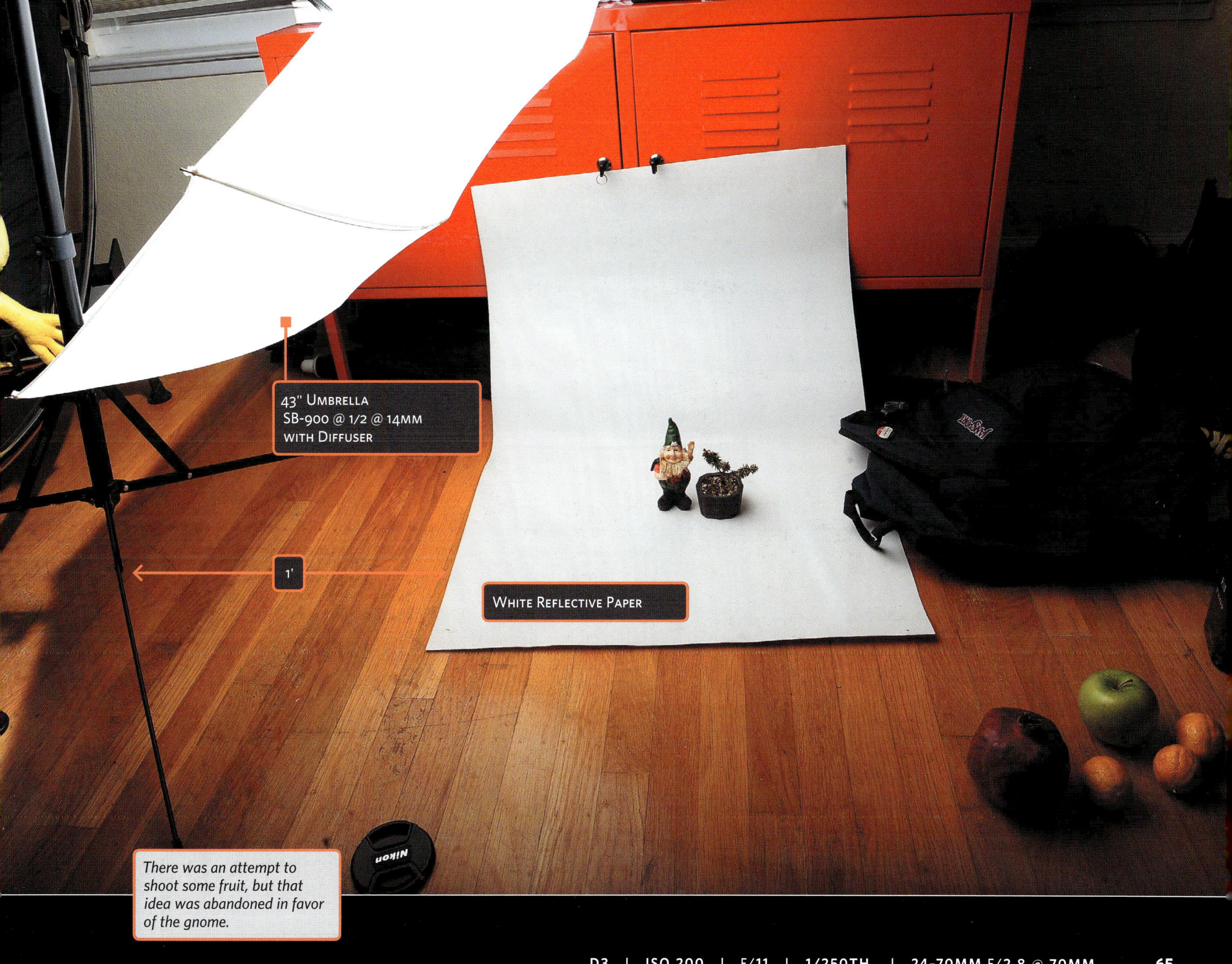

There was an attempt to shoot some fruit, but that idea was abandoned in favor of the gnome.

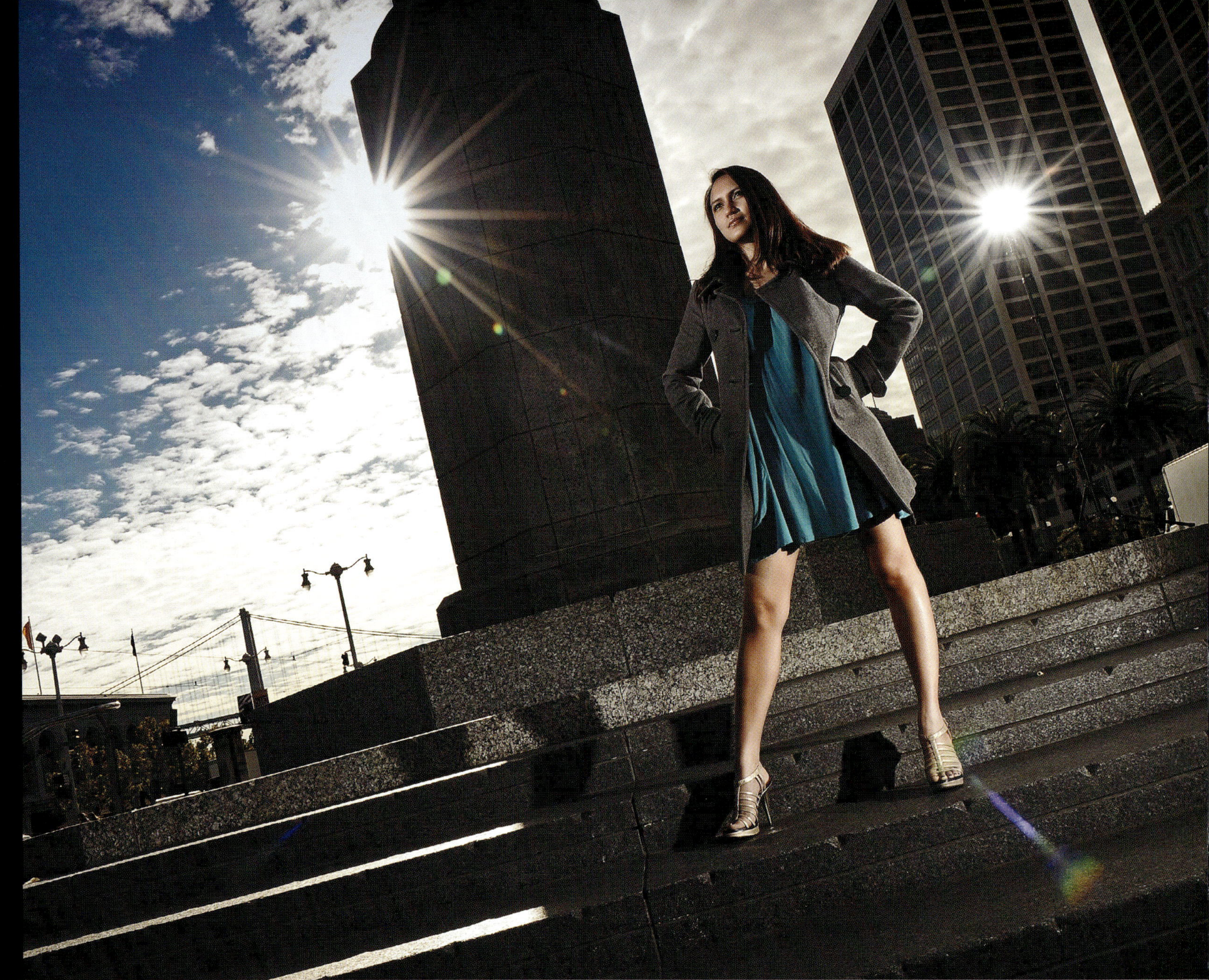

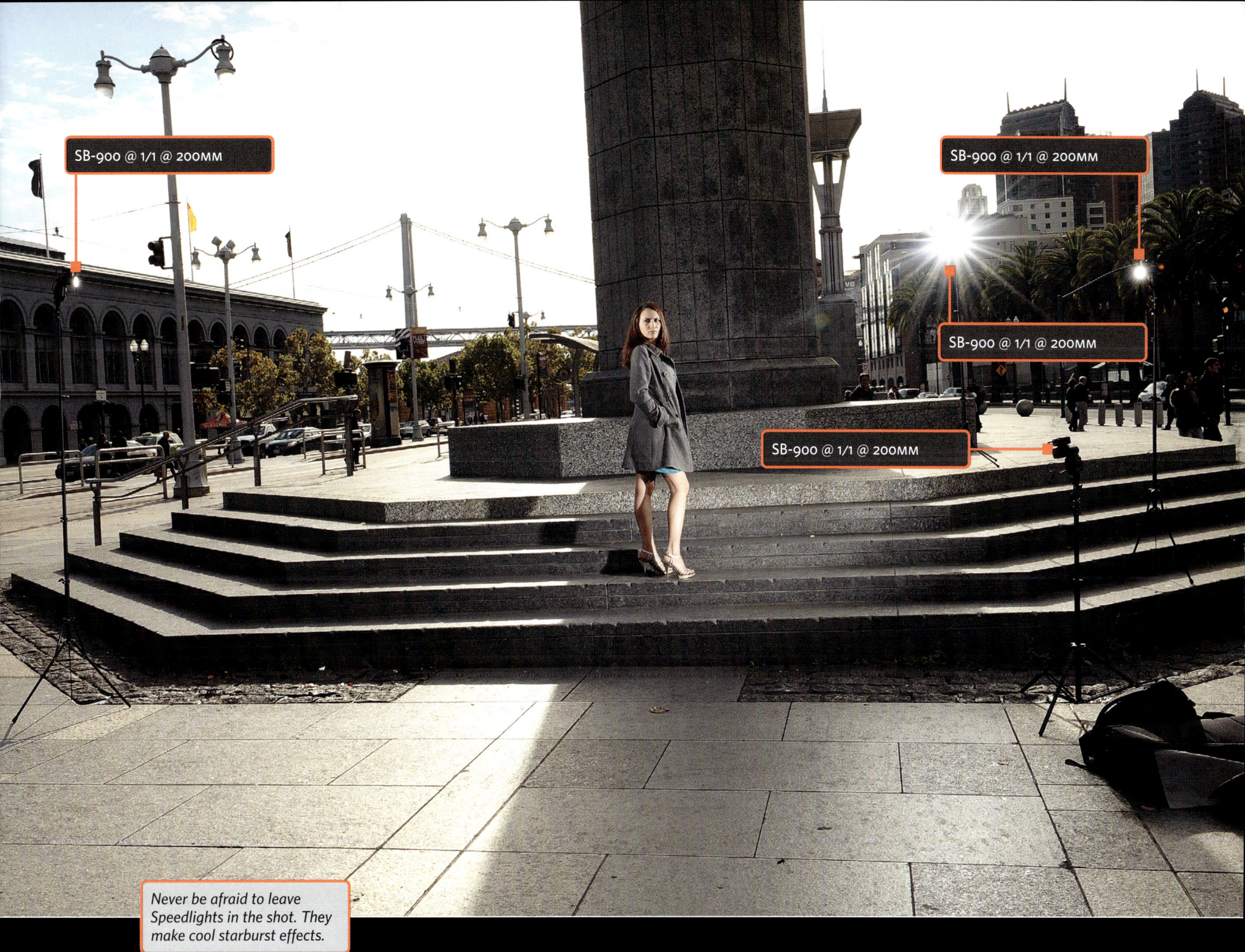

Never be afraid to leave Speedlights in the shot. They make cool starburst effects.

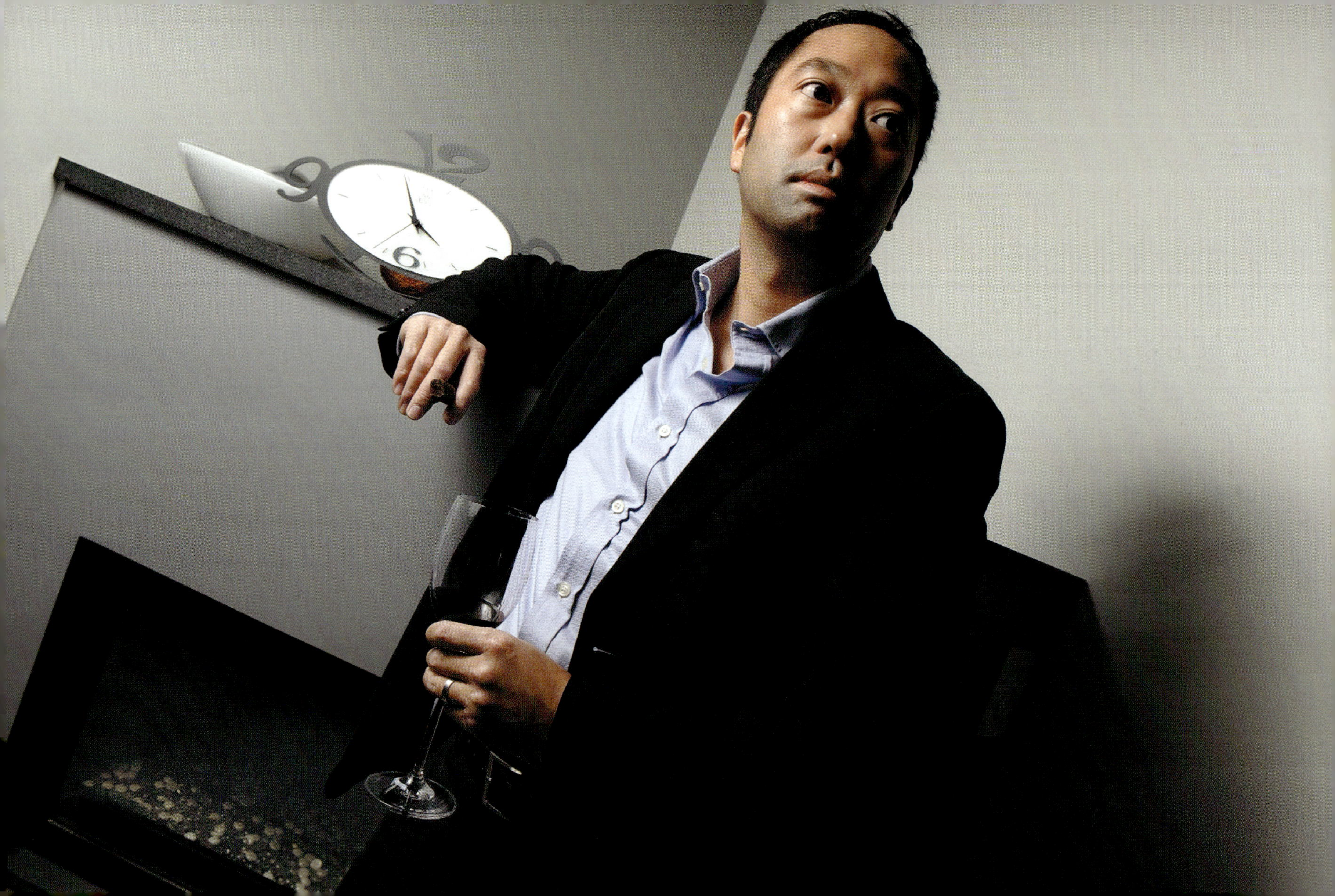

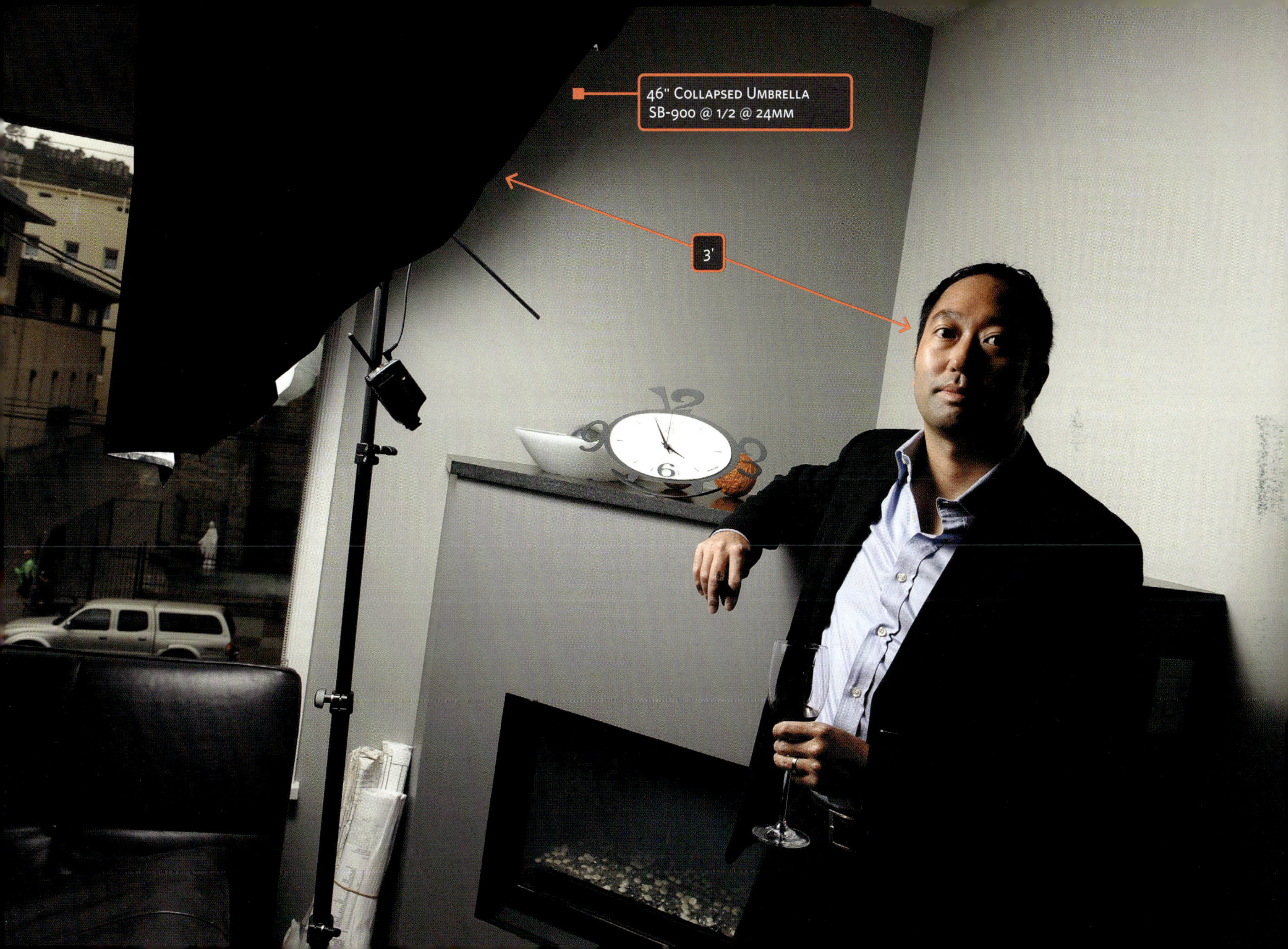
46" Collapsed Umbrella
SB-900 @ 1/2 @ 24mm
3'

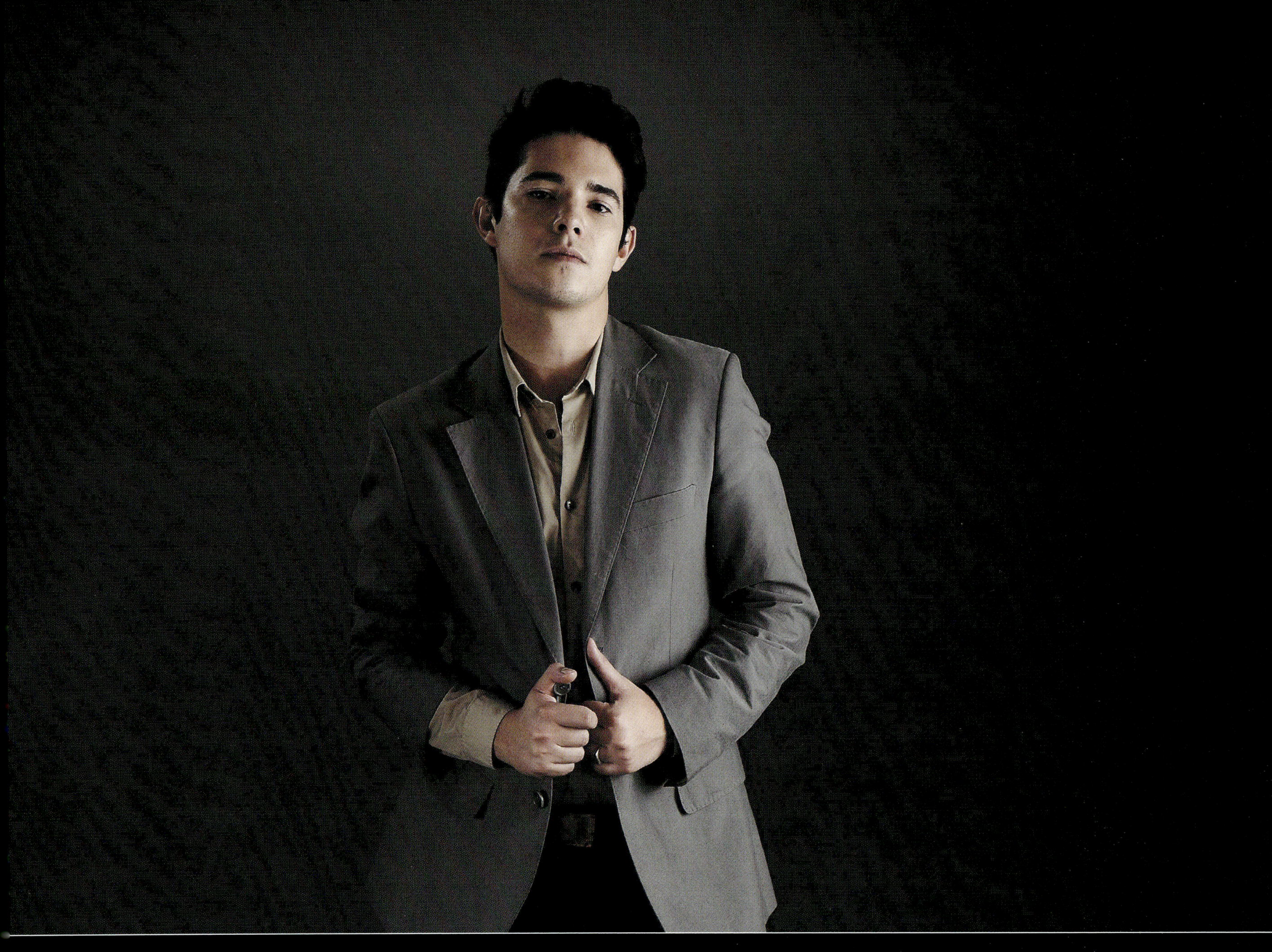

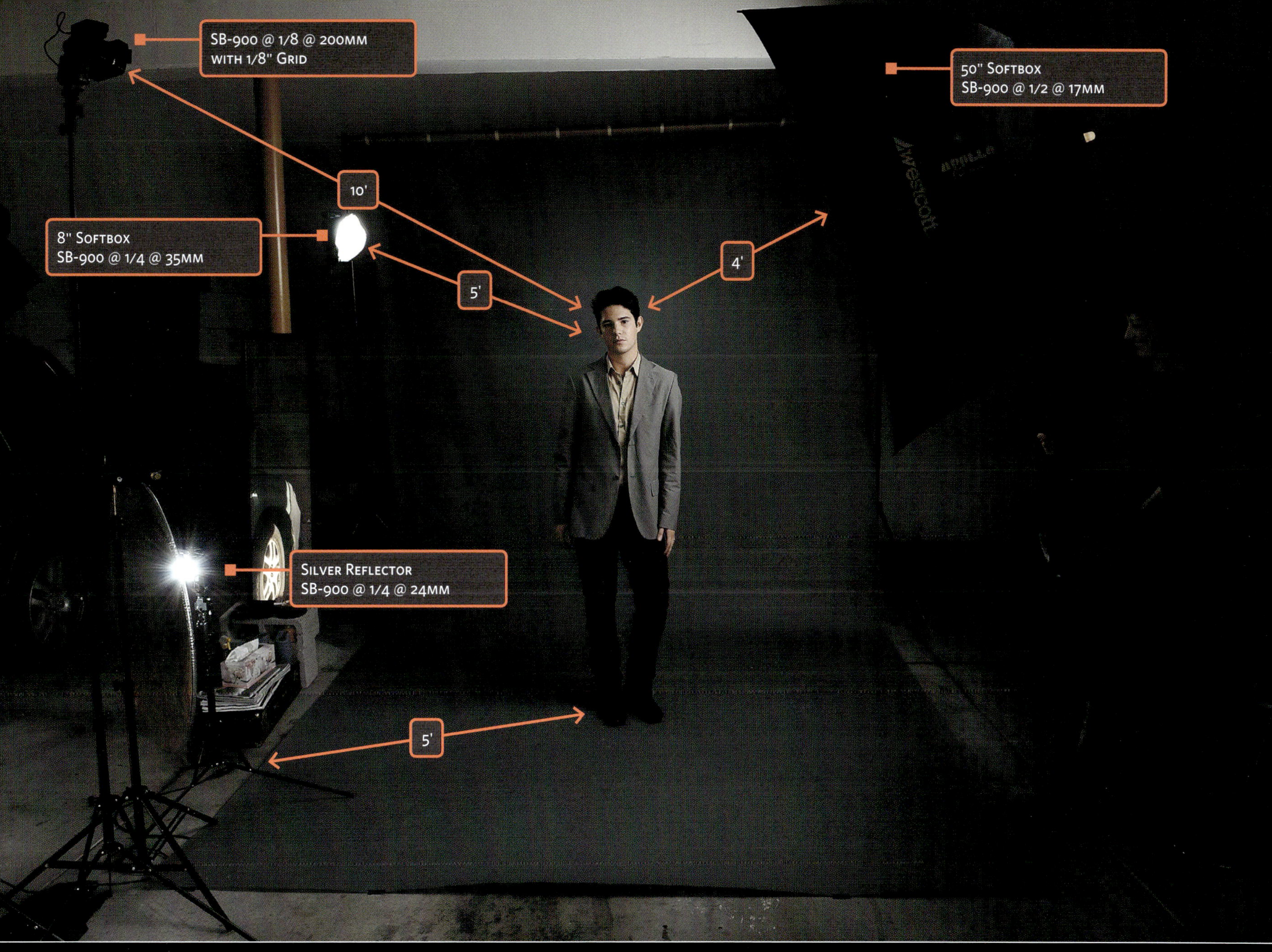

D3 | ISO 200 | F/6.3 | 1/125TH | 24-70MM F/2.8 @ 62MM

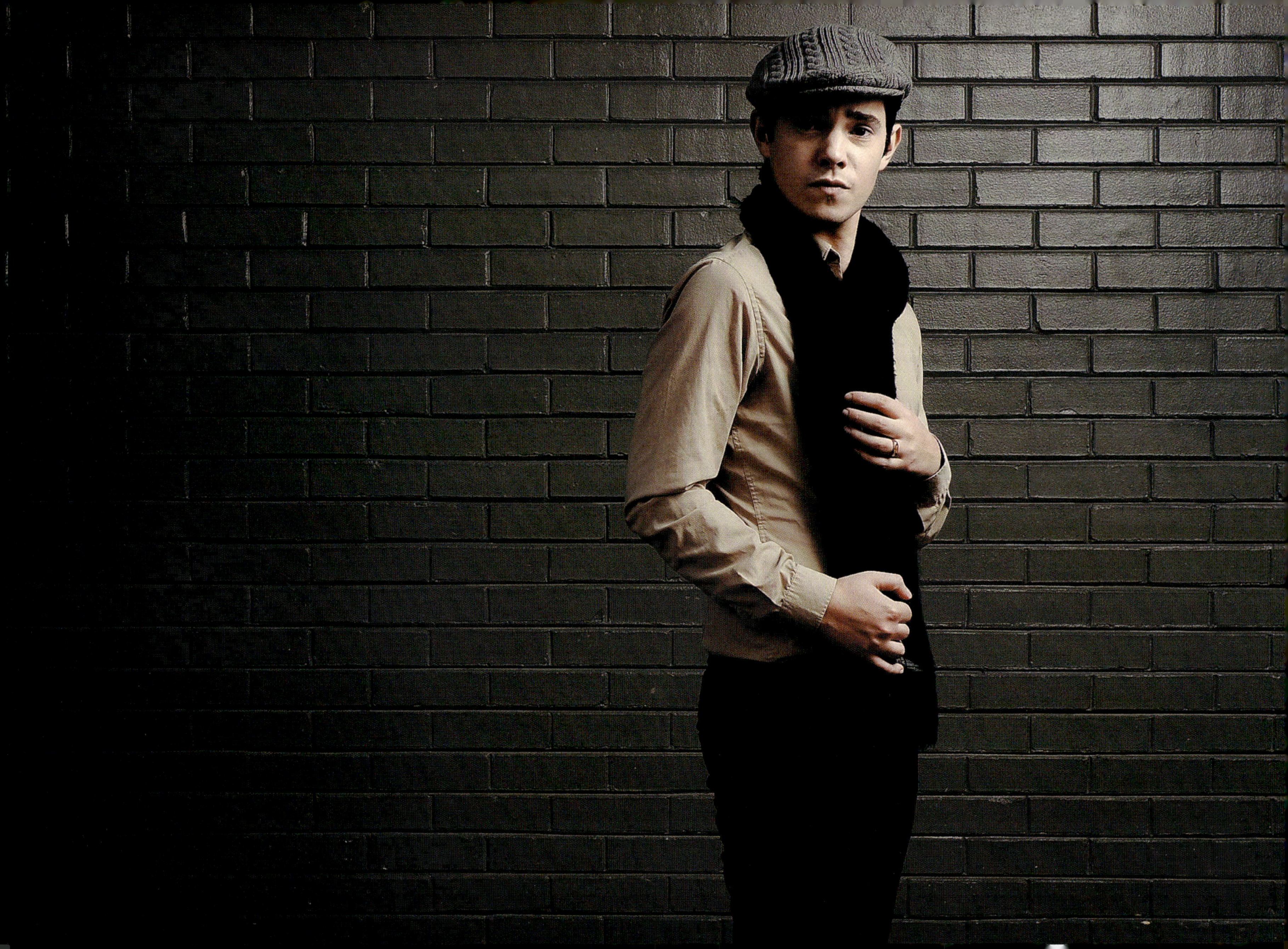

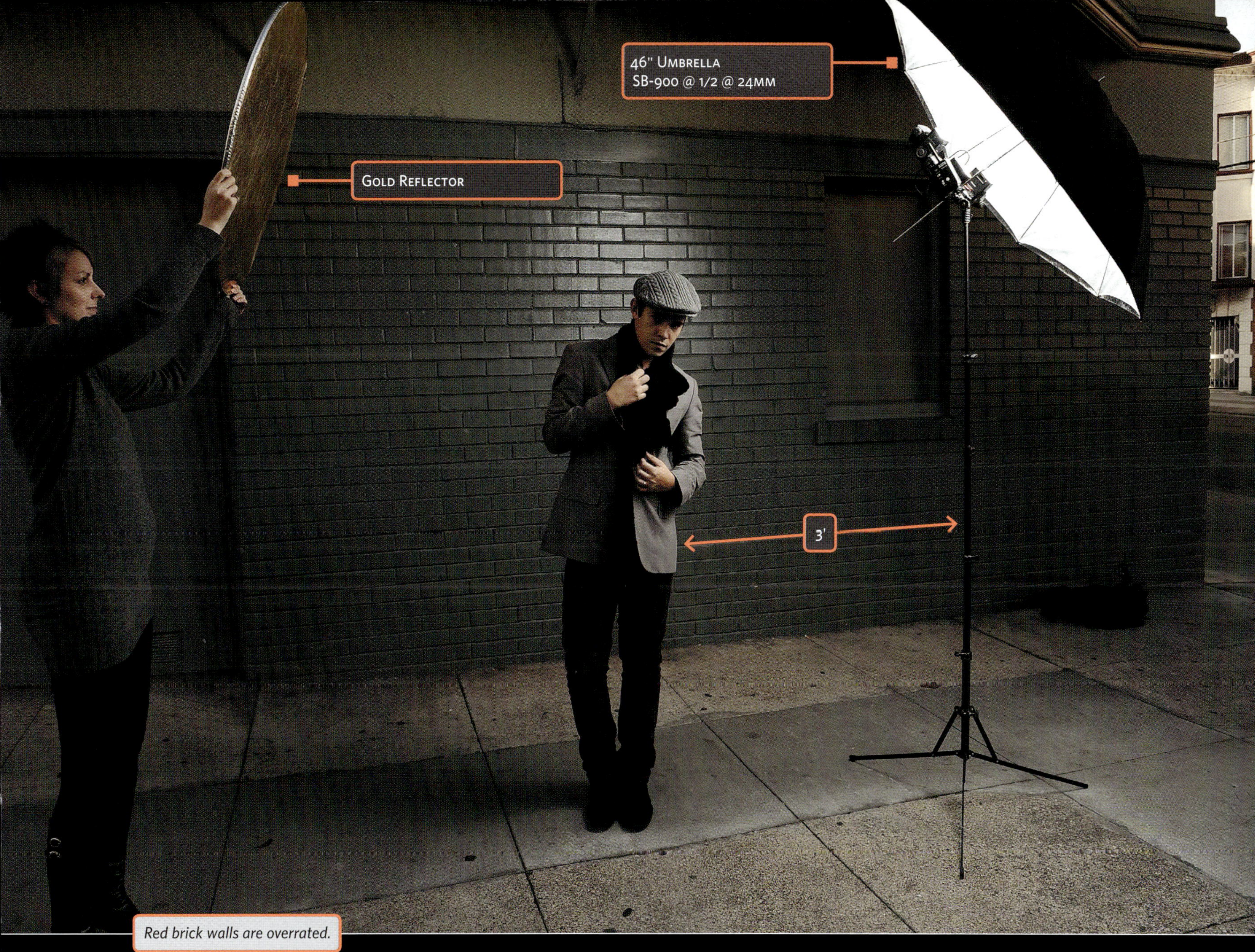

Red brick walls are overrated.

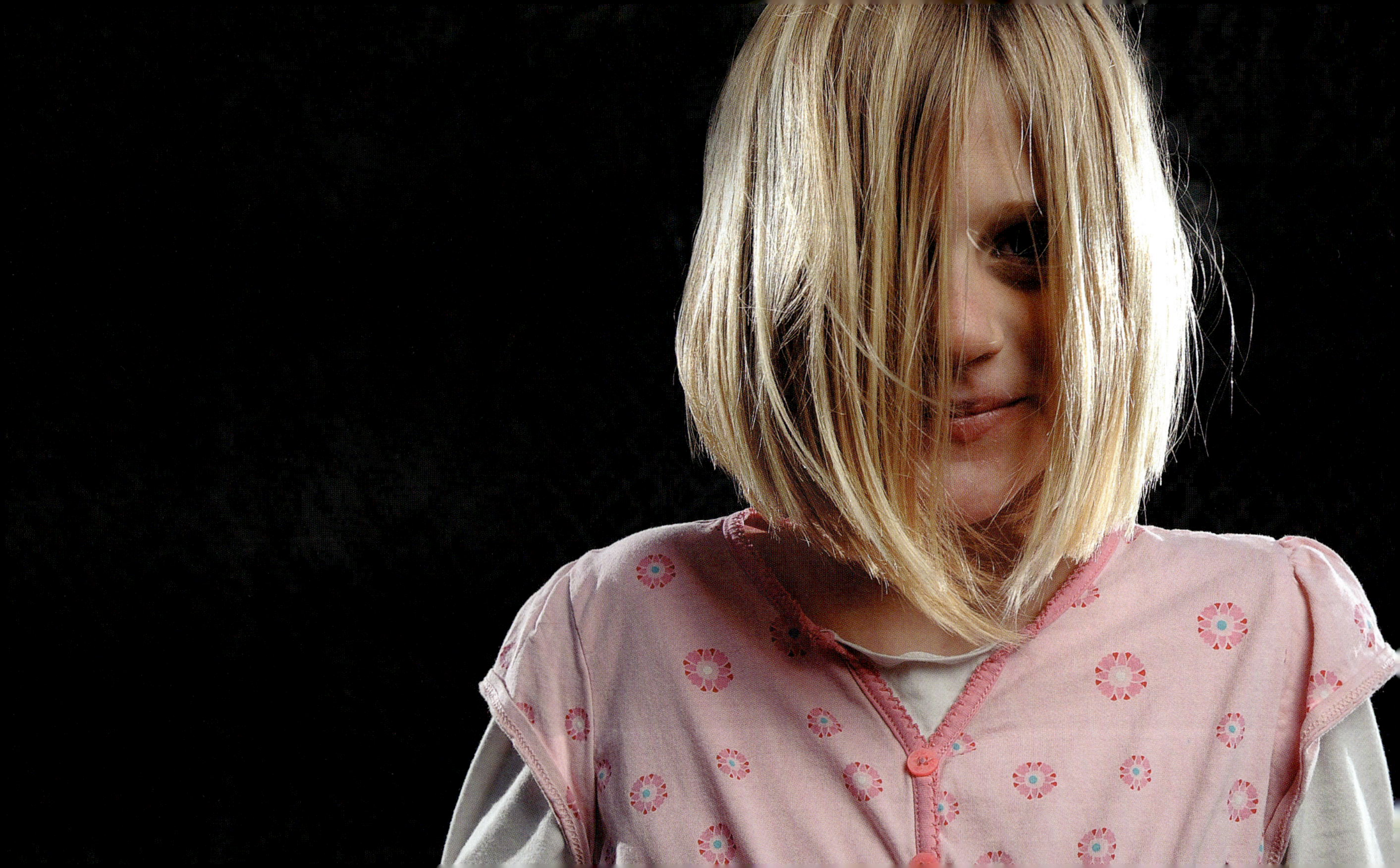

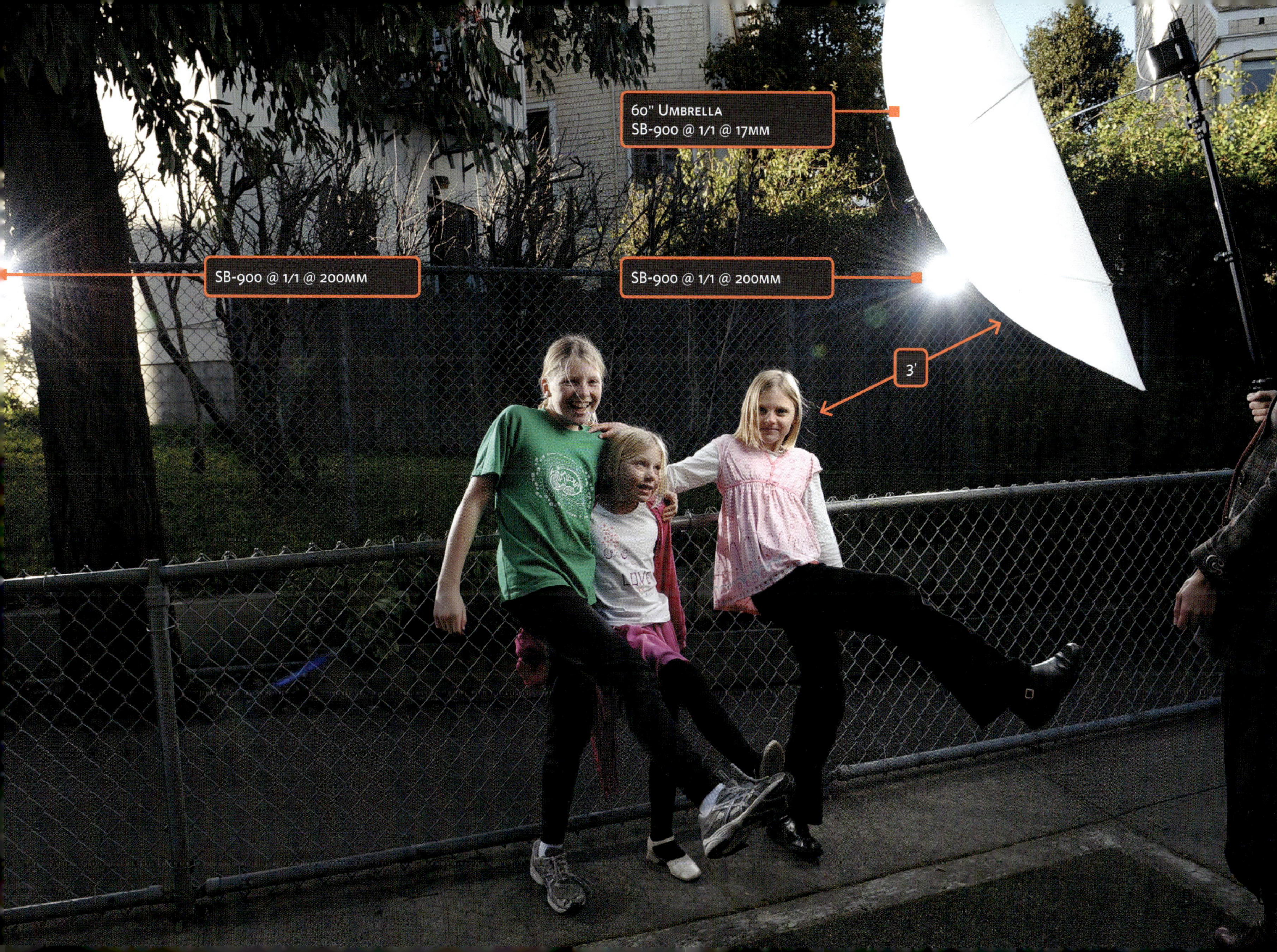
60" Umbrella
SB-900 @ 1/1 @ 17mm
SB-900 @ 1/1 @ 200mm
SB-900 @ 1/1 @ 200mm
3'

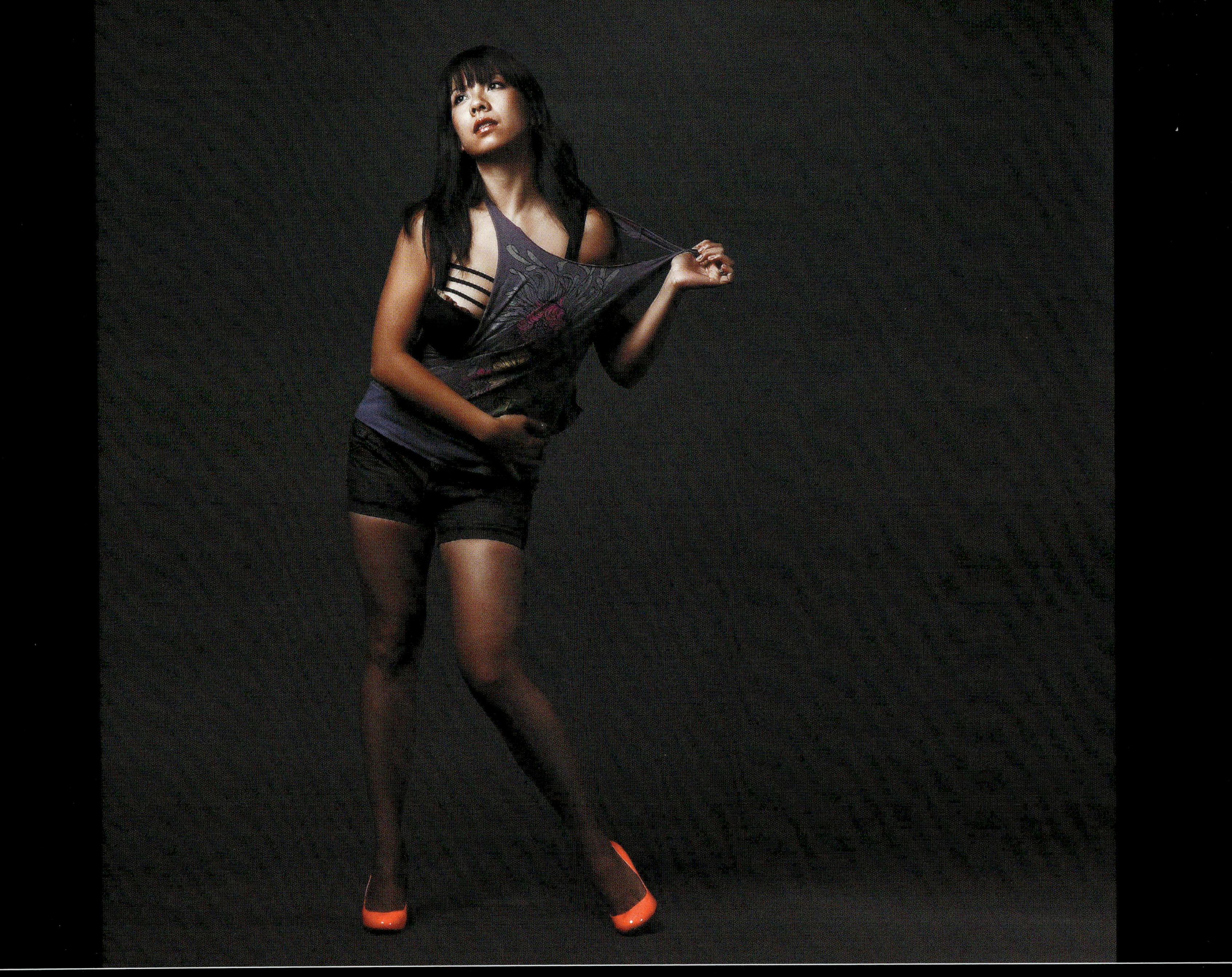

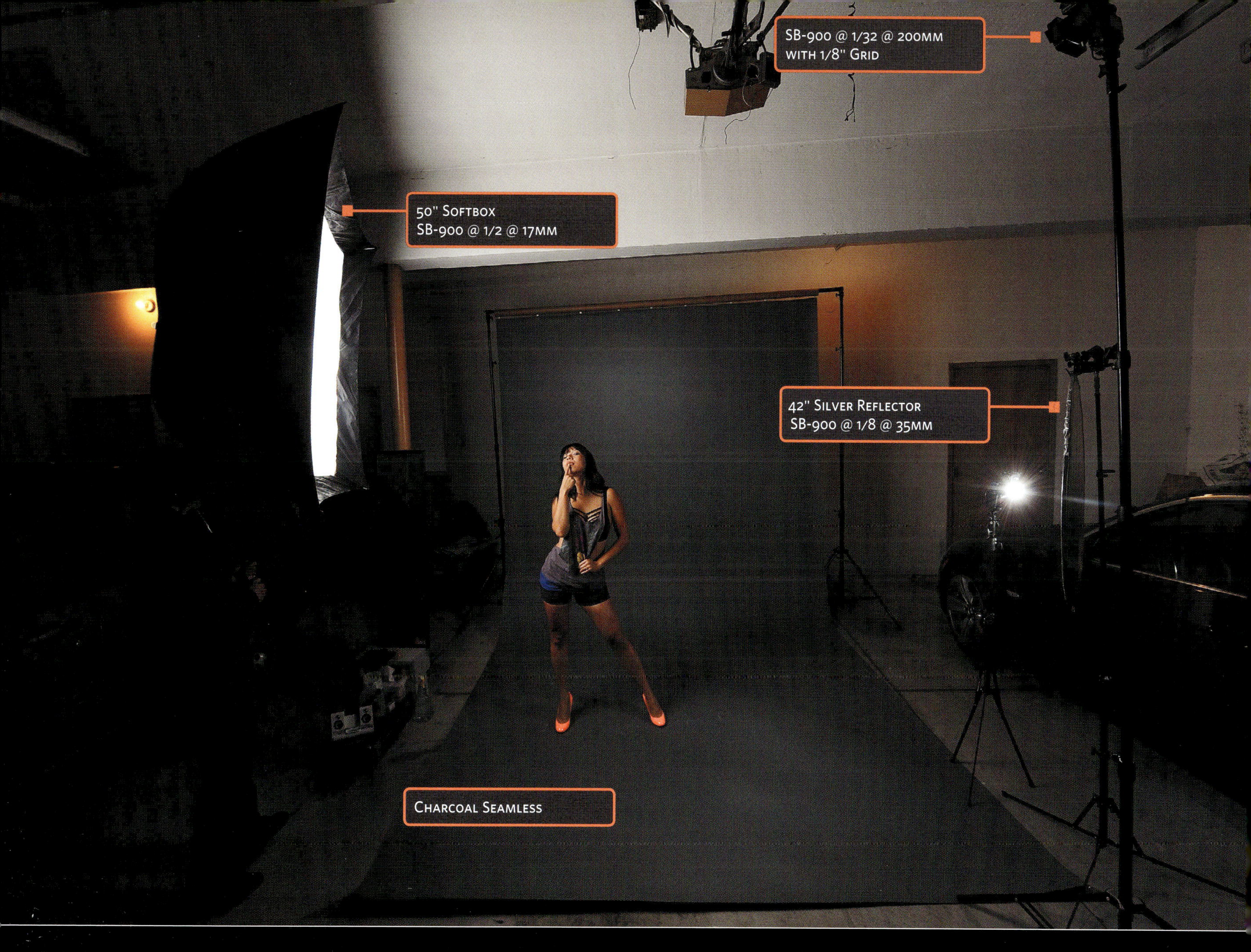

D3 | ISO 200 | F/8 | 1/250TH | 85MM F/1.4 @ 85MM

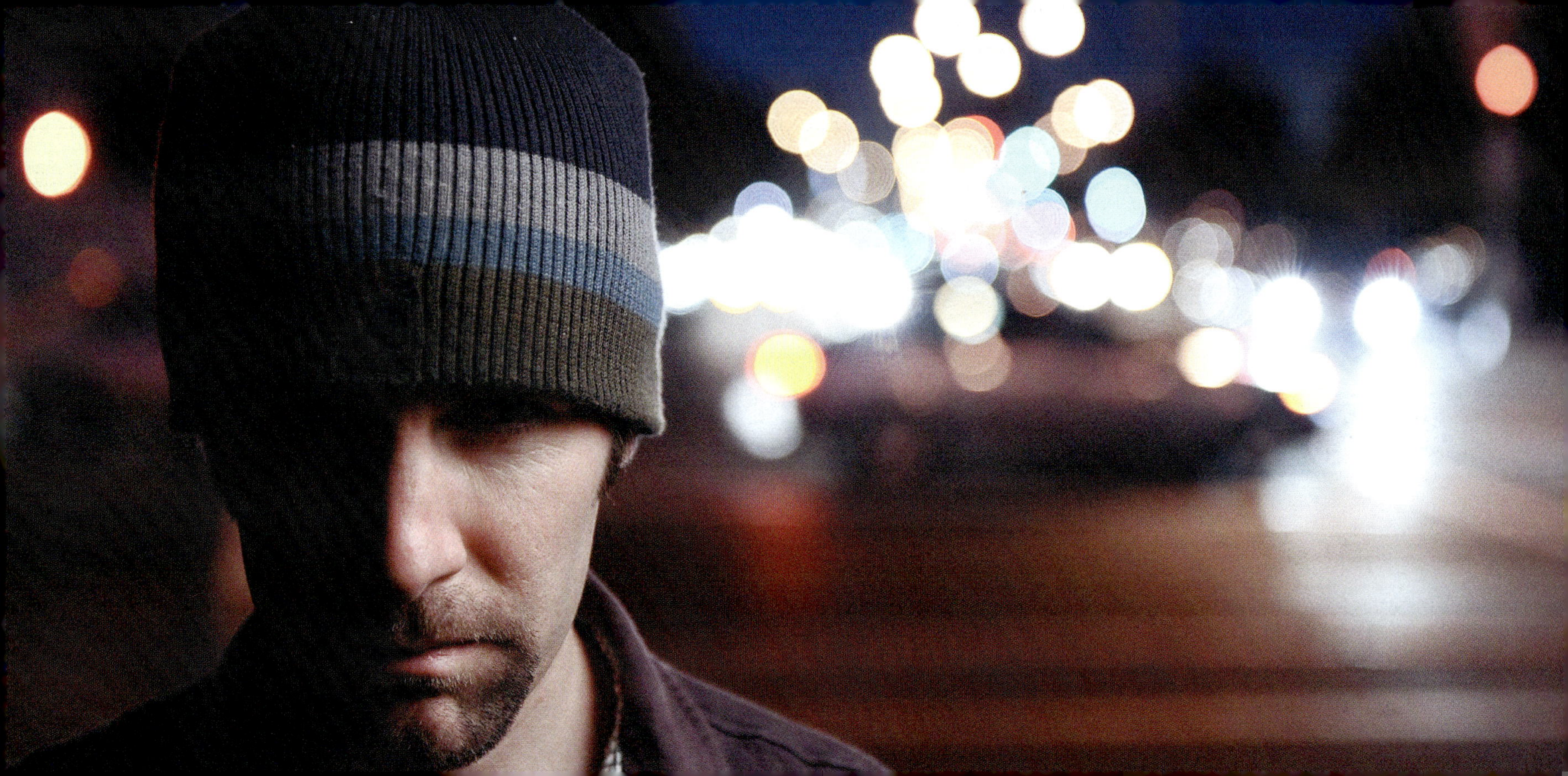

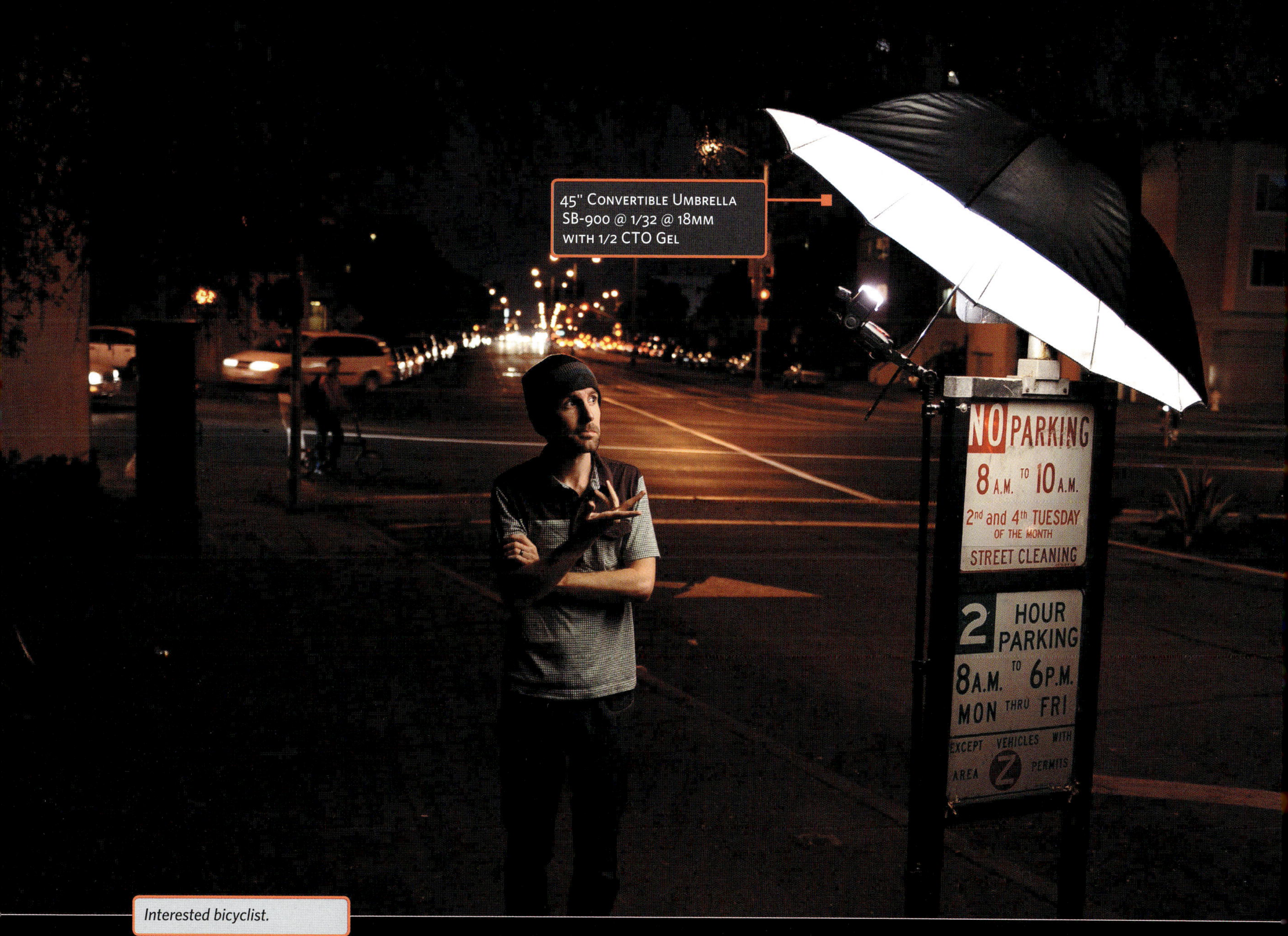

Interested bicyclist.

D3 | ISO 800 | F/2.8 | 1/15TH | 24-70MM F/2.8 @ 70MM

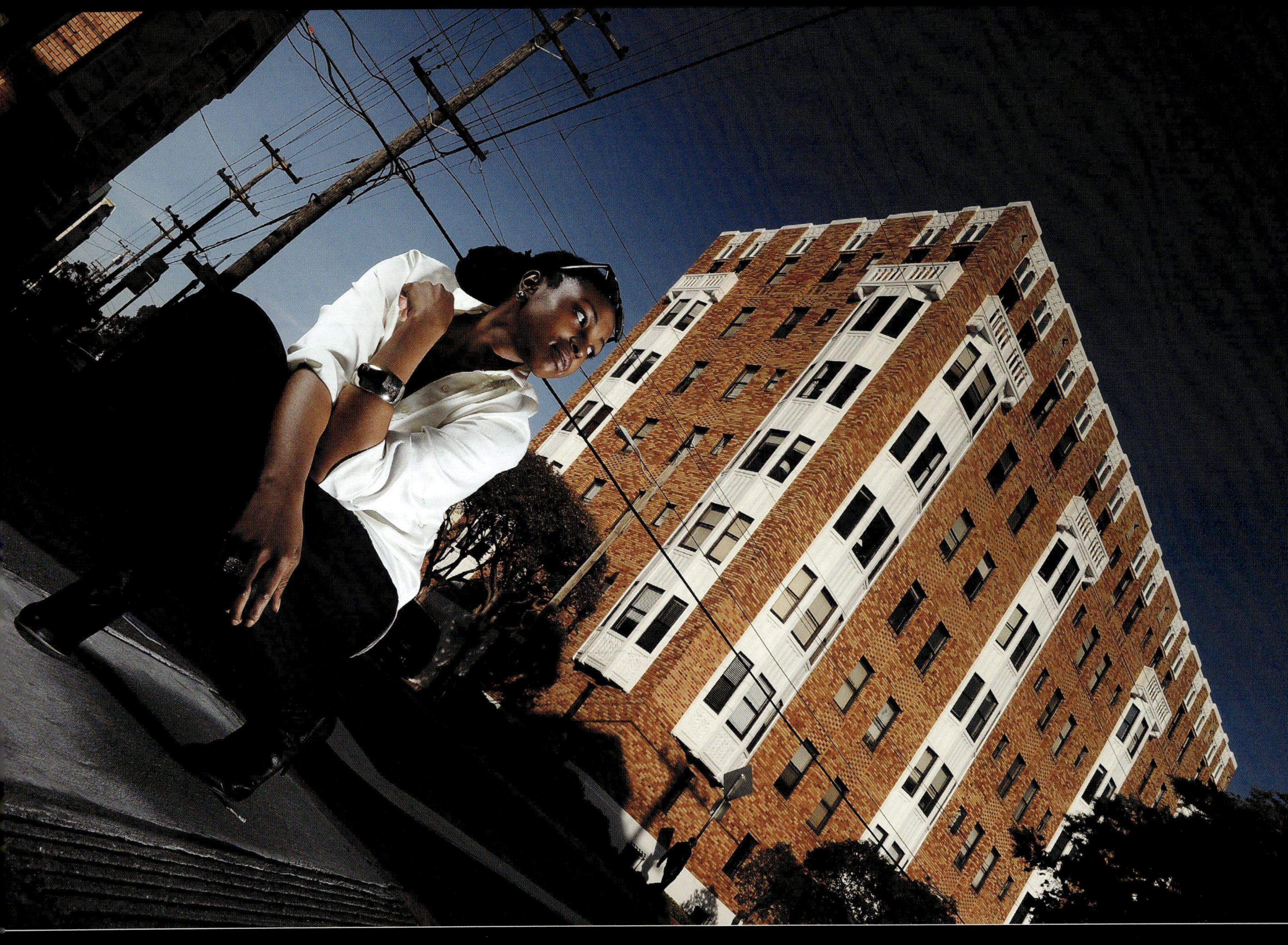

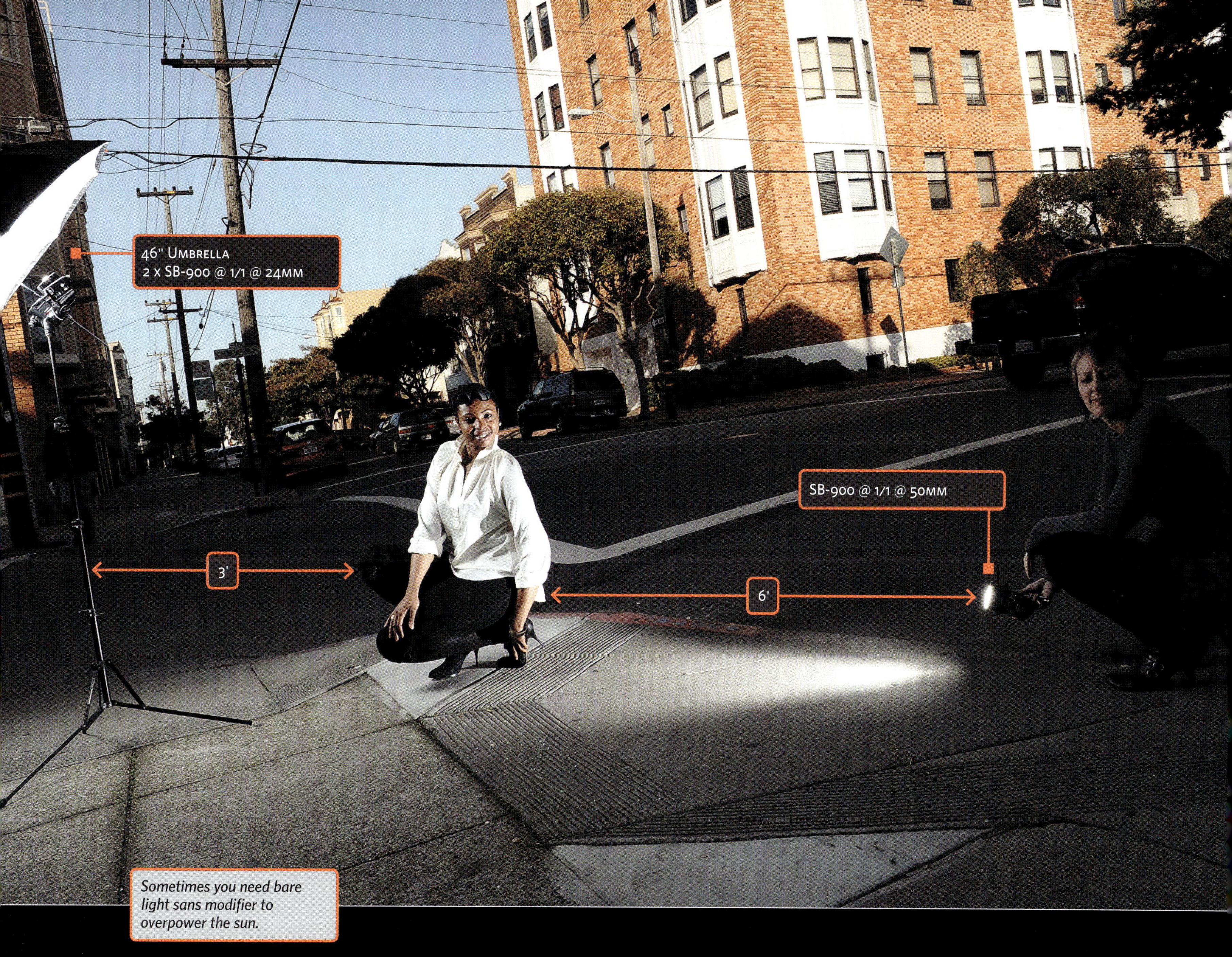

Sometimes you need bare light sans modifier to overpower the sun.

D3 | ISO 200 | F/14 | 1/250TH | 24-70MM F/2.8 @ 24MM

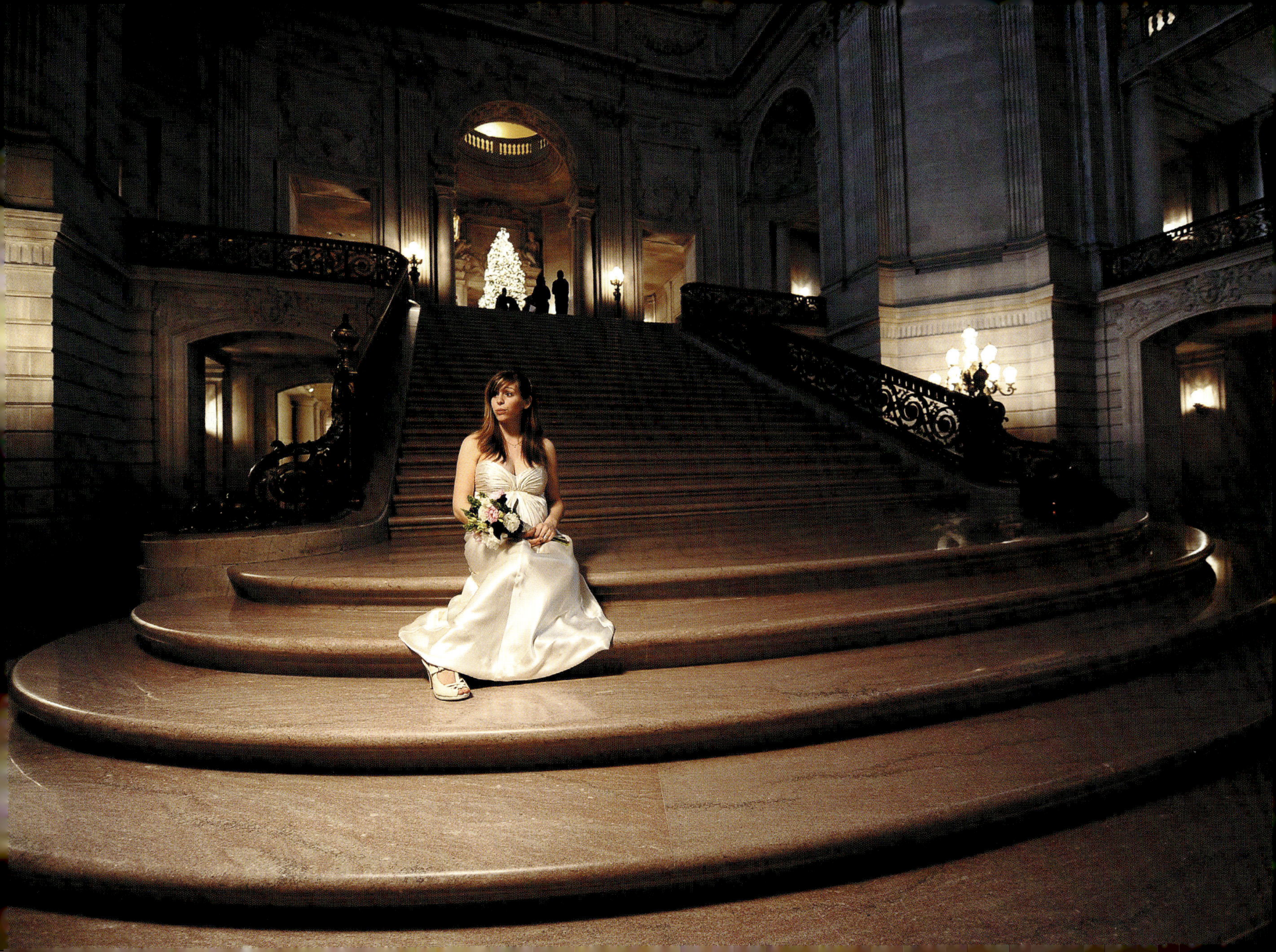

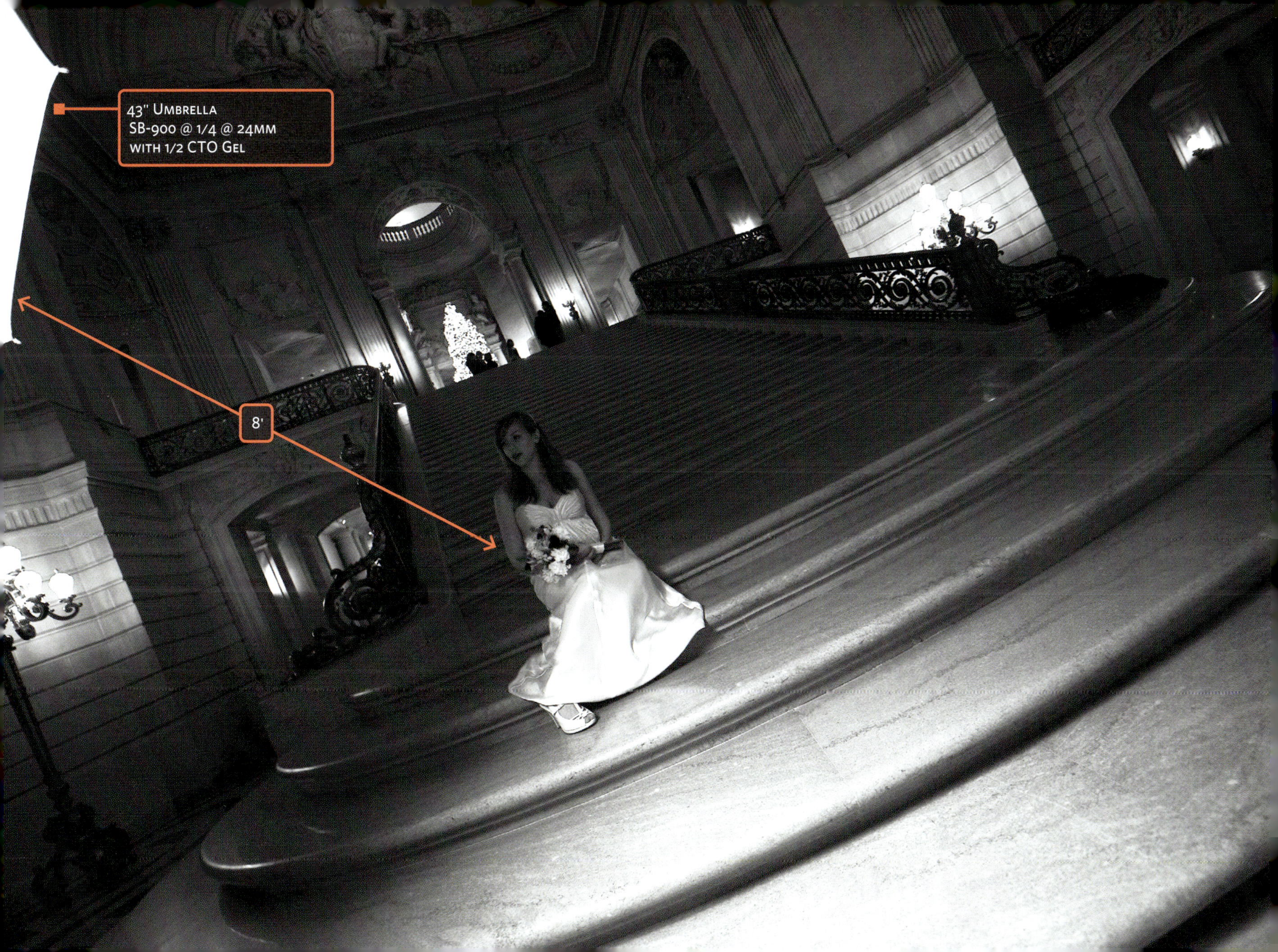
43" Umbrella
SB-900 @ 1/4 @ 24mm
with 1/2 CTO Gel
8'

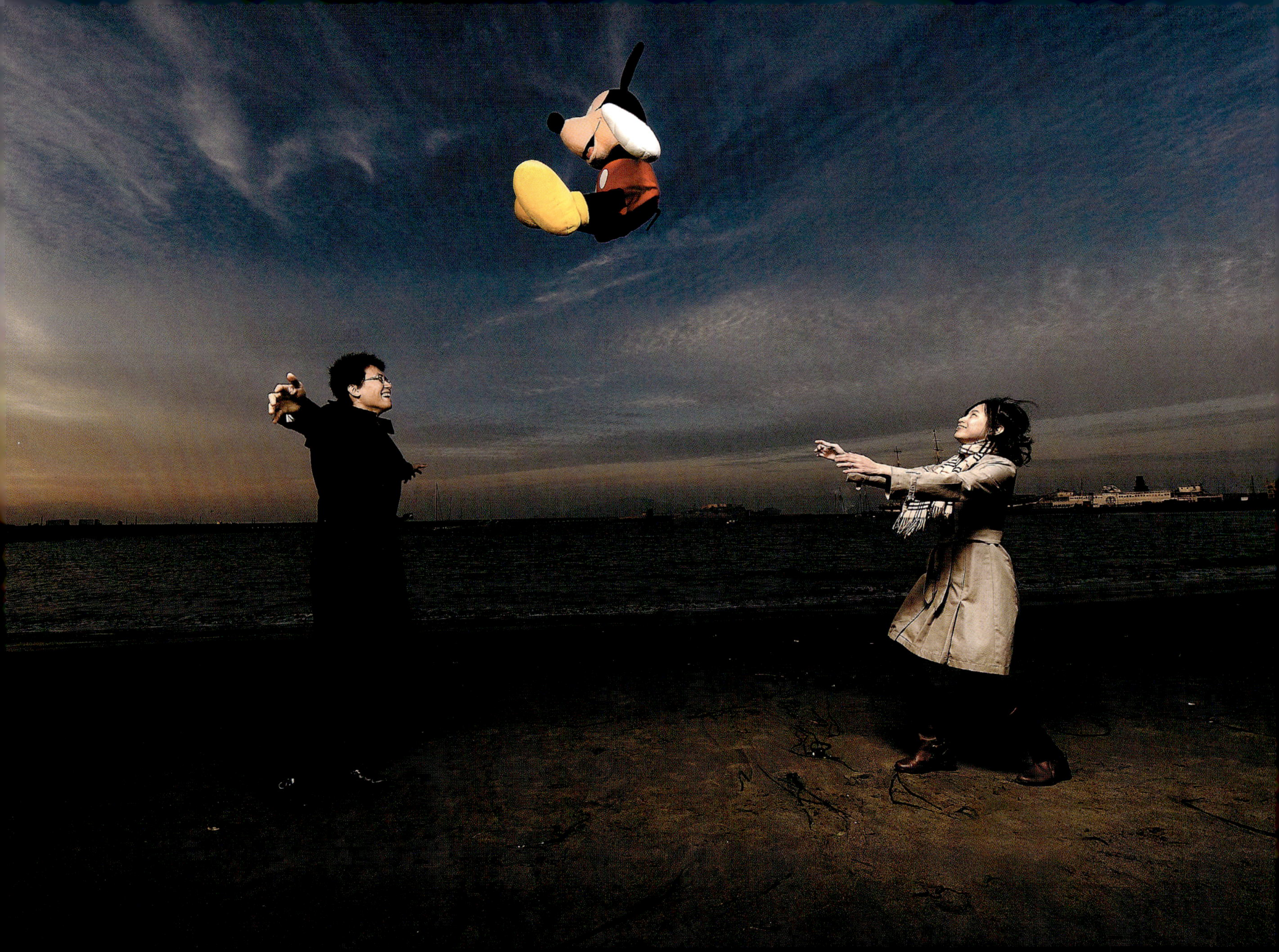

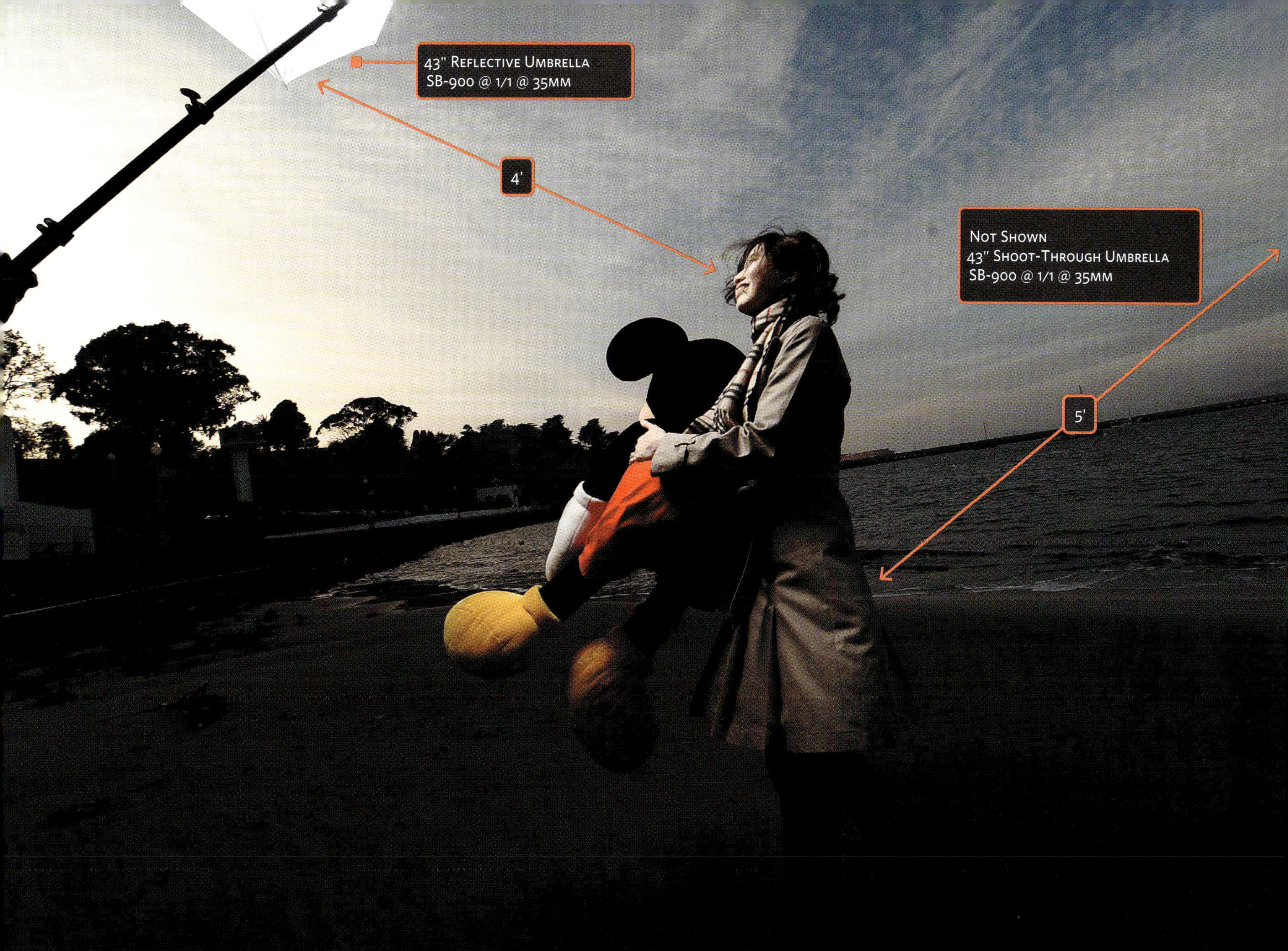
43" Reflective Umbrella
SB-900 @ 1/1 @ 35mm
4'
Not Shown
43" Shoot-Through Umbrella
SB-900 @ 1/1 @ 35mm
5'

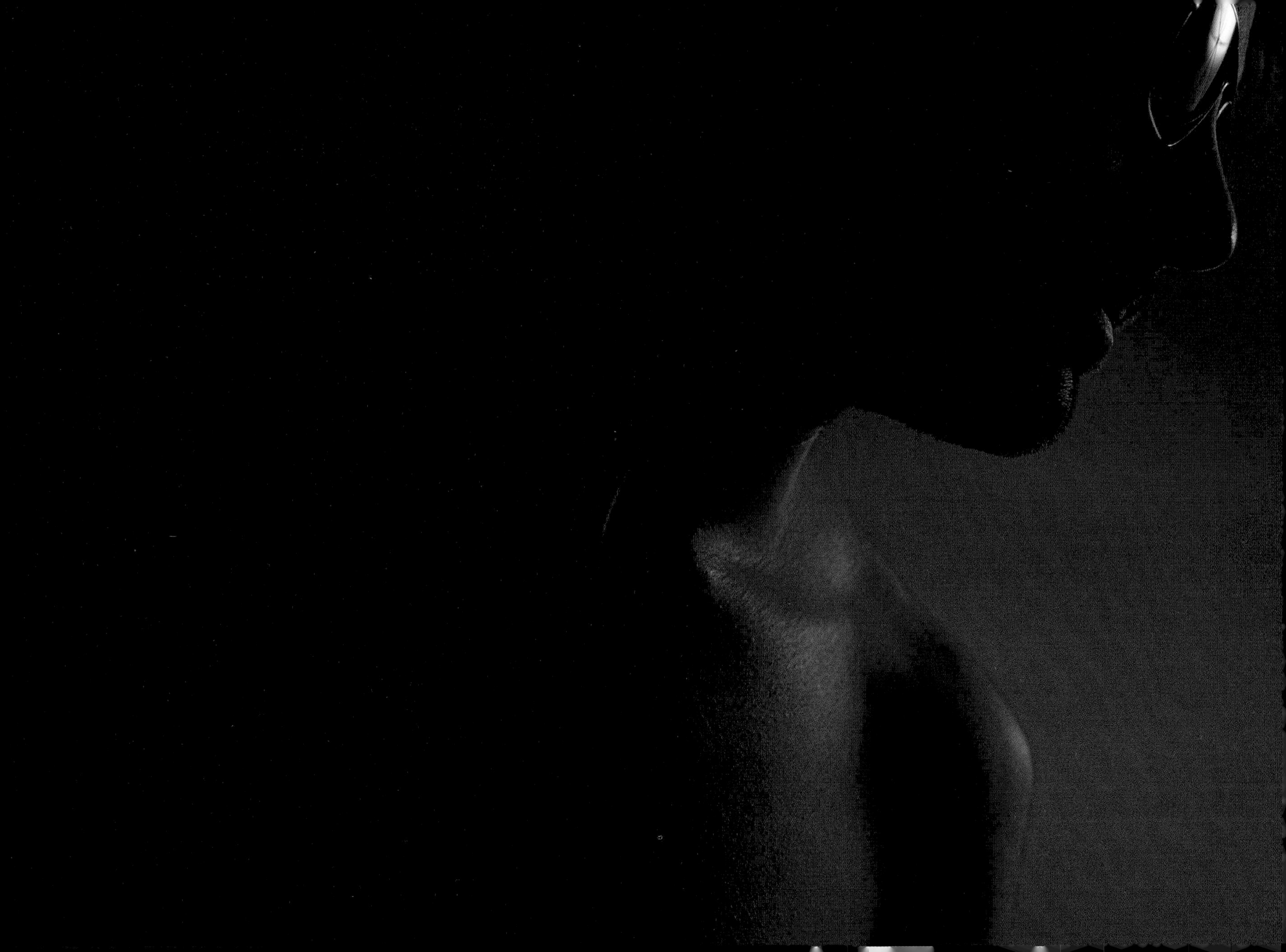

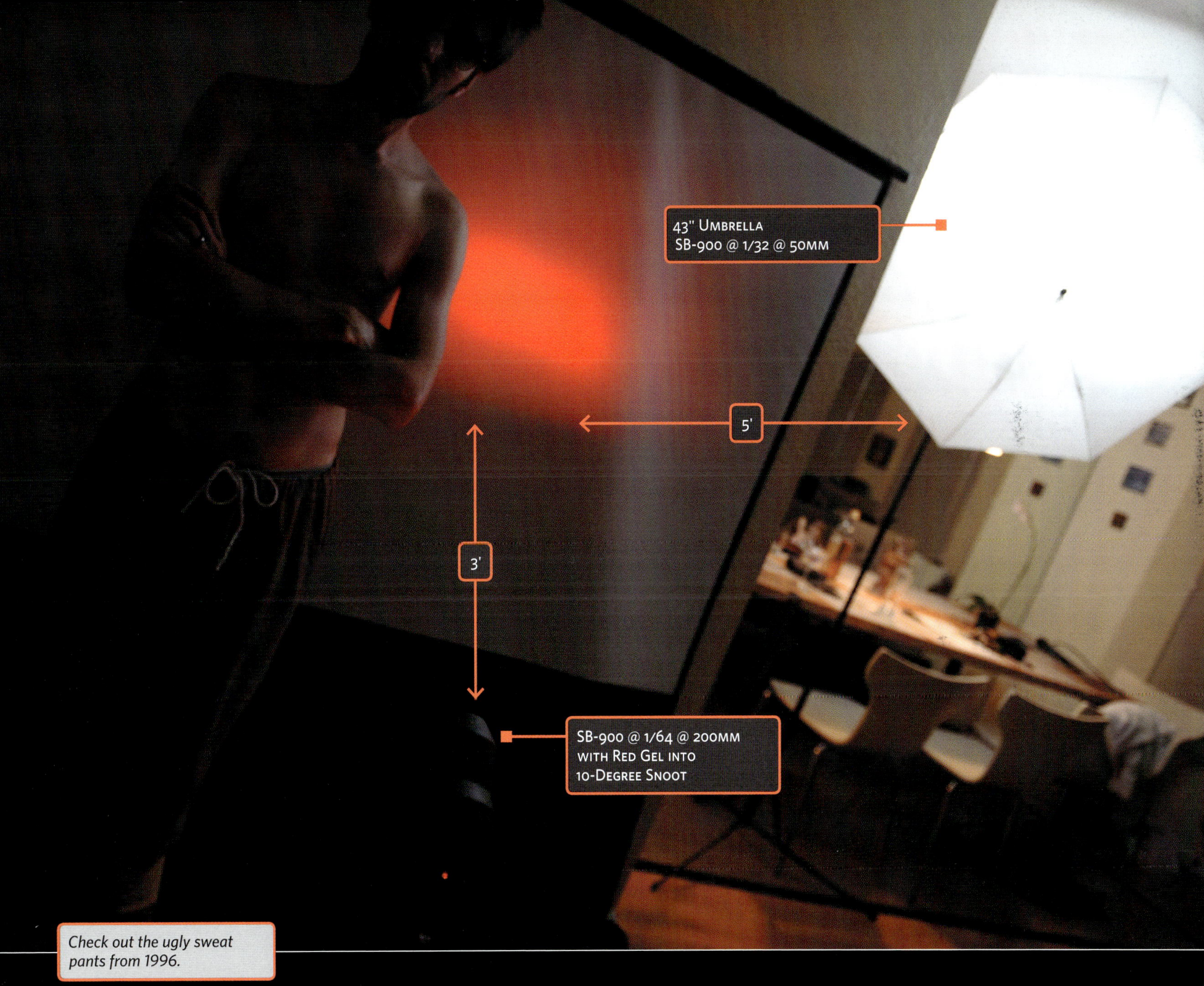

Check out the ugly sweat pants from 1996.

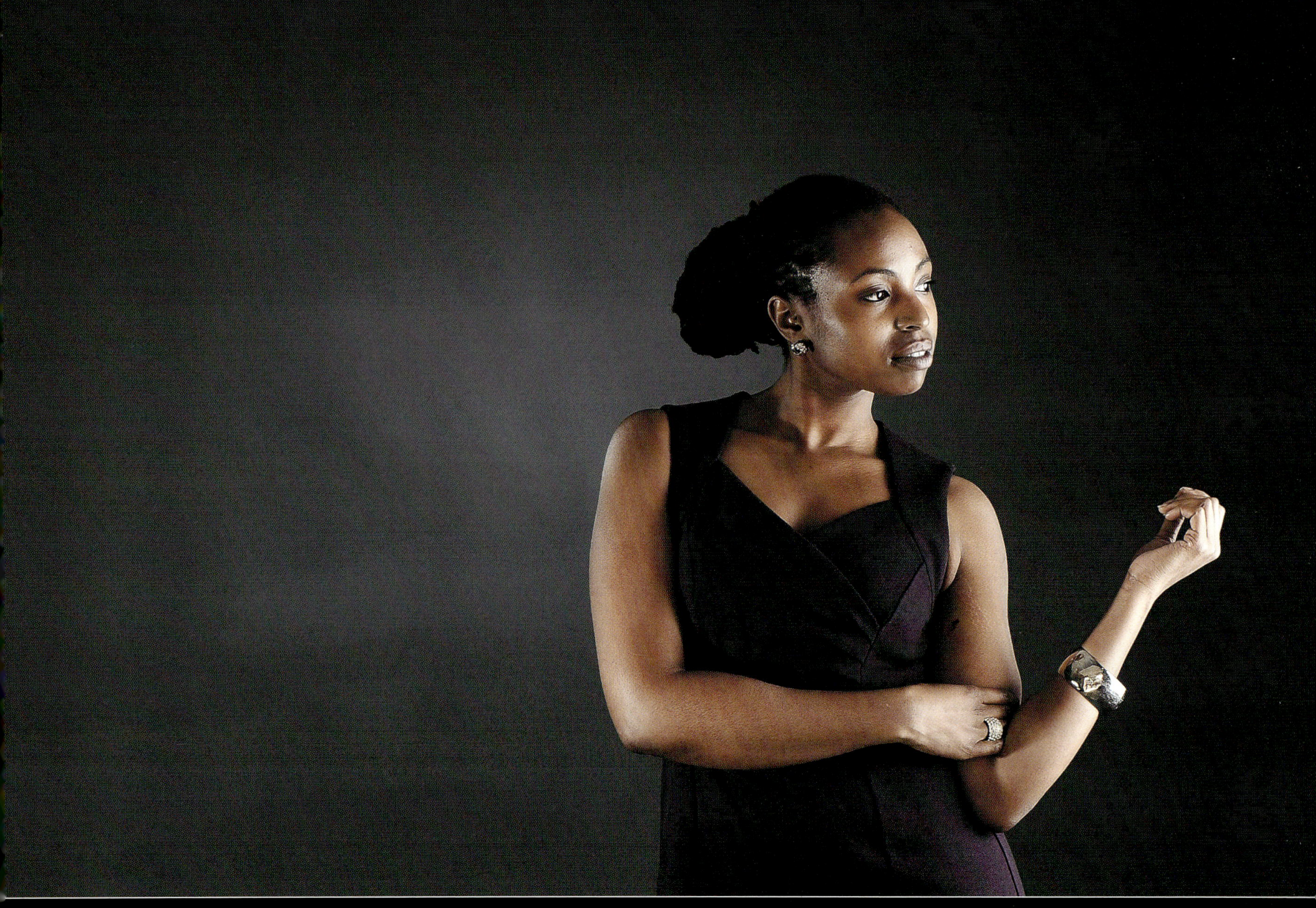

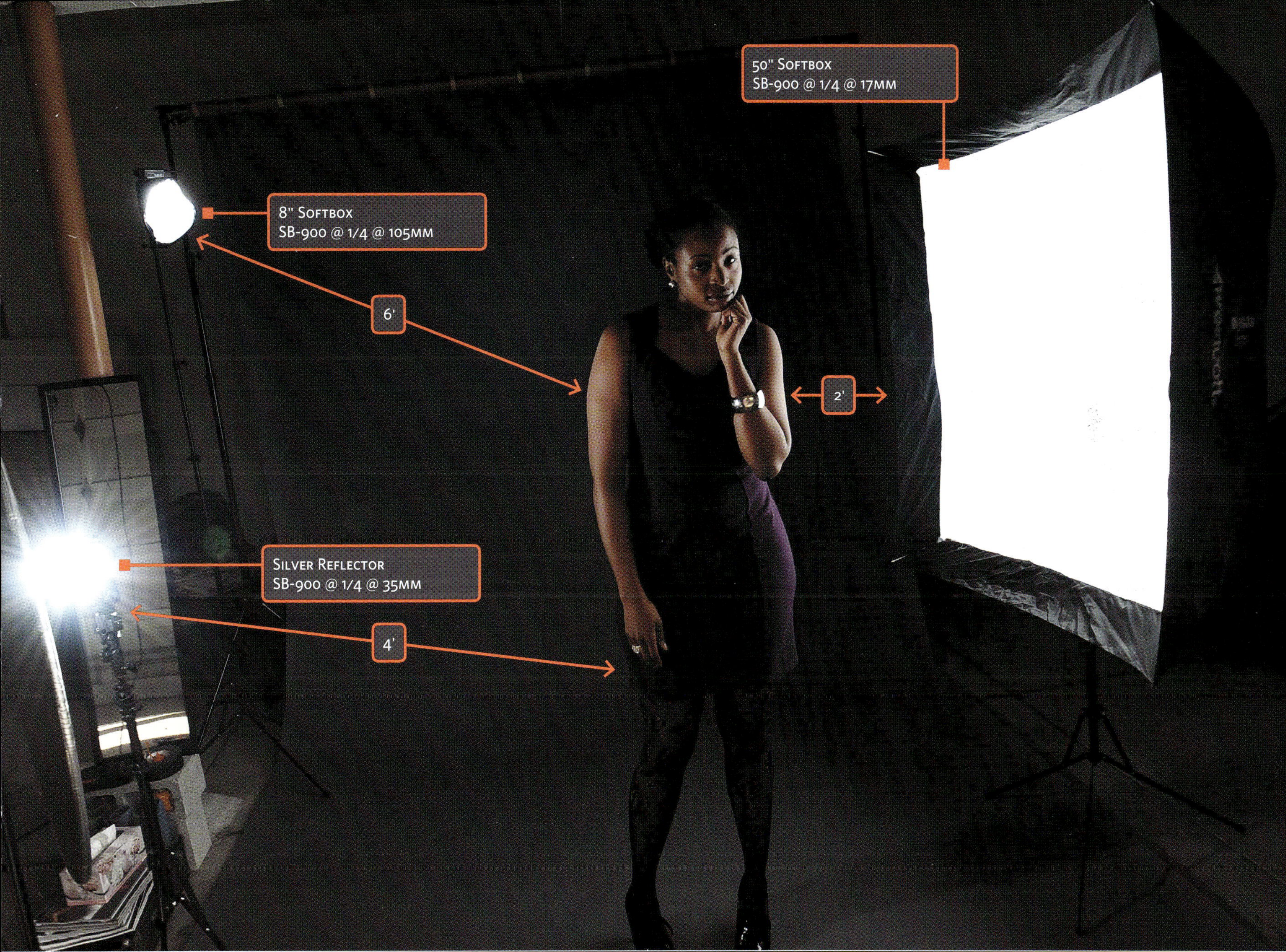

50" Softbox
SB-900 @ 1/4 @ 17mm
8" Softbox
SB-900 @ 1/4 @ 105mm
6'
2'
Silver Reflector
SB-900 @ 1/4 @ 35mm
4'

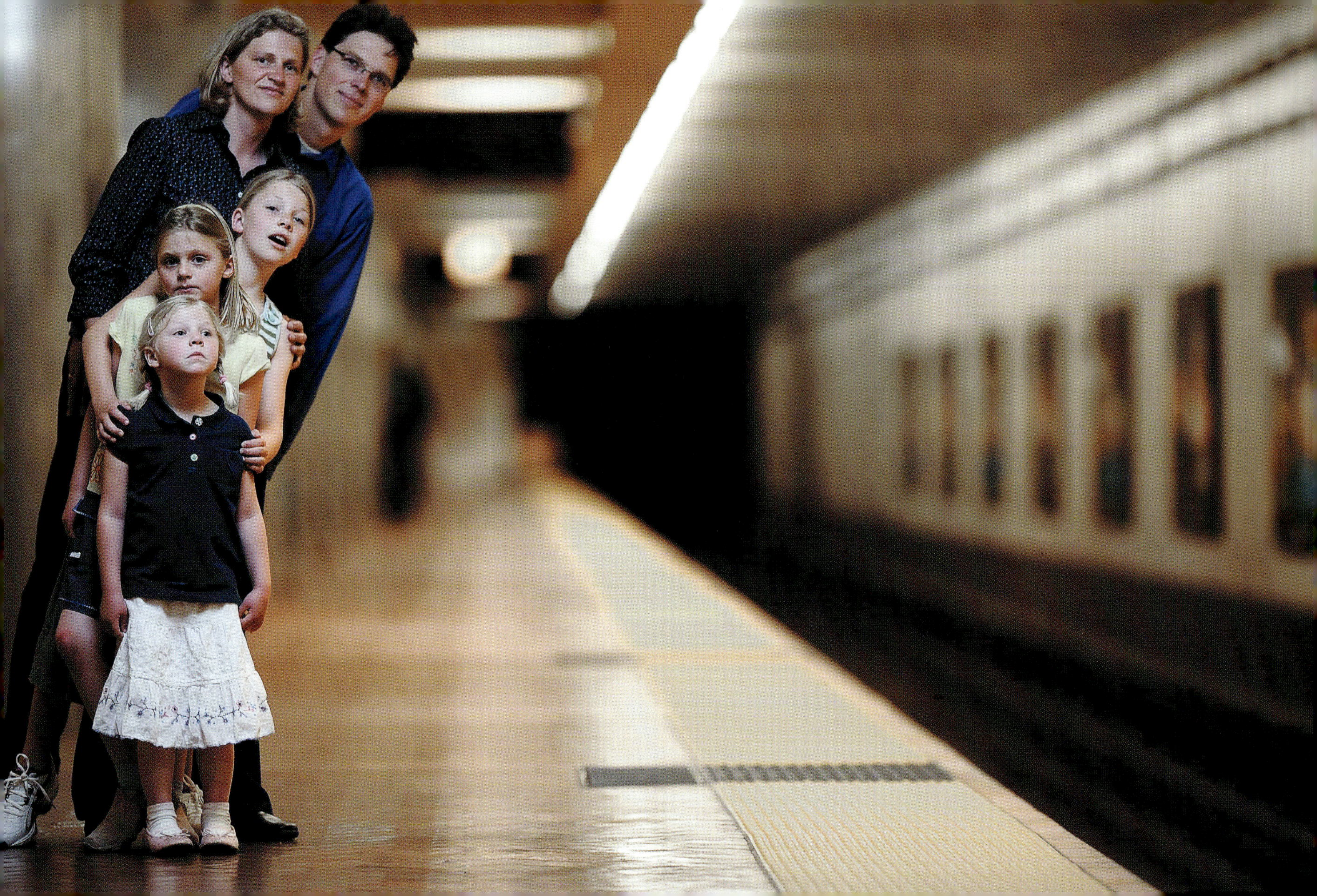

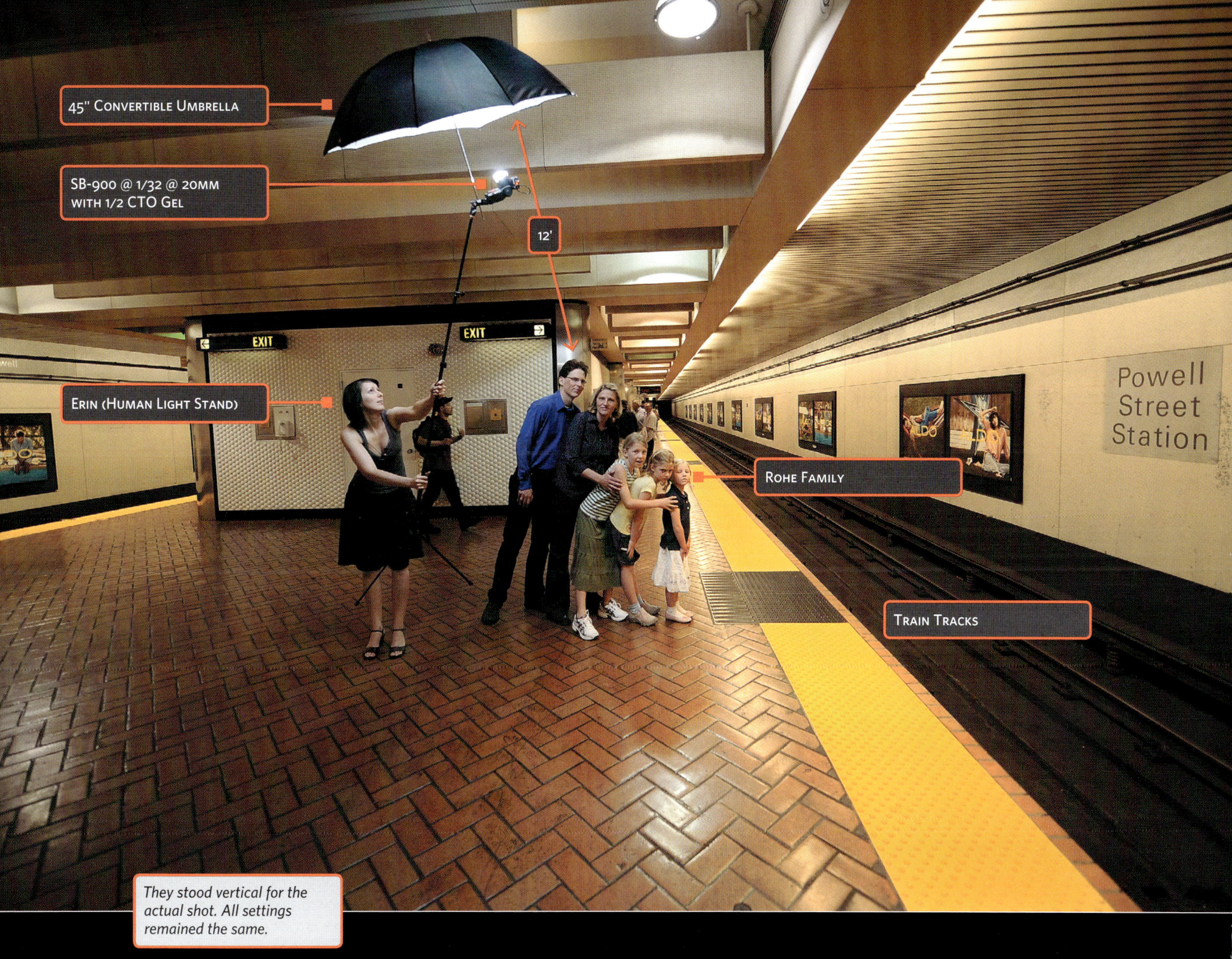

They stood vertical for the actual shot. All settings remained the same.

D700 | ISO 400 | F/2 | 1/60TH | 200MM F/2 @ 200MM

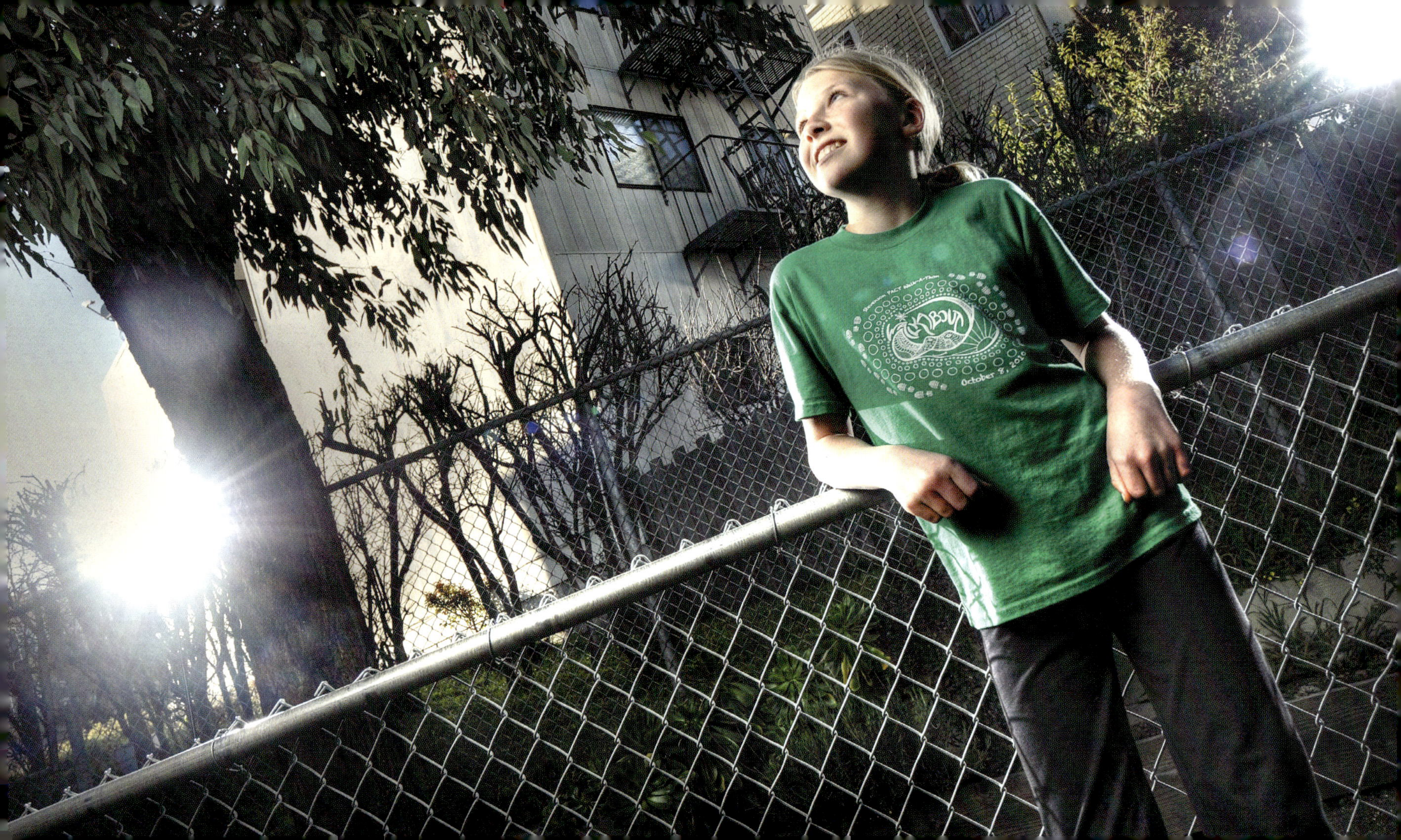

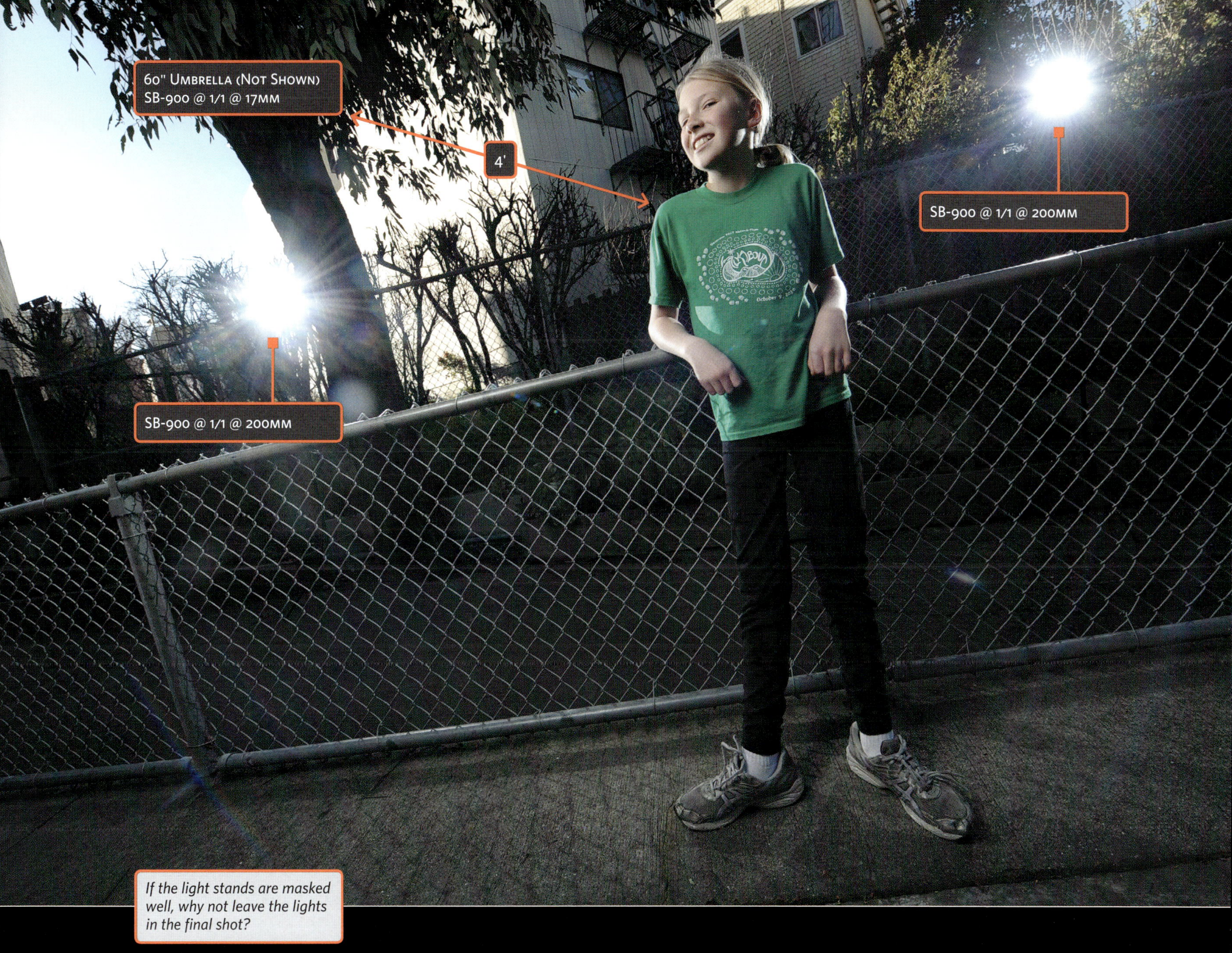

If the light stands are masked well, why not leave the lights in the final shot?

D3 | ISO 200 | F/8 | 1/250TH | 14–24MM F/2.8 @ 24MM

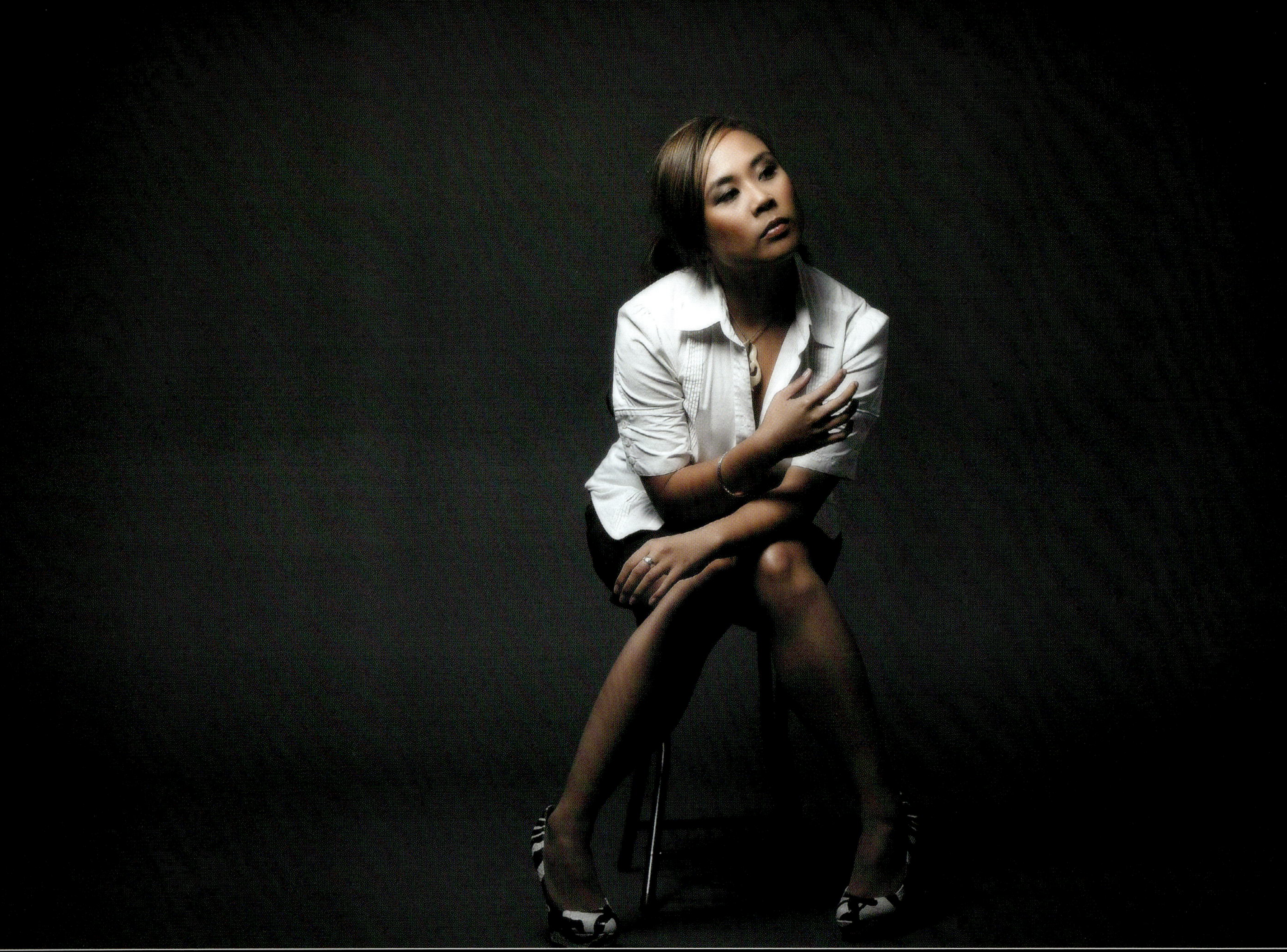

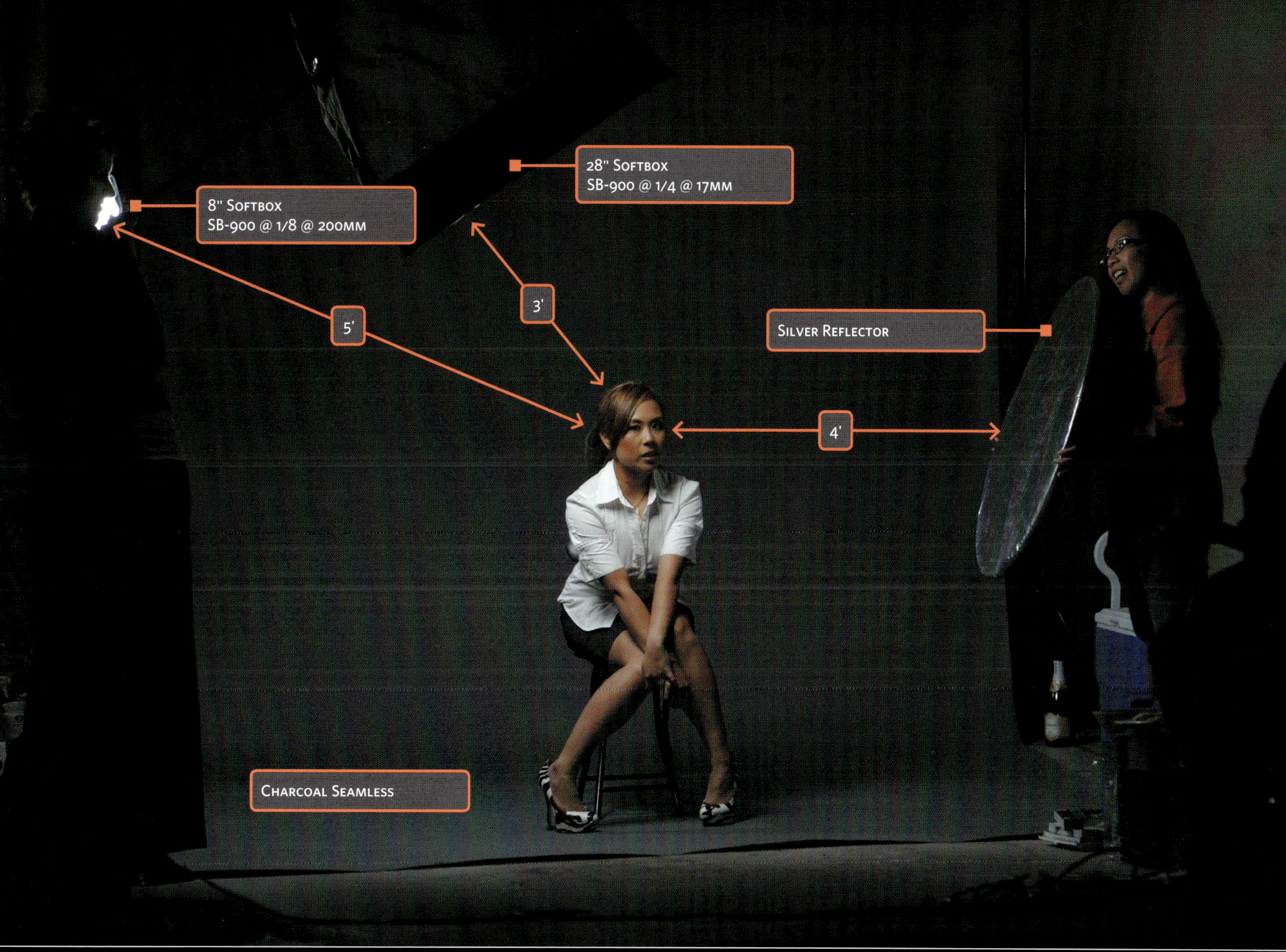

D3 | ISO 200 | F/5.6 | 1/200TH | 85MM F/1.4 @ 85MM

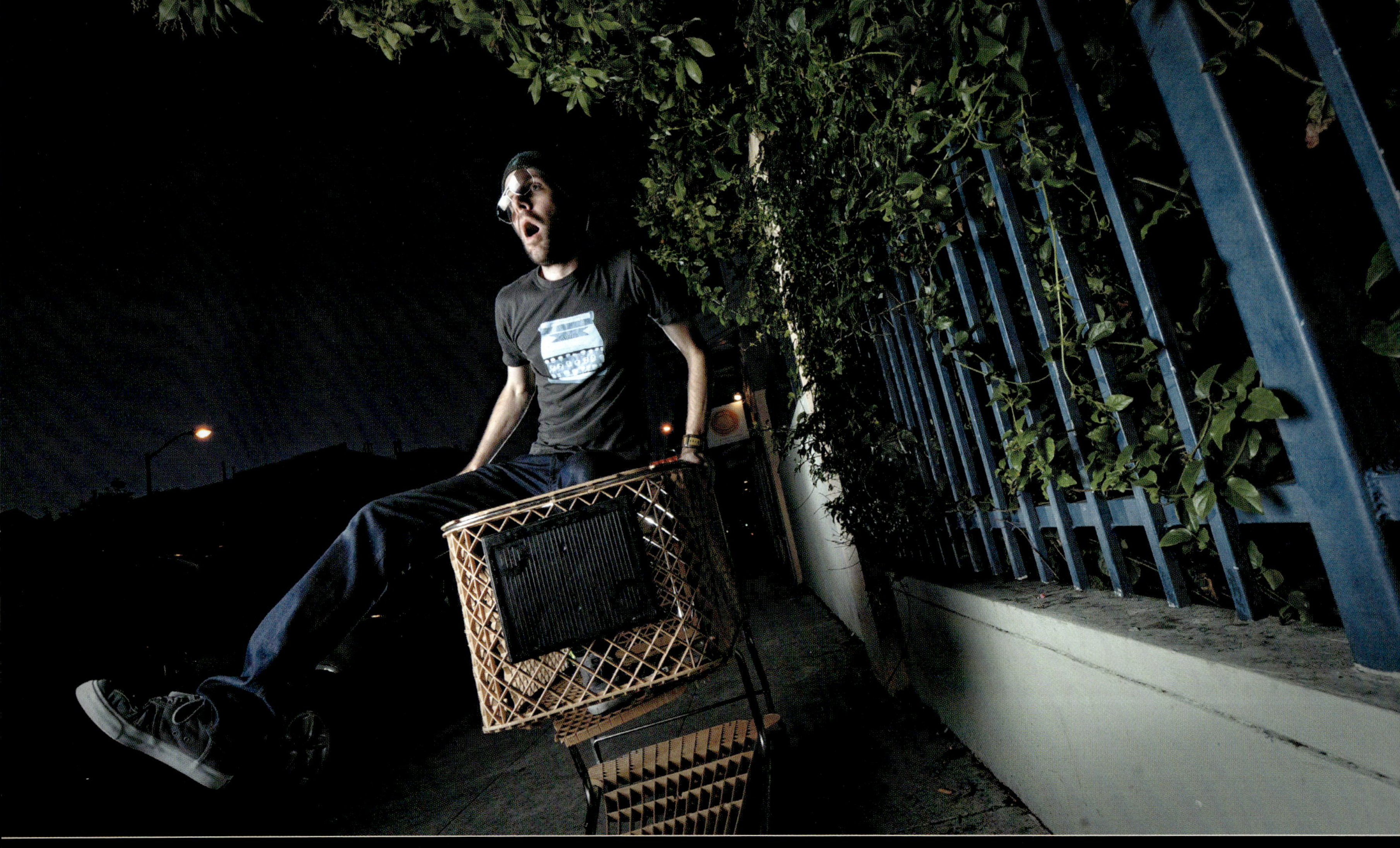

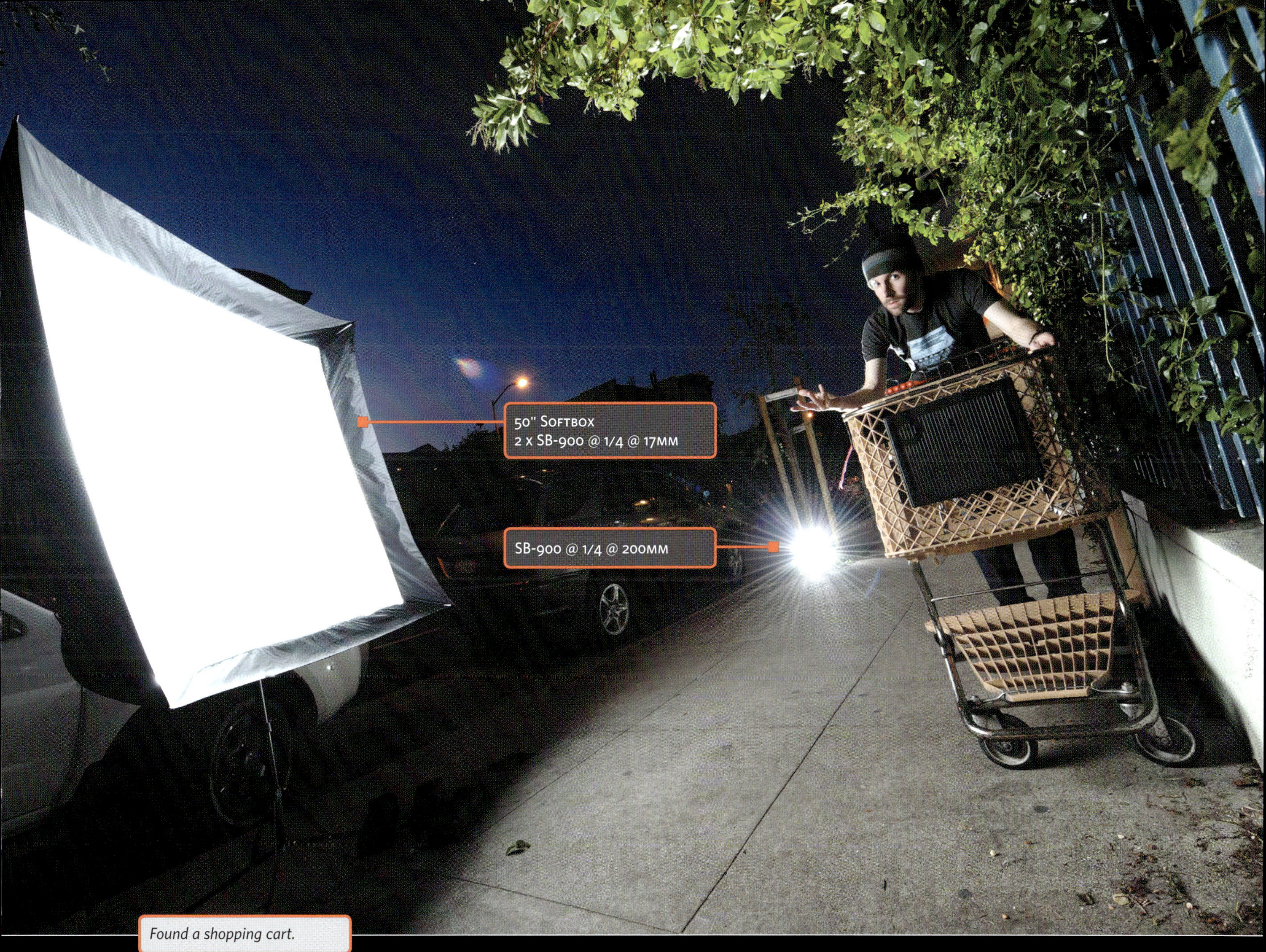

Found a shopping cart.

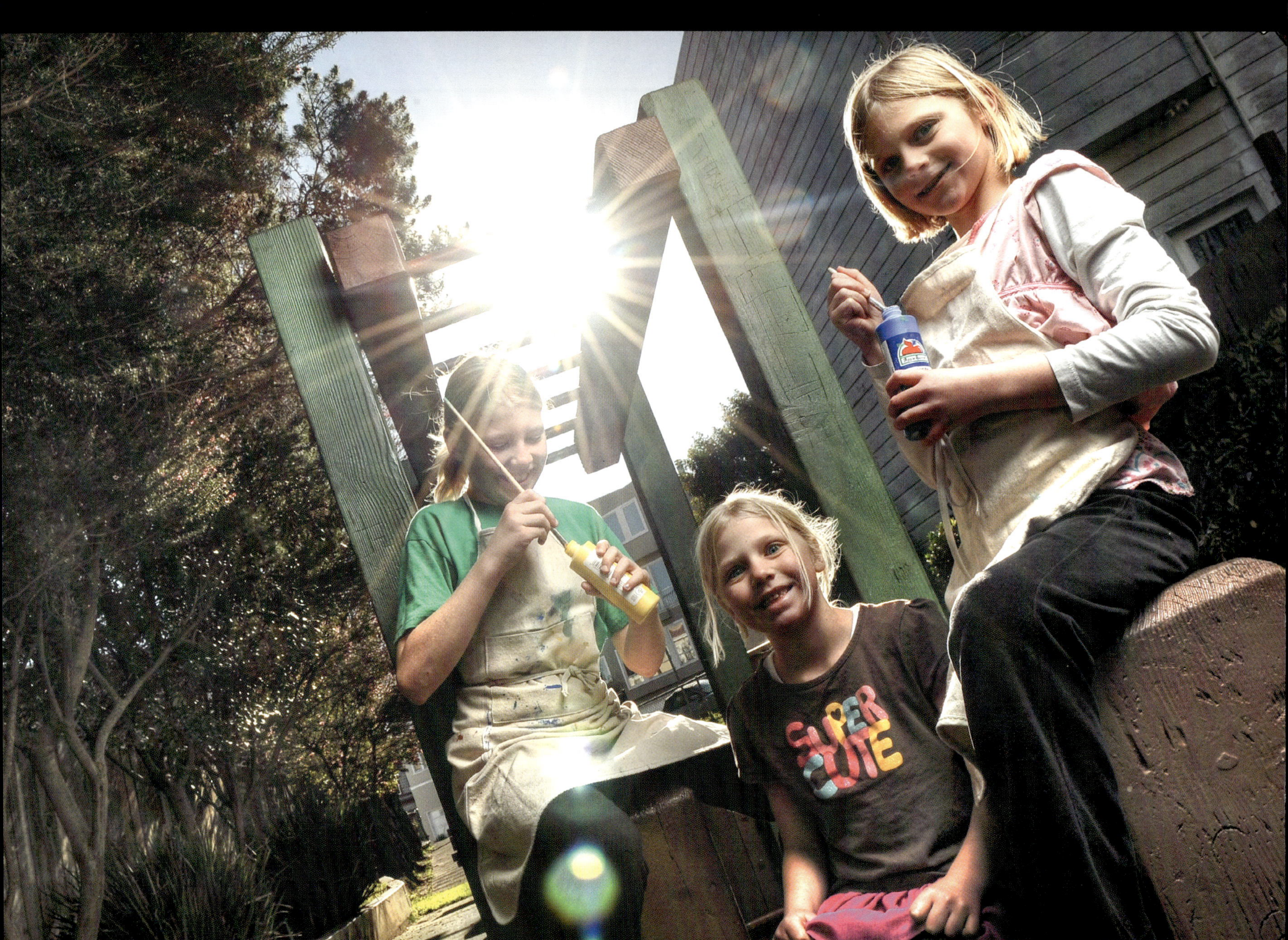
SUPER
CUTE

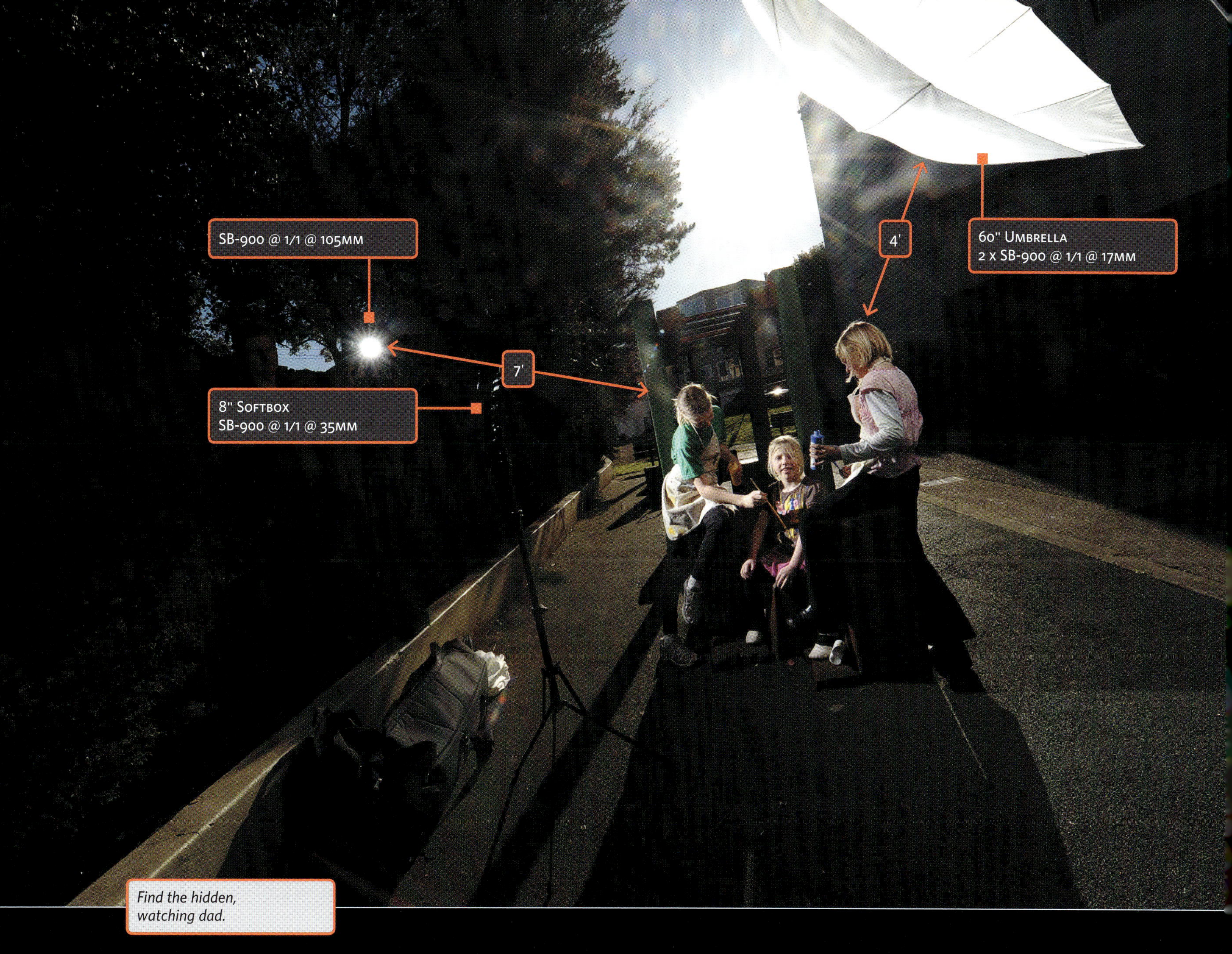

Find the hidden, watching dad.

D3 | ISO 200 | F/11 | 1/250TH | 24-70MM F/2.8 @ 24MM

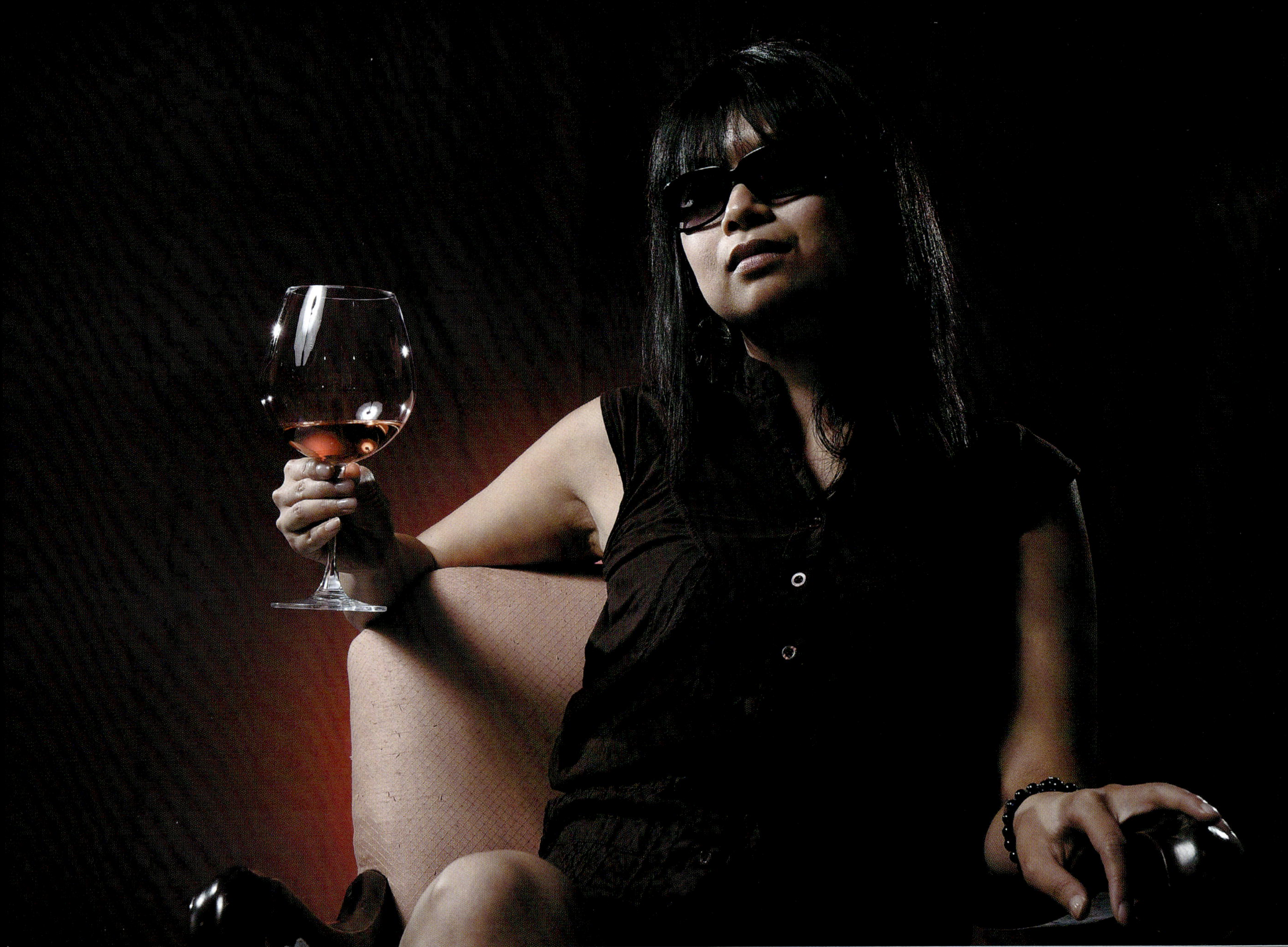

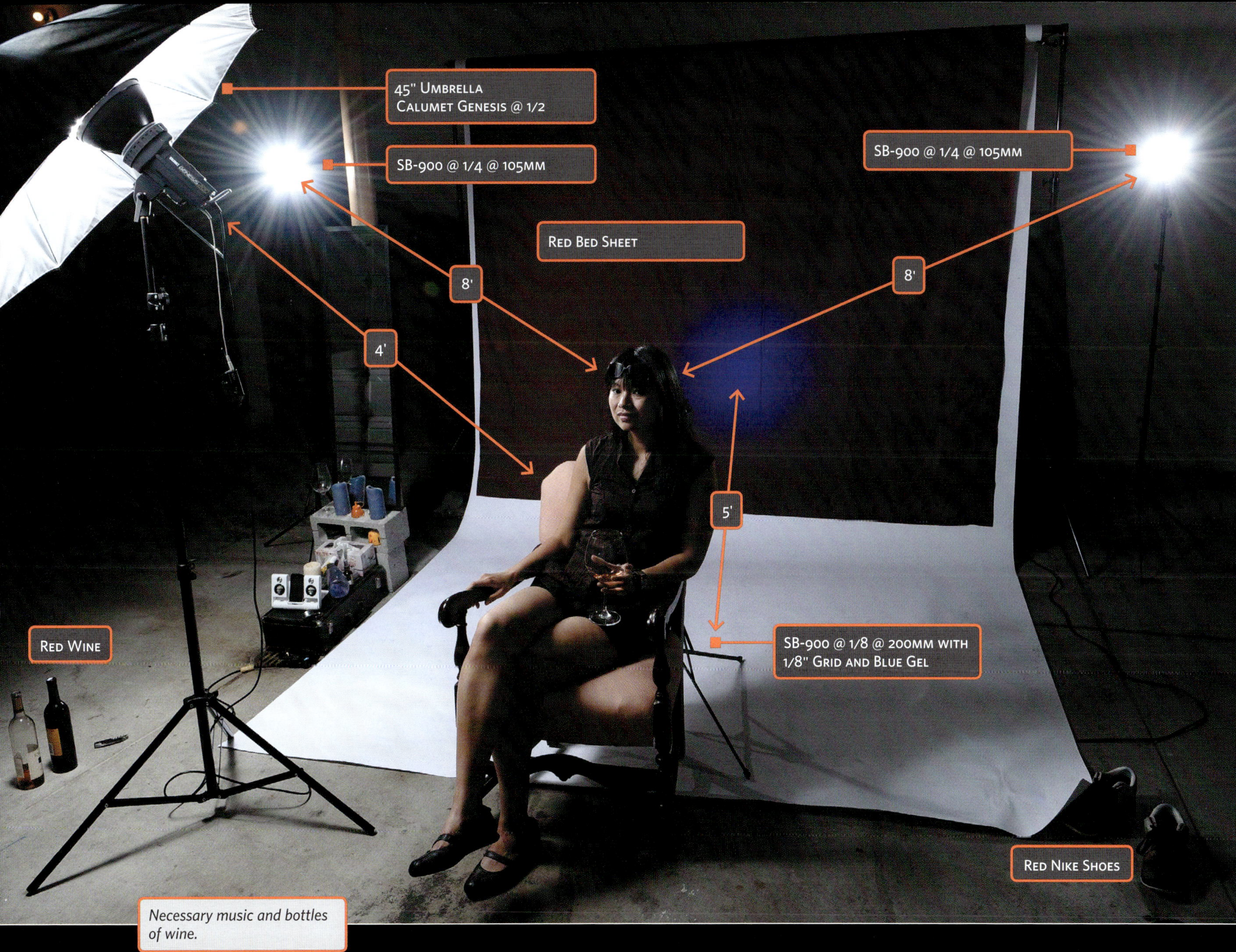

Necessary music and bottles of wine.

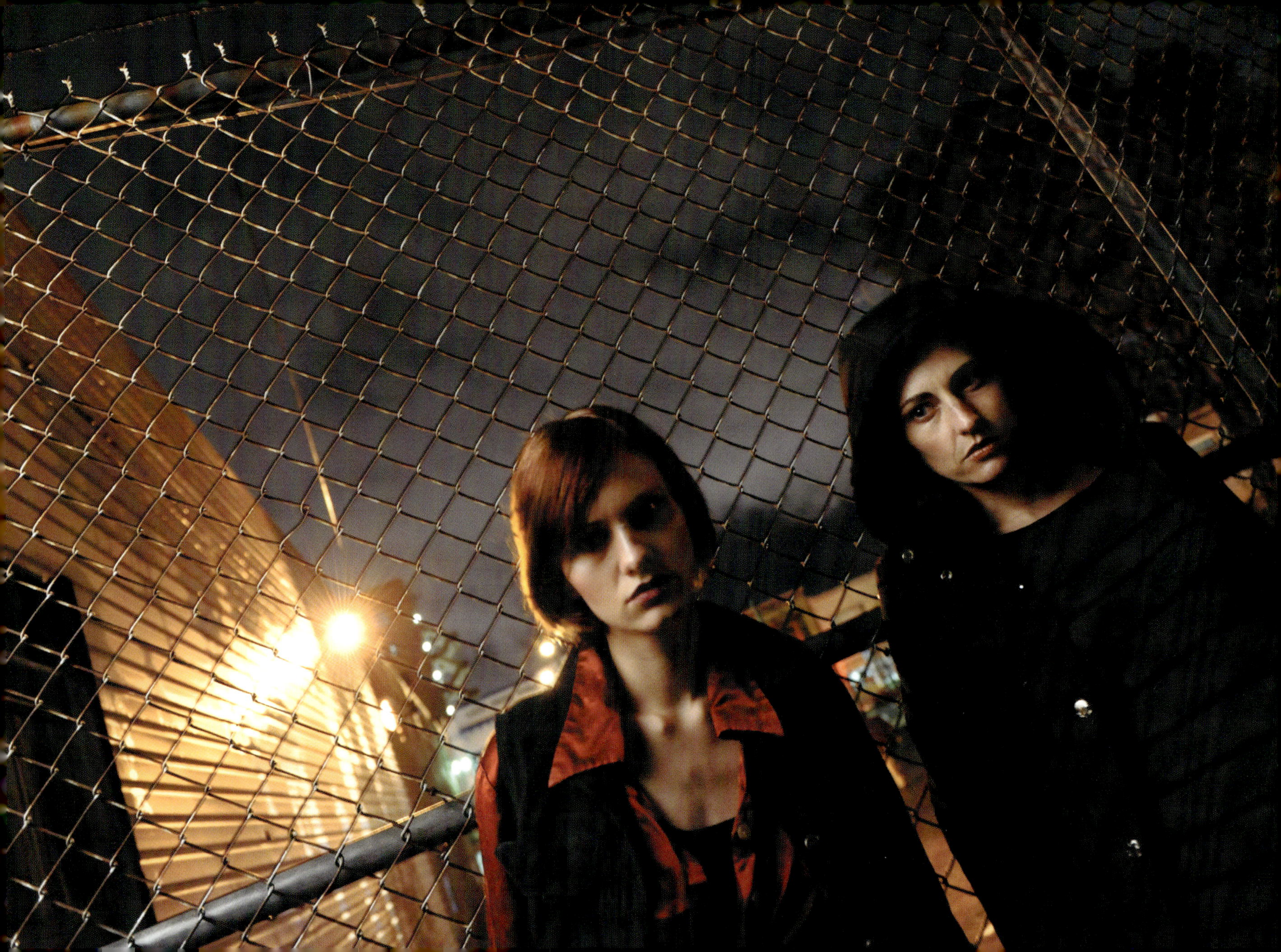

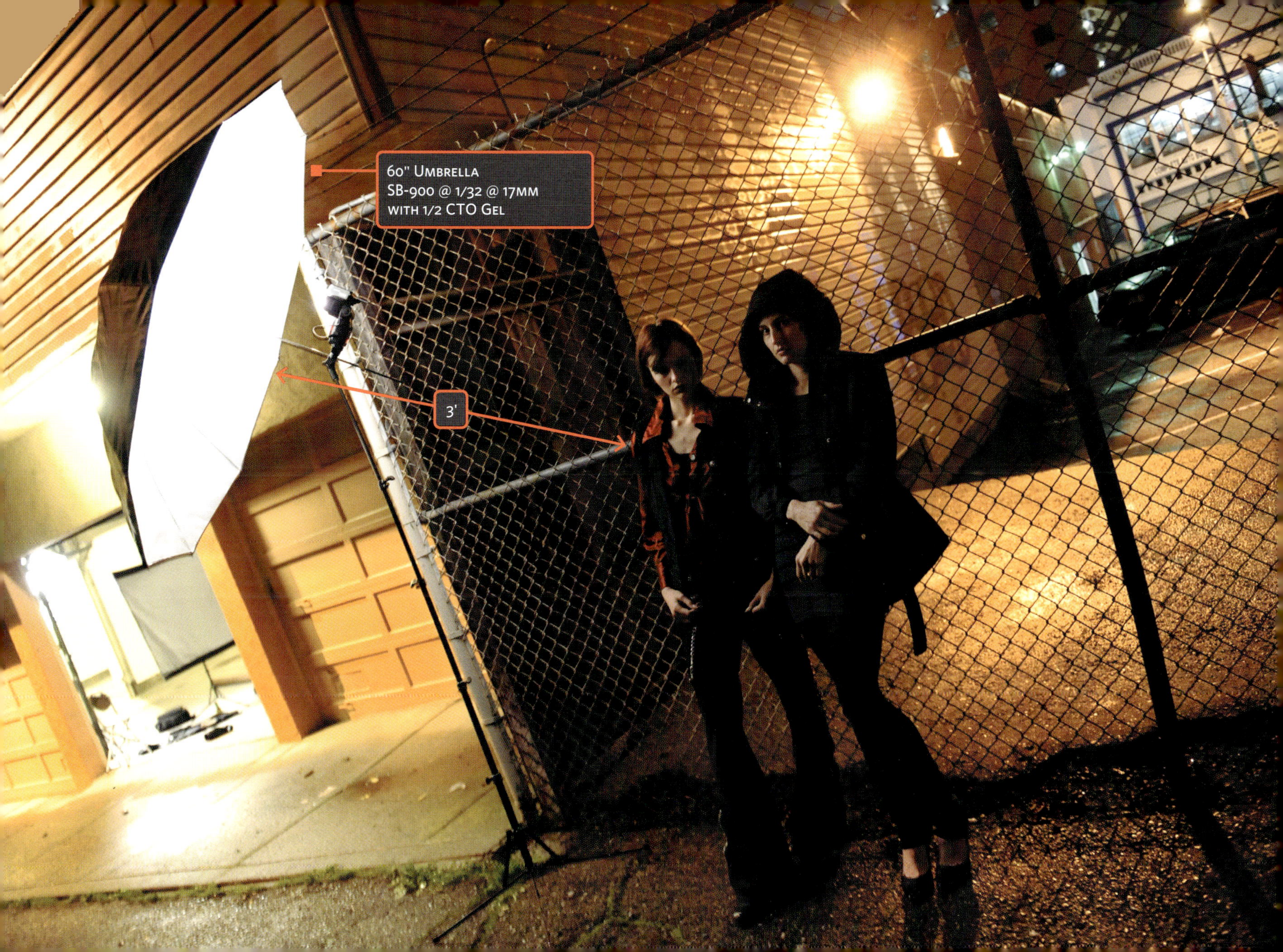
60" Umbrella
SB-900 @ 1/32 @ 17mm
with 1/2 CTO Gel
3'

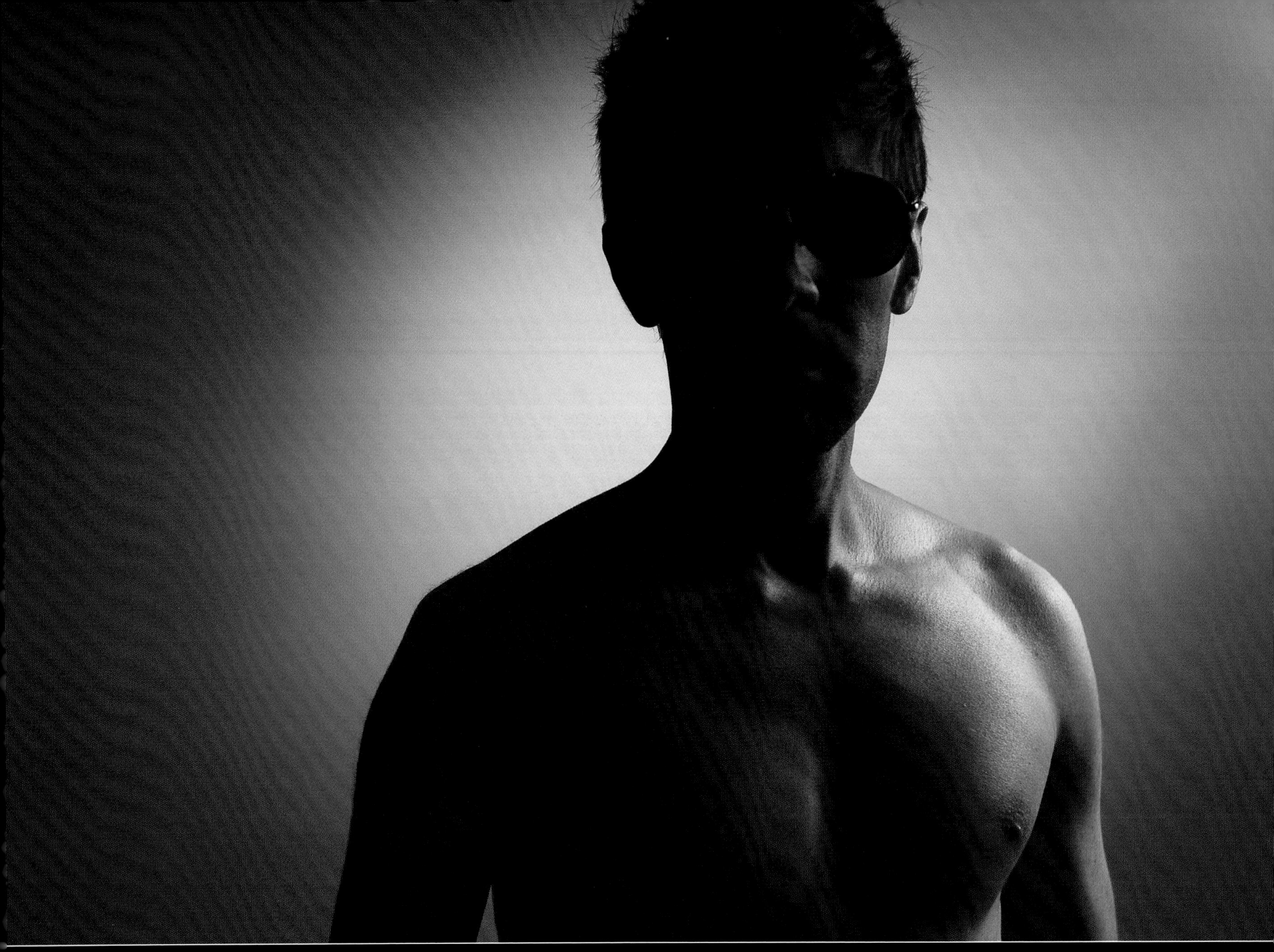

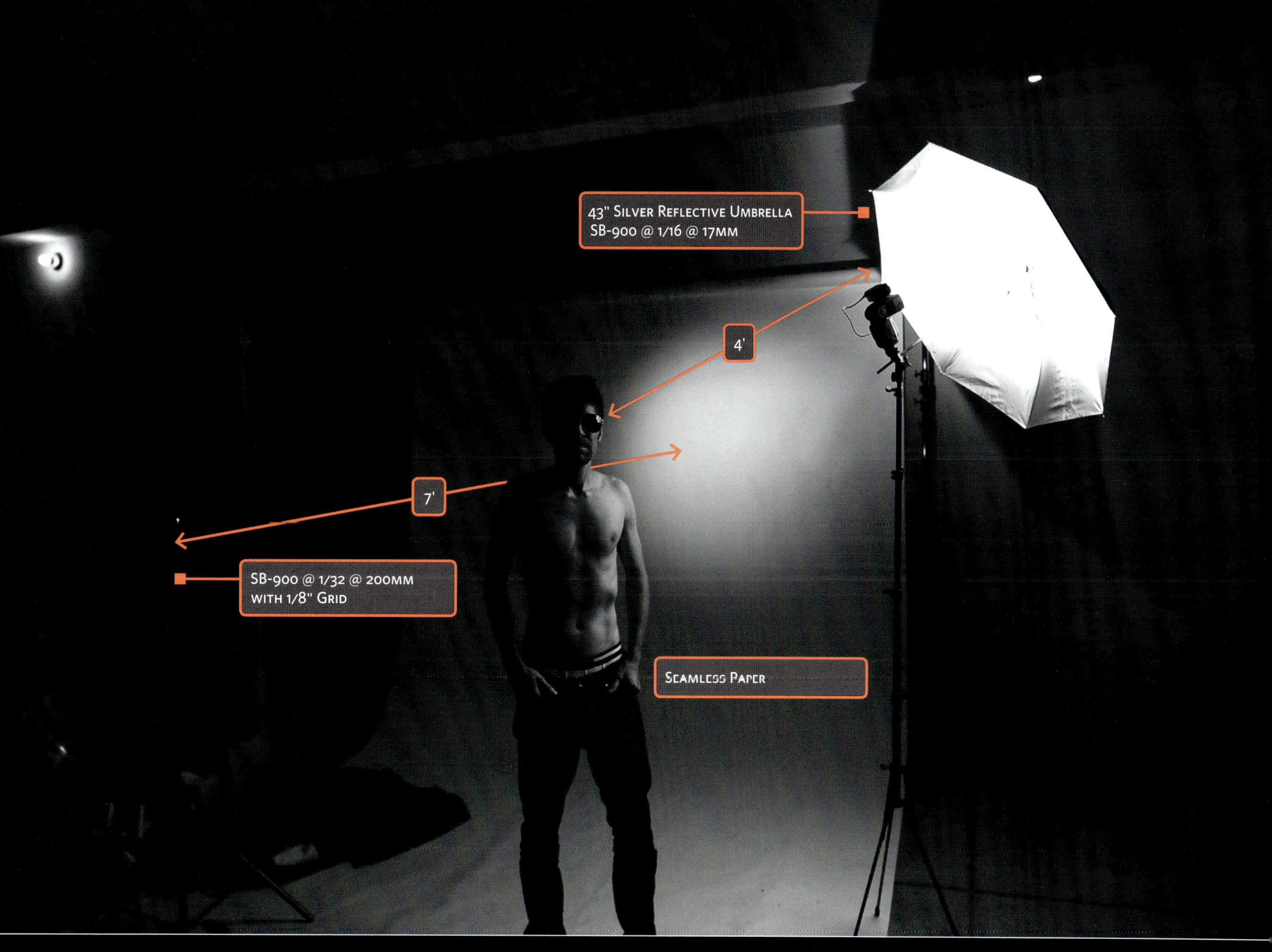

D3 | ISO 200 | F/3.5 | 1/125TH | 24-70MM F/2.8 @ 70MM

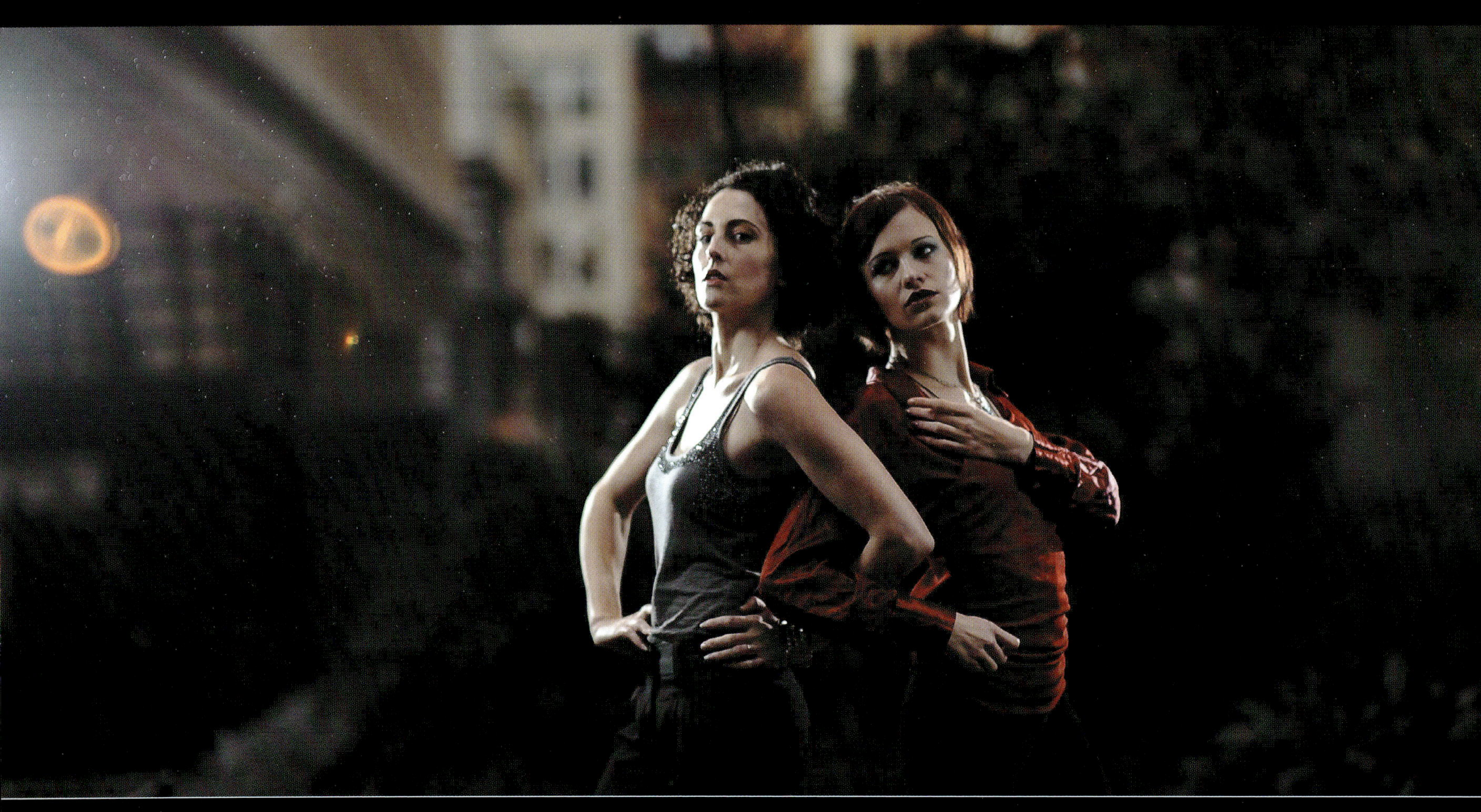

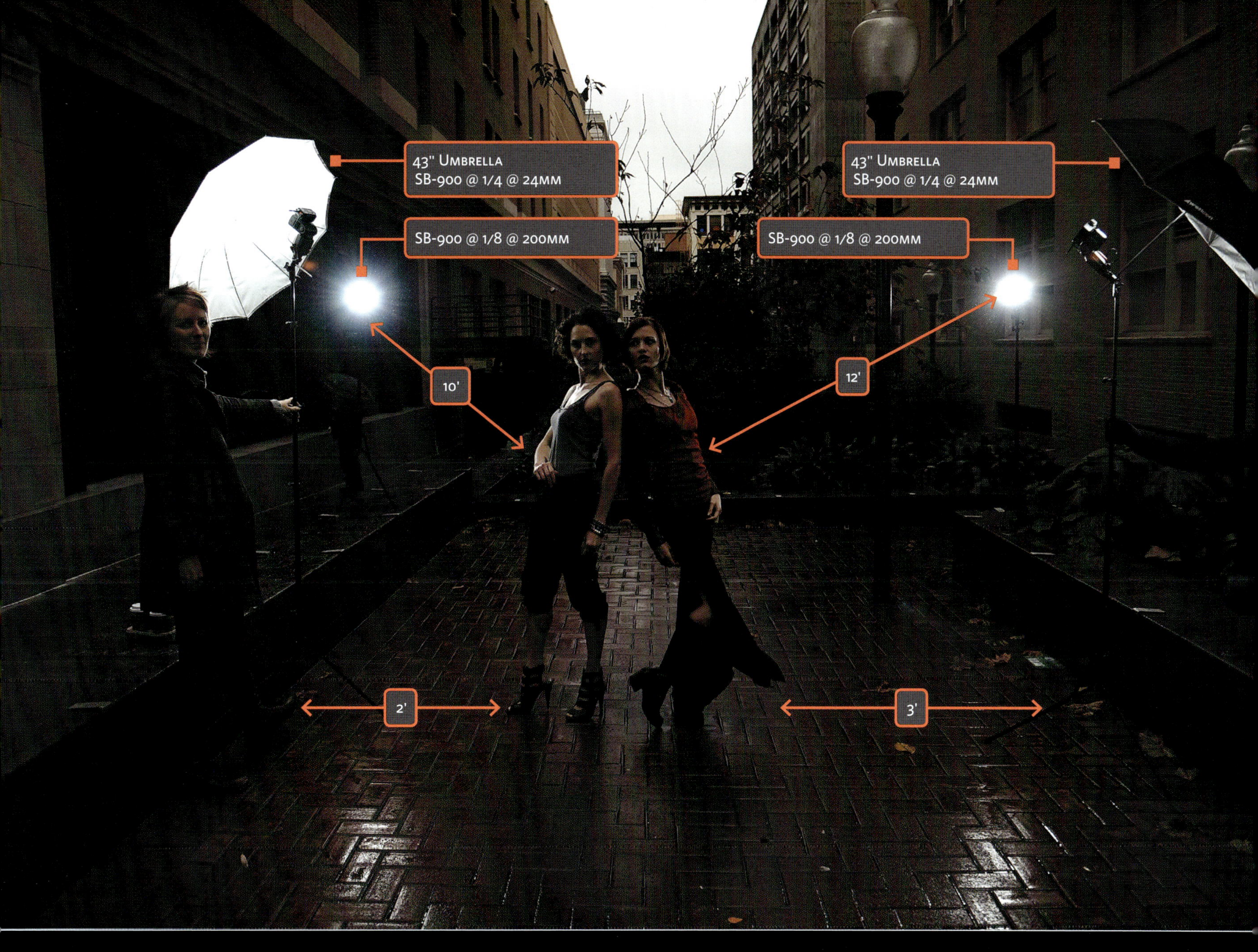

D3 | ISO 100 | F/1.8 | 1/250TH | 85MM F/1.4 @ 85MM

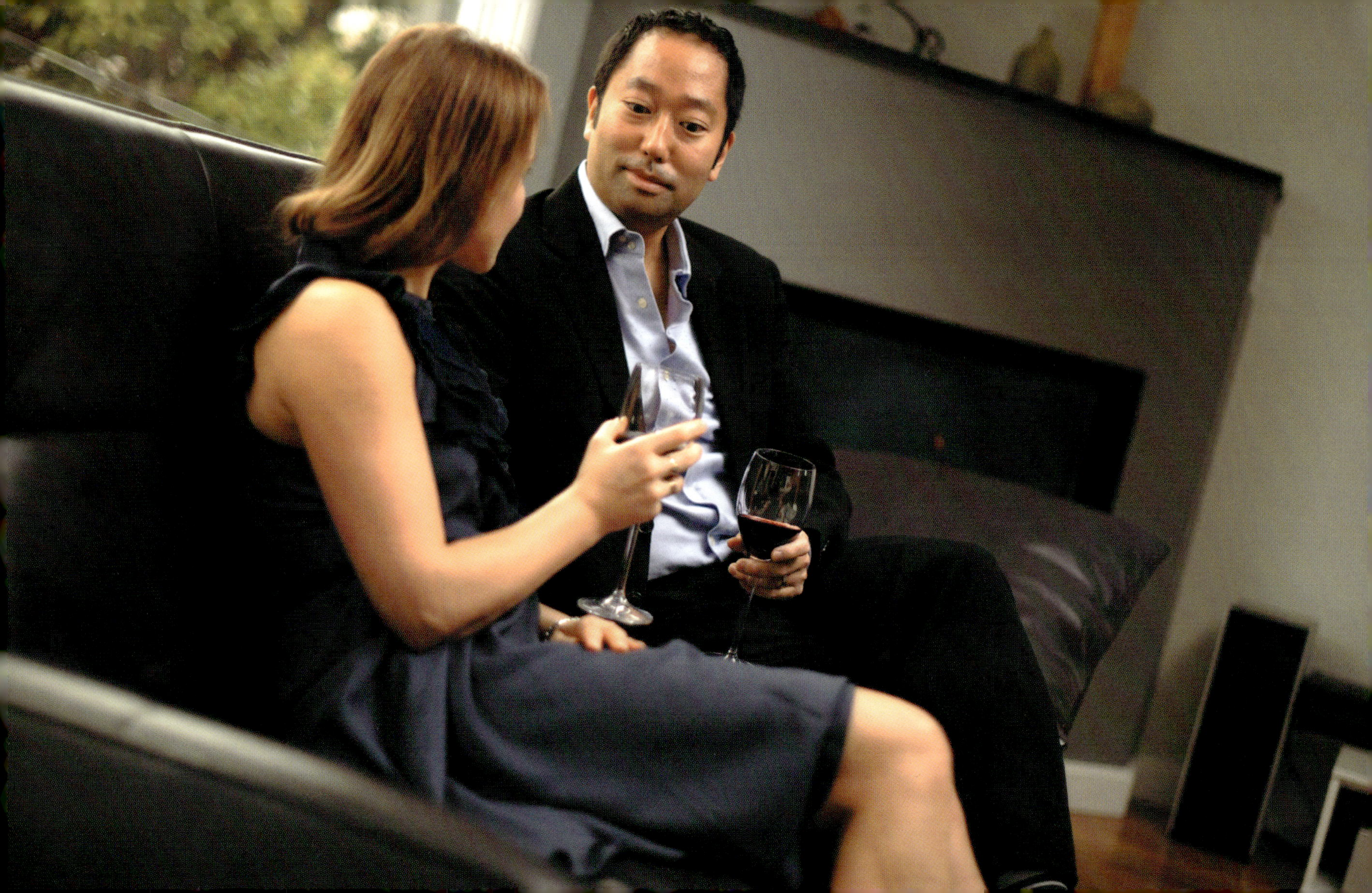

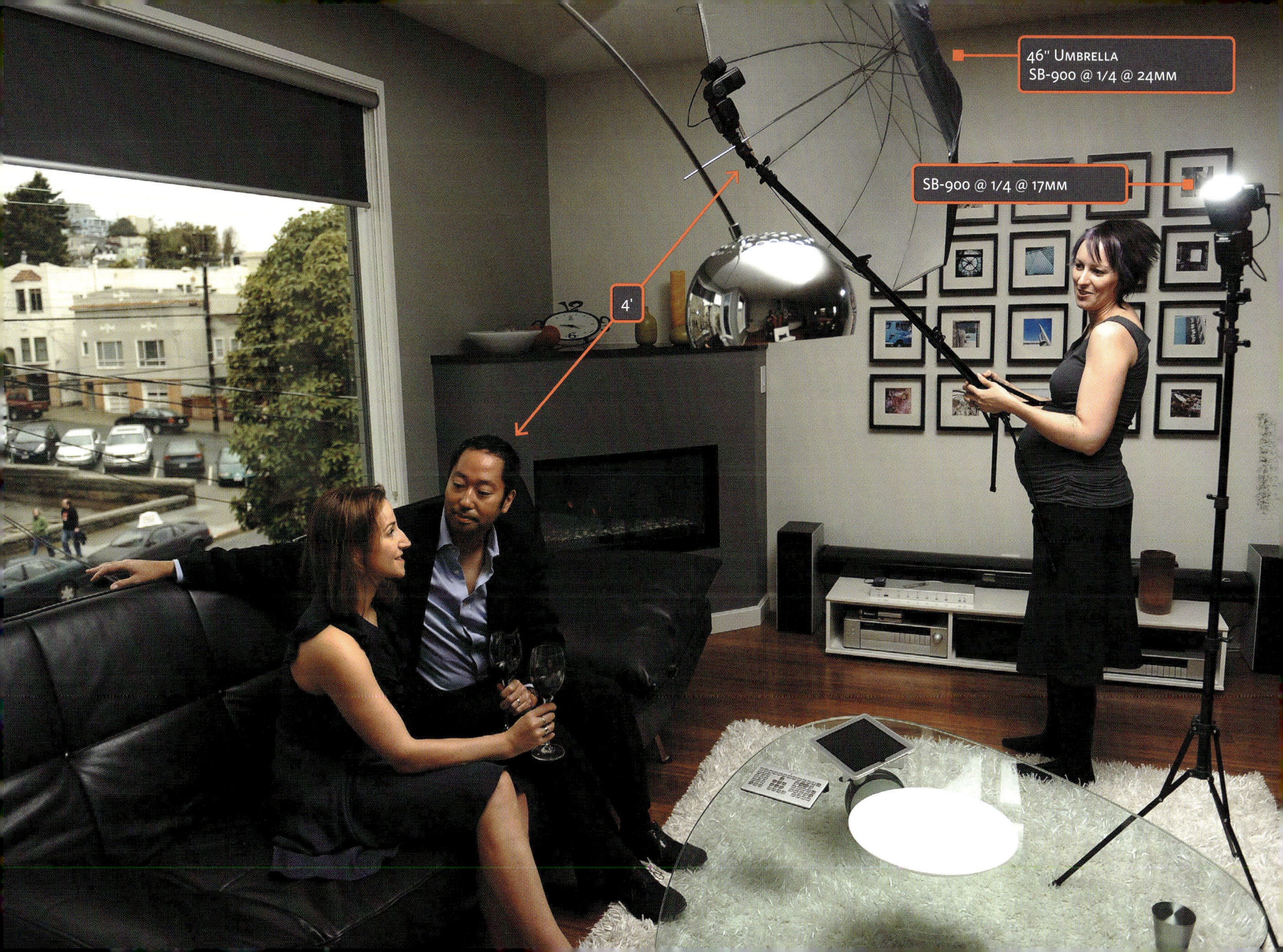
46" Umbrella
SB-900 @ 1/4 @ 24mm
SB-900 @ 1/4 @ 17mm
4'

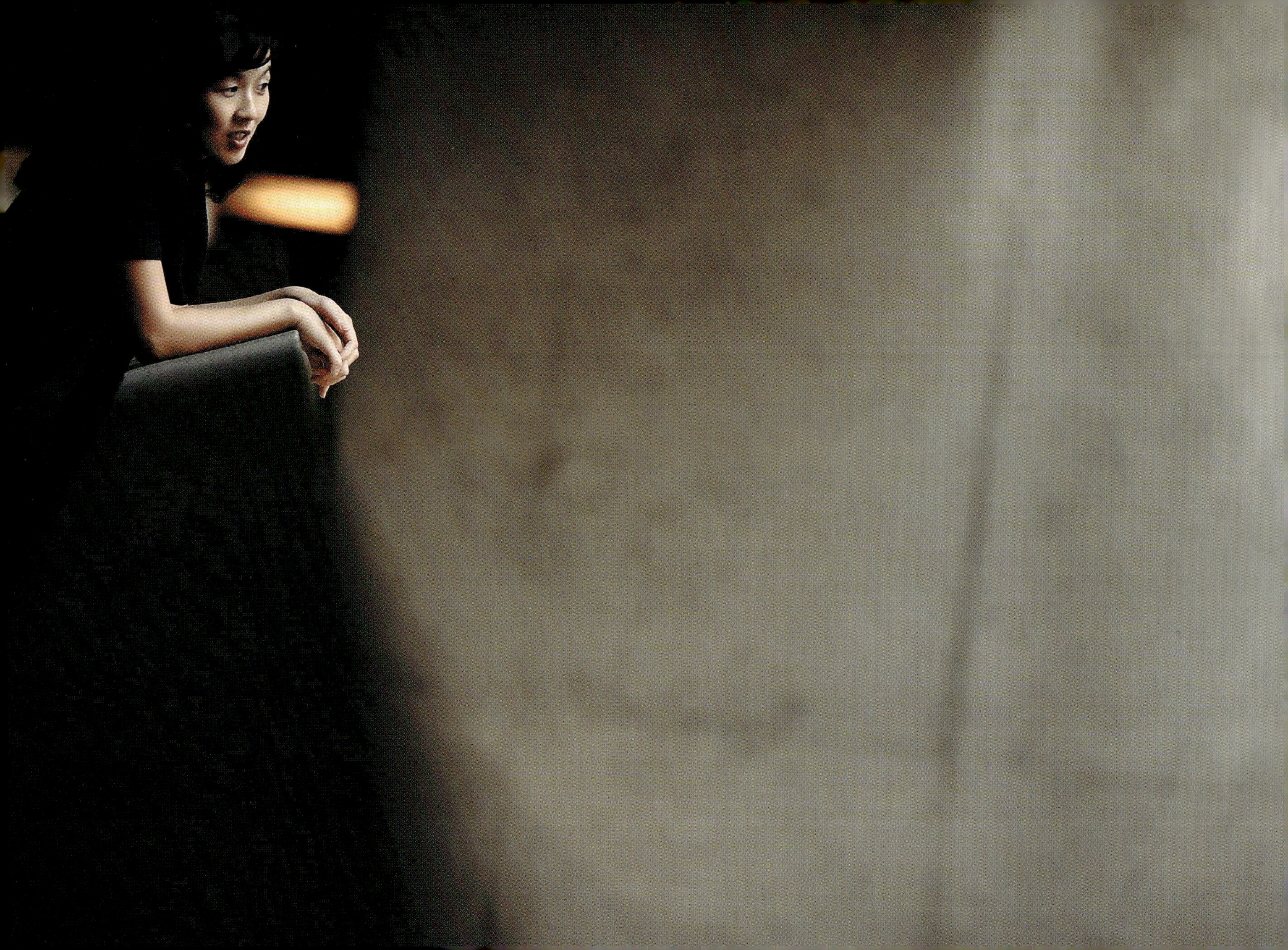

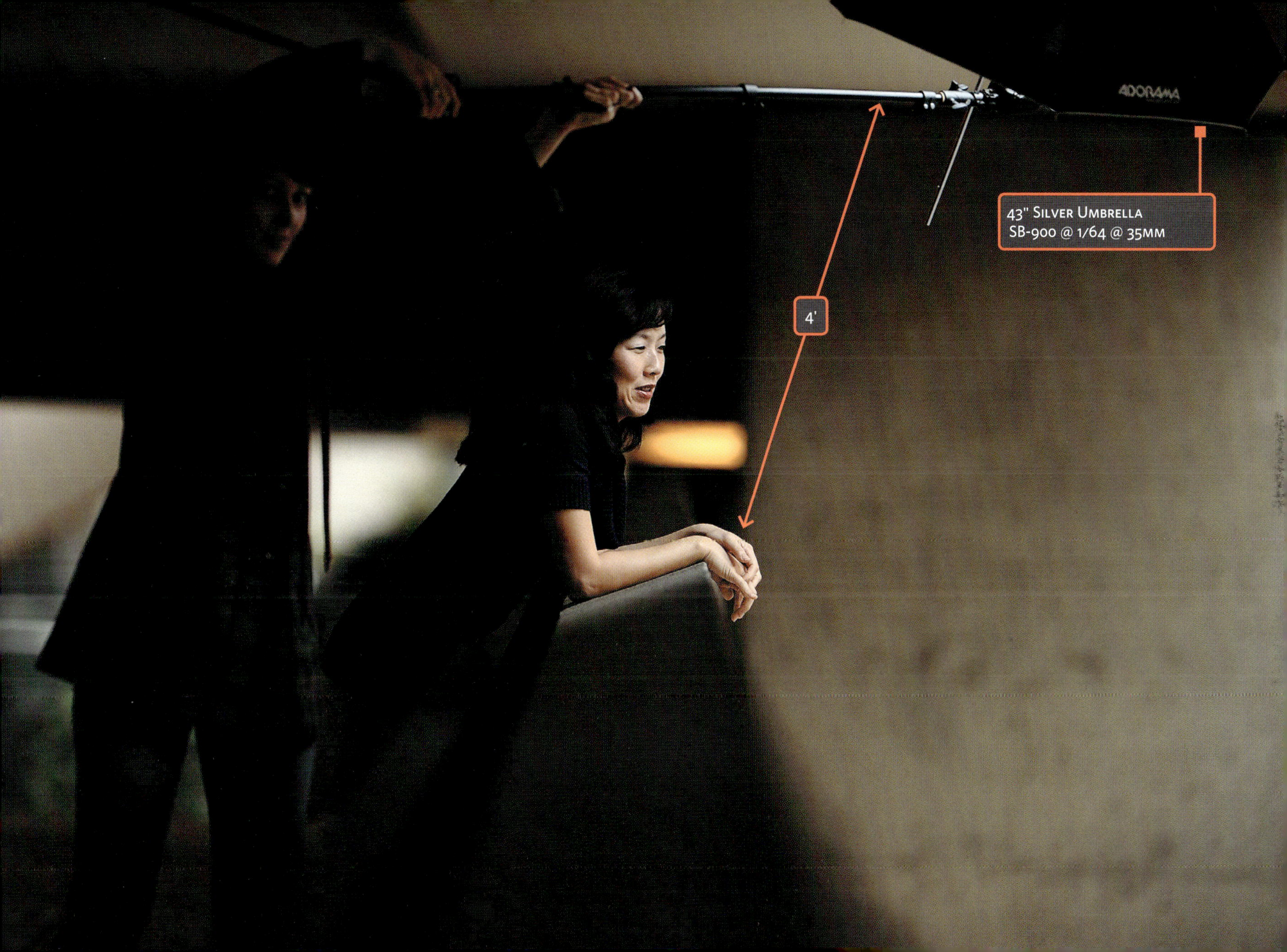

ADORAMA
43" Silver Umbrella
SB-900 @ 1/64 @ 35mm
4'

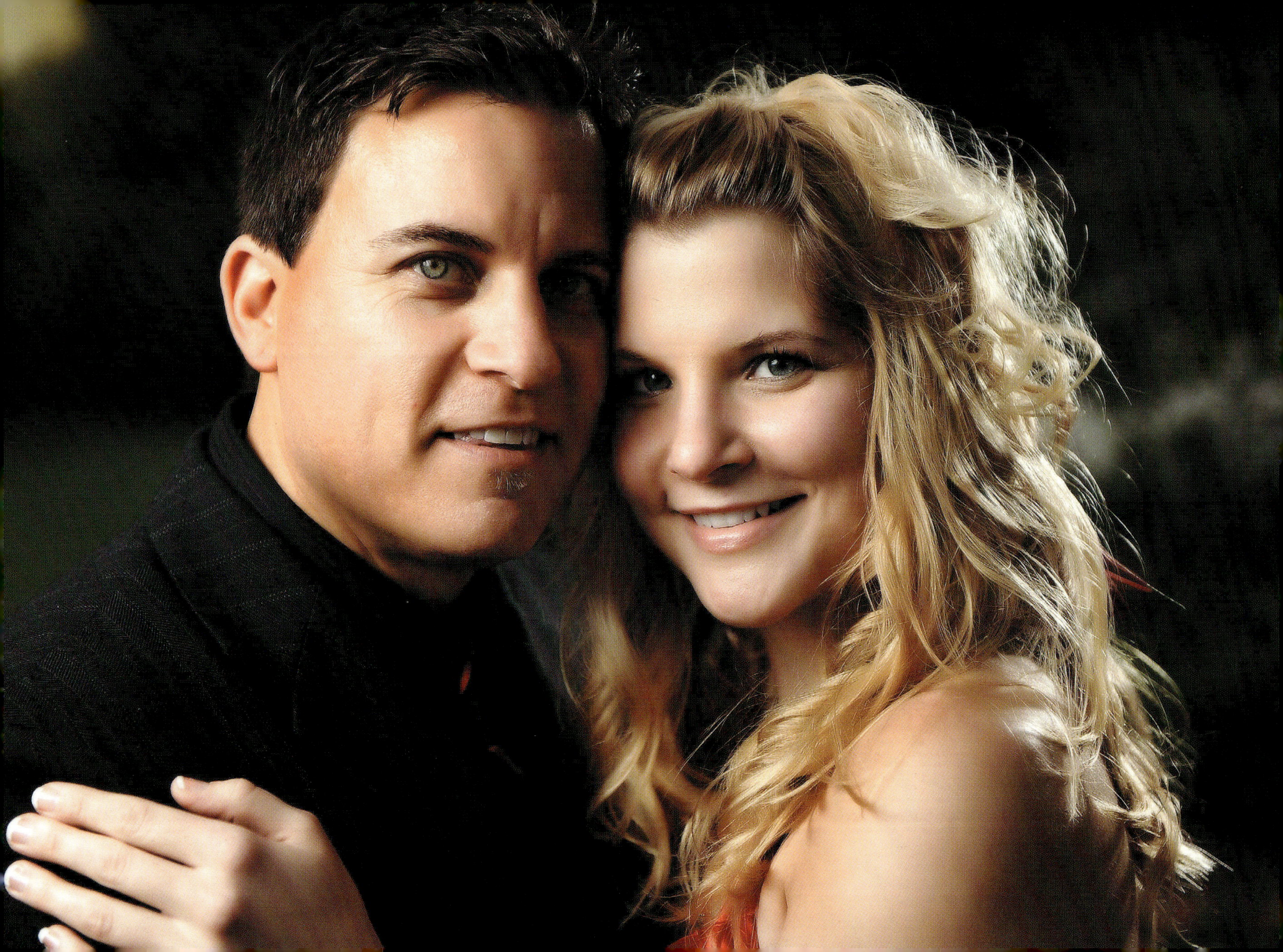

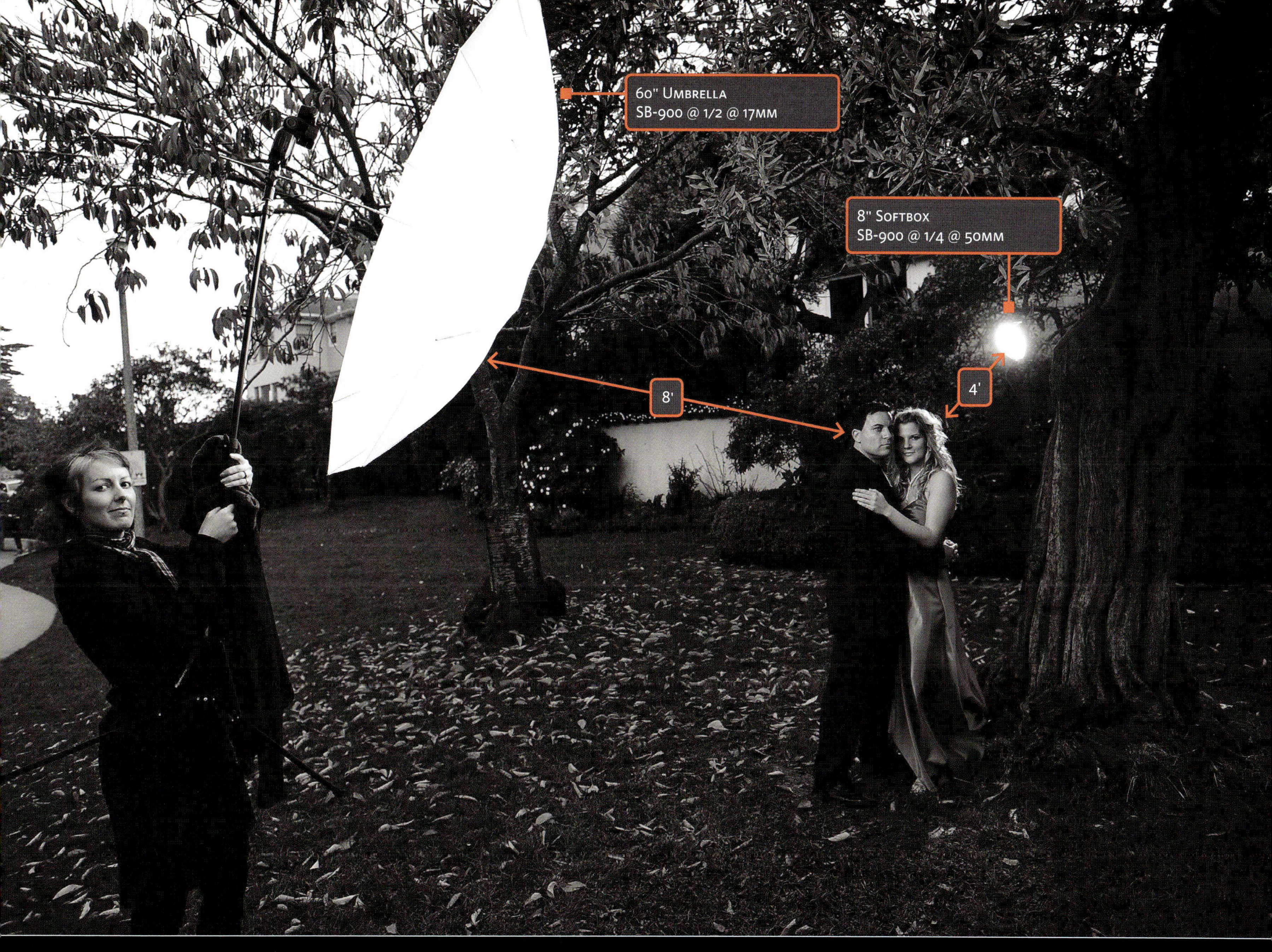

D3 | ISO 160 | F/2.8 | 1/250TH | 24-70MM F/2.8 @ 70MM

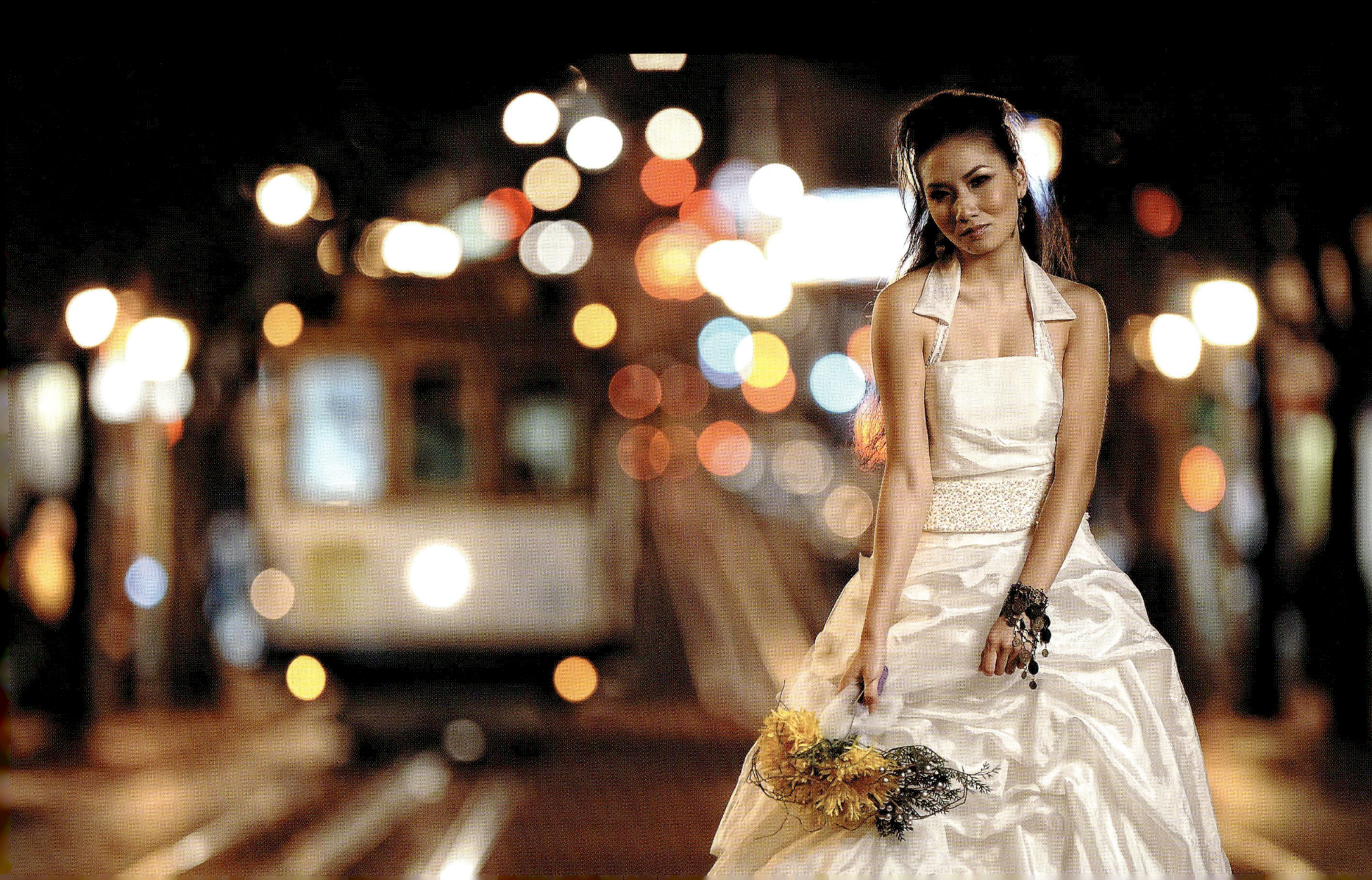

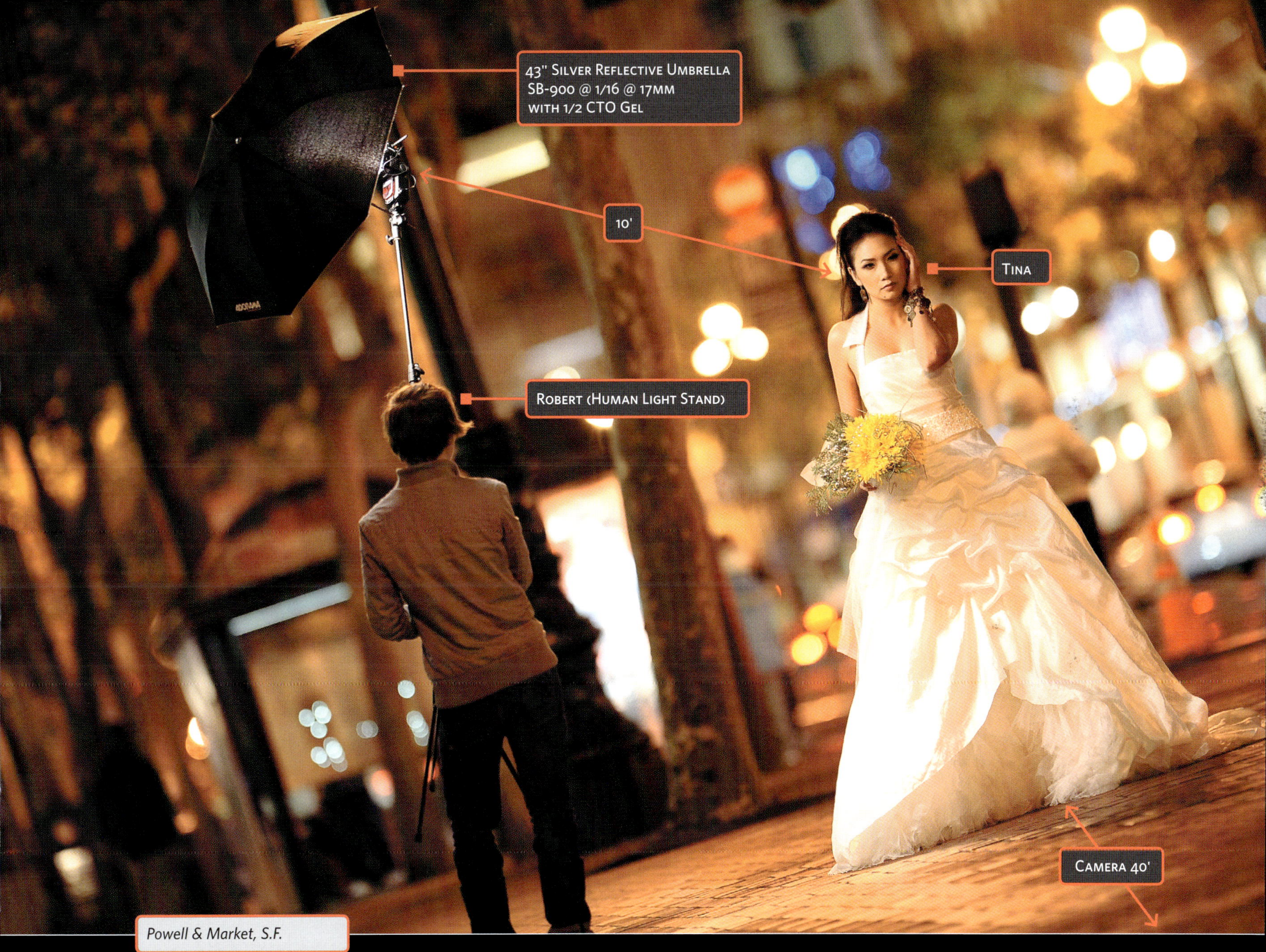
43" Silver Reflective Umbrella
SB-900 @ 1/16 @ 17mm
with 1/2 CTO Gel
10'
Tina
Robert (Human Light Stand)
Camera 40'
Powell & Market, S.F.

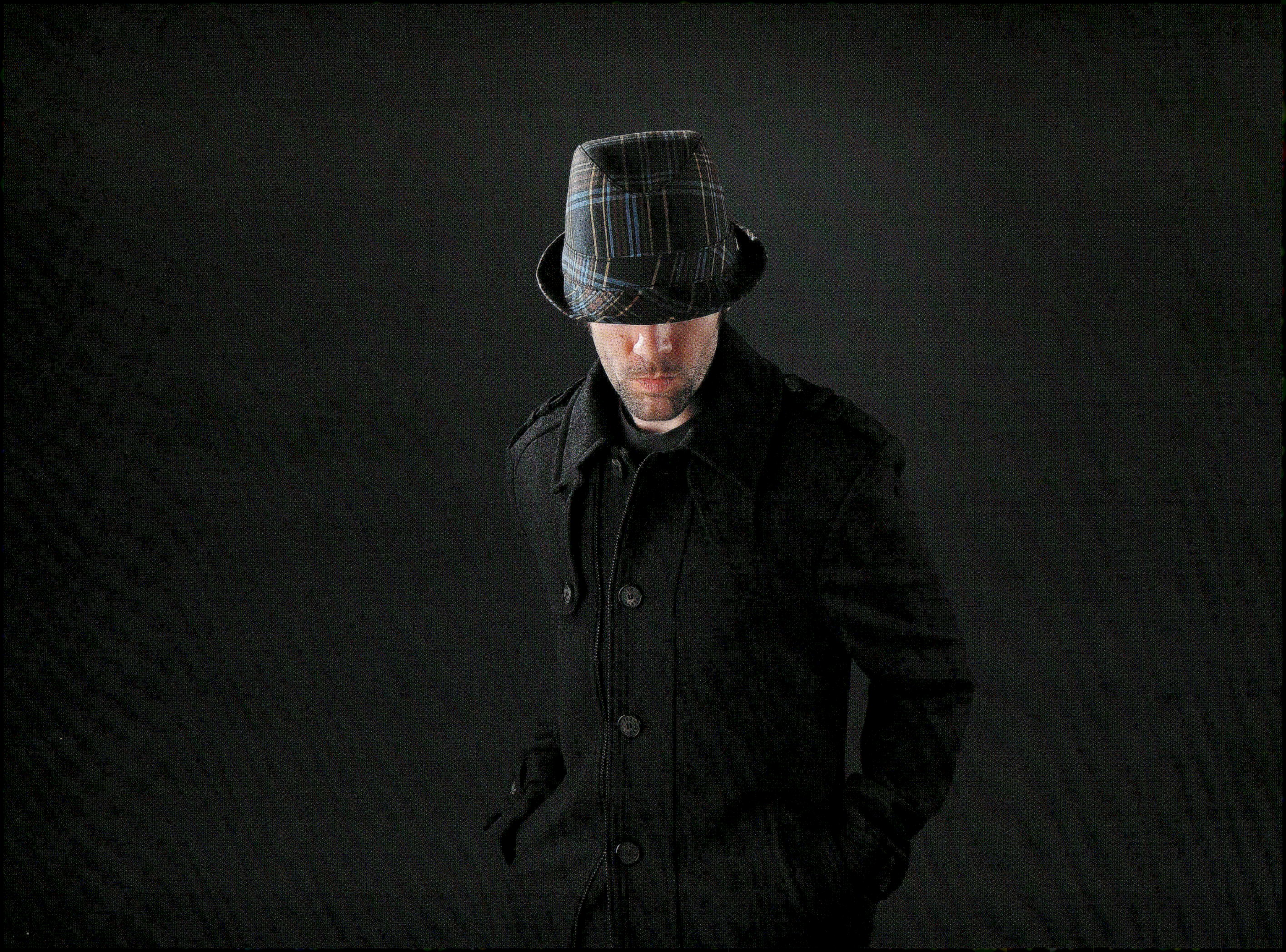

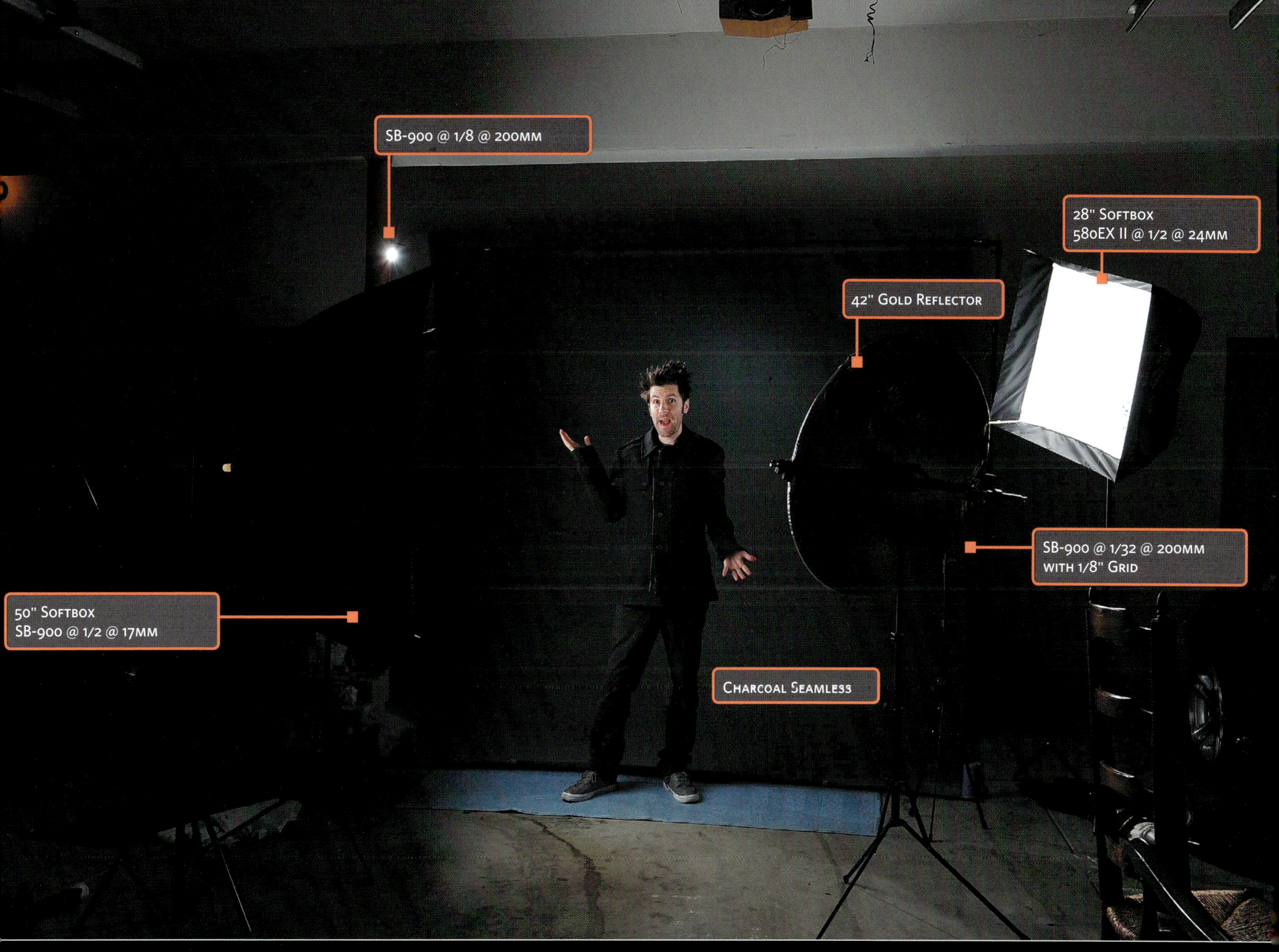

D3 | ISO 200 | F/8 | 1/250TH | 24-70MM F/2.8 @ 56MM

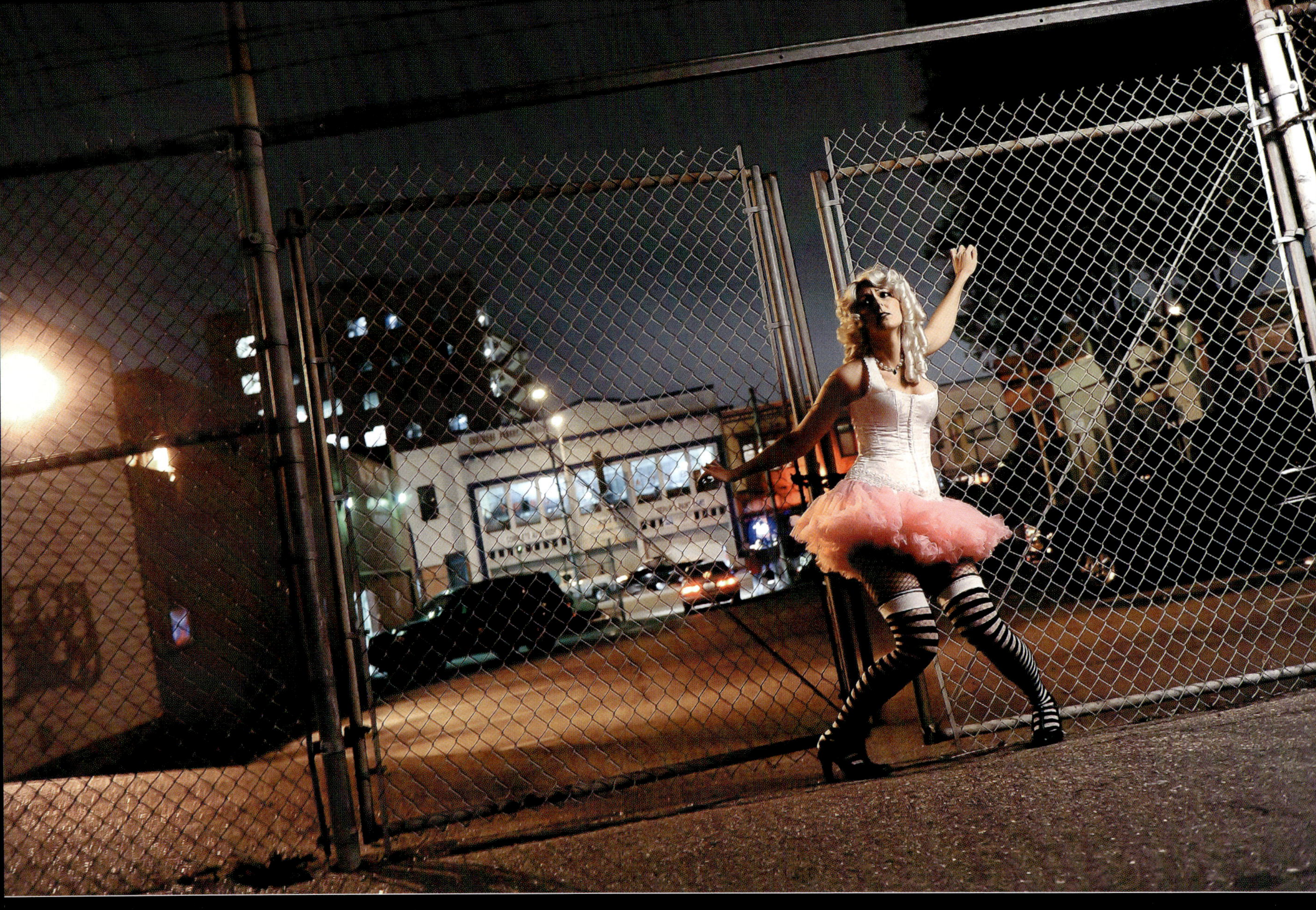

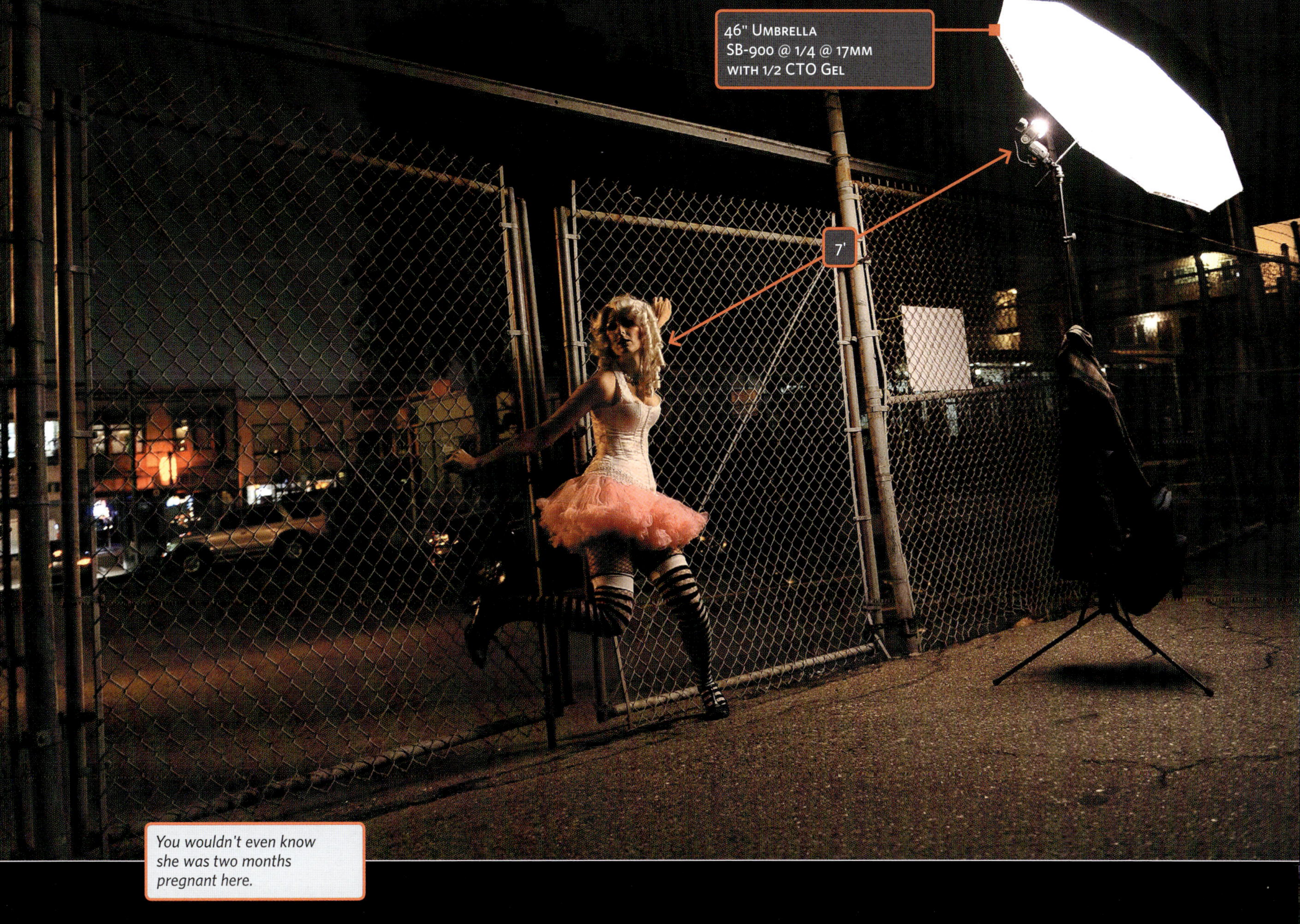

You wouldn't even know she was two months pregnant here.

D3 | ISO 1600 | F/2.8 | 1/10TH | 24-70MM F/2.8 @ 29MM

Index

W

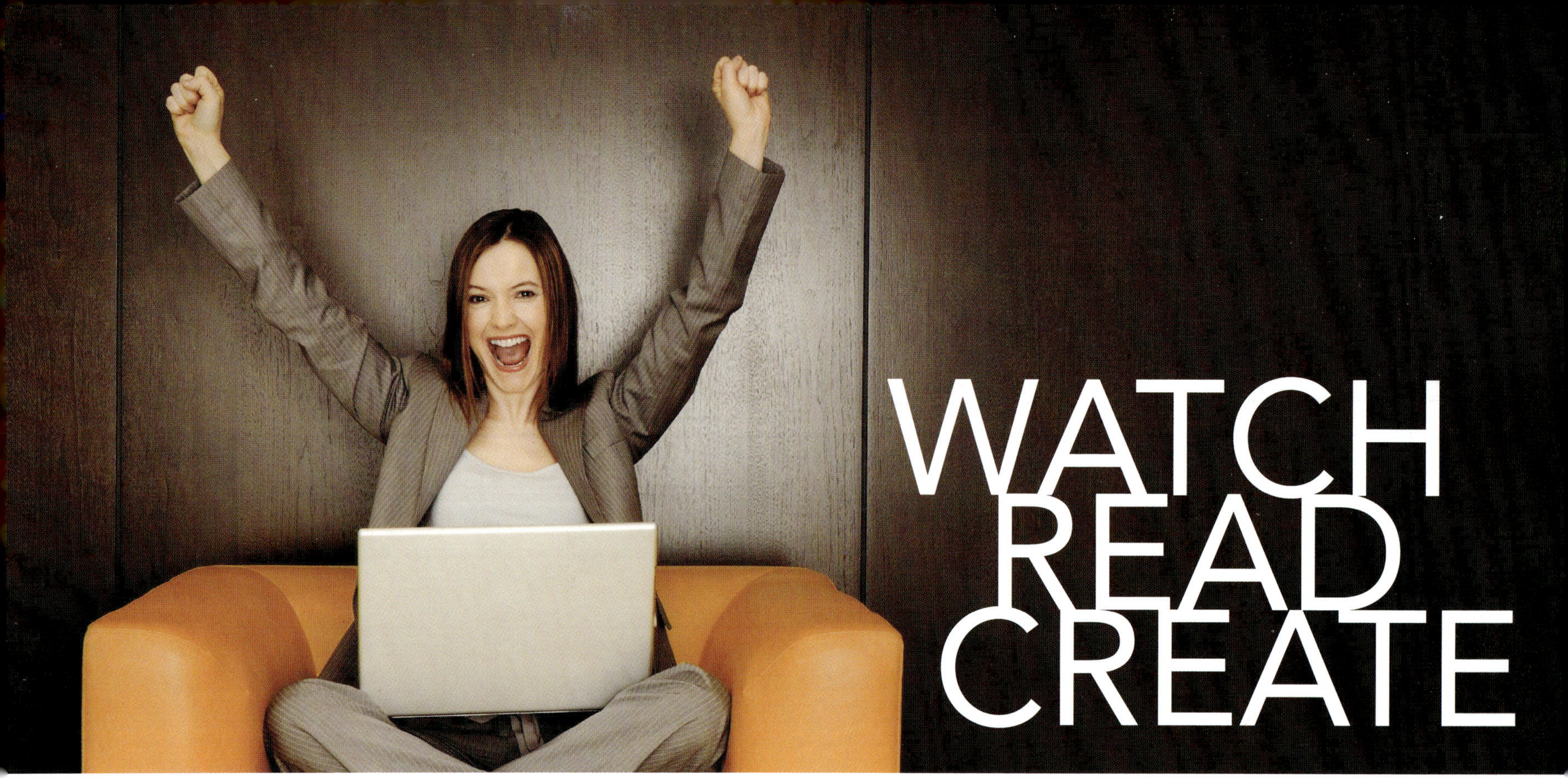